Women in Ancient Egypt

Women in Ancient Egypt

GAY ROBINS

HARVARD UNIVERSITY PRESS
CAMBRIDGE, MASSACHUSETTS

Printed in Great Britain

Third printing 1998

Library of Congress Cataloging-in-Publication Data
Robins, Gay.
  Women in Ancient Egypt/Gay Robins.
     p.   cm.
  Includes bibliographical references and index.
  ISBN 0-674-95468-8 (pbk).
    1. Women—Egypt—History.   2. Egypt—History—To 322 B.C.
I. Title.
HQ1137.E3R63   1993   92-38221 CIP
305. 4'0932—dc20

Cover: Gilded wooden inner coffin of the Theban priestess Henutmehit.

Contents

100827

Acknowledgements

I owe thanks to everyone who has in any way helped and encouraged me in writing this book. I am especially grateful to Vivian Davies and Celia Clear for suggesting that I undertake the project in the first place. In addition, I would like to thank John Baines for helpful discussions while I was working on the book in Oxford; Annette Depla for allowing me to read the draft of her paper 'Women in ancient Egyptian wisdom literature' before publication; Andrea McDowell for all her help in answering my questions and for letting me read prior to publication two papers of hers, 'Women's economic position in the New Kingdom' and 'Agricultural activity by the workmen of Deir el-Medina'; Malcolm Mosher, Jr. for information about Late Period *Books of the Dead* owned by women; Richard Parkinson for numerous interesting discussions; Geraldine Pinch for all her help and stimulating discussions, and for providing me with a copy of her paper 'Fertility magic' before publication; Stephen Quirke who provided me with many interesting insights while helping me on another project connected with women in ancient Egypt; Jim Romano who kindly gave me a copy of his lecture on 'Mother and child in ancient Egypt' delivered at the Metropolitan Museum of Art, New York; Donald Spanel for his helpfulness in providing references and answering questions, and who, as always whatever aspect of ancient Egypt is under discussion, offered interesting and valuable comments. Finally, I must thank my husband, Charles Shute, for reading the various drafts of the typescript innumerable times and making many important suggestions for improvement, and my editor, Carolyn Jones, for seeing the project through to fruition.

Chronology

(after J. Baines and J. Málek *Atlas of Ancient Egypt*, Oxford, 1980, 36–37. All dates are BC. Those before 664 are approximate.)

2920–2649	Early Dynastic Period (First – Second Dynasties)
2649–2150	Old Kingdom (Third – Sixth Dynasties)
2649–2575	*Third Dynasty*
2575–2465	*Fourth Dynasty*
2465–2323	*Fifth Dynasty*
2323–2150	*Sixth Dynasty (including Nitiqret)*
2289–2255	*Pepy I*
2150–2040	First Intermediate Period (Seventh – Theban Eleventh Dynasties)
2040–1640	Middle Kingdom
2040–1991	*Eleventh Dynasty*
1991–1783	*Twelfth Dynasty*
1991–1962	*Amenemhat I*
1971–1926	*Senusret I*
1929–1892	*Amenemhat II*
1897–1878	*Senusret II*
1878–1841	*Senusret III*
1844–1797	*Amenemhat III*
1799–1787	*Amenemhat IV*
1787–1783	*Nefrusobk*
1783–1640	*Thirteenth Dynasty*
1640–1550	Second Intermediate Period (Fifteenth – Seventeenth Dynasties)
1555–1550	*Kamose*

1550–1070	**New Kingdom (Eighteenth – Twentieth Dynasties)**
1550–1307	*Eighteenth Dynasty*
1550–1525	*Ahmose*
1525–1504	*Amenhotep I*
1504–1492	*Thutmose I*
1492–1479	*Thutmose II*
1479–1425	*Thutmose III*
1473–1458	*Hatshepsut*
1427–1401	*Amenhotep II*
1401–1391	*Thutmose IV*
1391–1353	*Amenhotep III*
1353–1335	*Amenhotep IV/Akhenaten*
1335–1333	*Smenkhkara*
1333–1323	*Tutankhamun*
1323–1319	*Ay*
1319–1307	*Horemheb*
1307–1196	*Nineteenth Dynasty*
1307–1306	*Ramses I*
1306–1290	*Sety I*
1290–1224	*Ramses II*
1224–1214	*Merenptah*
1214–1204	*Sety II*
	Amenmessu (usurper during reign of Sety II)
1204–1198	*Saptah*
1198–1196	*Tausret*
1196–1070	*Twentieth Dynasty*
1196–1194	*Setnakht*
1194–1163	*Ramses III*
1163–1156	*Ramses IV*
1156–1151	*Ramses V*
1151–1143	*Ramses VI*
1143–1070	*Ramses VII–XI*

1070–712	**Third Intermediate Period (Twenty-First – Theban Twenty-Fifth Dynasties)**
978–959	*Saamun (Twenty-First Dynasty)*
777–749	*Osorkon III/ IV (Twenty-Third Dynasty)*
770–750	*Kashta (Theban Twenty-Fifth Dynasty)*
750–712	*Piy (Theban Twenty-Fifth Dynasty)*
712–332	**Late Period (Twenty-Fifth – Thirty-First Dynasties)**
712–657	*Twenty-Fifth Dynasty*
712–698	*Shabako*
698–690	*Shabitko*
690–664	*Taharqo*
664–657	*Tanutamani*
664–525	*Twenty-Sixth Dynasty*
664–610	*Psamtek I*
525–404	*Twenty-Seventh Dynasty (Persian)*
404–399	*Twenty-Eighth Dynasty*
399–380	*Twenty-Ninth Dynasty*
380–343	*Thirtieth Dynasty*
343–332	*Thirty-First Dynasty (Persian)*
332	**Conquest of Alexander**

Introduction

The aim of this book is to provide a study of women in ancient Egypt which is accessible to the general reader. This raises the question: why is such a book necessary? We do not, after all, find books specifically on men in ancient Egypt. Since women must have formed approximately half the population of Egypt, any book concerned with ancient Egypt should automatically be concerned with women. Why then single women out as though they formed some special group within society, as one might write about mourners, weavers, or dancers? The explanation is to be found in the political structure of ancient Egypt, which was dominated by a king, governing through an all-male bureaucracy. Thus women scarcely get a mention in political histories of Egypt, which have been the staple of Egyptological research since the discipline began last century. This did not seem odd to scholars in whose own societies the whole of public life (political, religious, military, and academic) was dominated by men, and where the affairs of men represented the norm which could be taken for granted. Women were regarded as deviating from this norm, and so were to be treated as a special case. Any study of ancient Egypt could also be assumed to be concerned with the male norm unless otherwise stated.

Prevailing attitudes are hard to change, but challenges to this domination of the male have gathered momentum during the twentieth century, giving rise to the feminist movement and to the academic discipline of women's studies. This has led to a continuing reassessment of the roles of women both in the past and today, and to a new understanding of the vital contributions they have made in the history of humankind. The present book is an attempt to extend this newly awakened interest to the parts played by women in the world of ancient Egypt.

A number of difficulties hamper this endeavour. One very fundamental problem is that, despite the wealth of source material, Egyptologists still lack a total understanding of the workings of Egyptian society, of the general functioning of government, law and the economy. It is hard to examine the place and importance of women in a system we do not fully comprehend. We can, though, draw some meaningful conclusions and the picture of women's lives which emerges is vivid and fascinating, if necessarily incomplete.

It is helpful to begin with a brief account of the main problems which arise in any study of ancient Egypt. There are two: first, the nature of the source material; second, the interests and biases of Egyptologists.

The major sources for any study of ancient Egypt divide into three main types: archaeological, textual, and representational. All three contain in-built biases and lacunae which have to be circumvented before the material can be meaningfully used. Archaeological evidence consists of the physical remains of a culture that can be retrieved through excavation. Scholars can only study what is recovered, so we begin with a gap in our knowledge left by the disappearance of perishable items. Archaeology is essentially a destructive pursuit, although in recent times an emphasis on non-destructive methods has been developing. As soon as the ground is in any way disturbed, however, evidence begins to be destroyed. To put it simplistically, the past is buried in the ground in layers which increase in age with depth, so that the lower one digs, the further back in time one goes. In the excavation of a site these layers must be peeled off one by one until the bottom is reached. The modern discipline of archaeology demands that every stage of the process is meticulously recorded so that future scholars can turn to the written report and find all the information that was revealed in the course of the excavation, since by the very act of excavating, the site itself has been irretrievably destroyed.

Unfortunately, archaeology as a scientific discipline is relatively recent, and is still developing and refining its methods. The history of archaeology began with looting and treasure hunting, and only gradually did the idea of controlled excavation develop. Thus many sites in Egypt were plundered in the last century, and the evidence that they might have yielded was destroyed. Even when Sir Flinders Petrie introduced a more scientific approach at the end of last century and the beginning of this, many of his colleagues ignored it. Slowly, Petrie's ideas took a hold, but in spite of this, much archaeological evidence has been lost, partly because the interests and questions asked about the past by each generation change, and partly because it is only in recent years that more refined archaeological techniques have been developed. So evidence now thought important was ignored or discarded in earlier decades. The vast number of small undecorated pottery sherds which turn up on most sites seemed to have no interest: now there are sophisticated methods for extracting a wide variety of information from these fragments, which can help, for example, in establishing the functions of different parts of a site. At one time animal bones were hardly rated as important finds, while the idea of taking soil samples to look for plant remains or the presence of parasites that could have been passed in human or animal faeces was unknown. Now most digs include specialists whose function is to study just these things. From them we can obtain evidence concerning animal husbandry, slaughtering practices, animal and human food supplies, parasite infestation in a population, and information concerning site function. Where excavations were conducted before such questions were even considered, this information has been lost forever.

Other gaps in our archaeological knowledge come from the geographical peculiarities of Egypt. The Delta, in the north, is a well-watered, fertile, flat area, which during much of its history formed the economic centre of the land. However, it is very poorly known archaeologically since the high water table makes excavation difficult and expensive, and access is limited by present-day occupation. A similar problem afflicts attempts to dig in the cultivated area of the Nile valley. Yet it is precisely in these agricultural areas of the Delta and the valley that ancient towns and villages were situated. Even the great southern city of Thebes, of which we seem to know so much, has only yielded knowledge about its temples and tombs; virtually nothing is known of the city's living quarters. The story is the same everywhere: there is no lack of excavations of temples and tombs but a dearth of settlement sites. The reason lies in the fact that the Egyptians built their temples and tombs at the edge of the desert, not in the cultivated area. Here, in the dry sand, it is not only easy to excavate, but the immediate rewards seem greater because of the splendour of the stone monuments unearthed, the chances of discovering rich tomb goods, and the generally good preservative properties of the sand. How much more rewarding this appears compared to digging a water-logged site with unimpressive, poorly preserved mud-brick buildings and little likelihood of precious or artistic finds. We should be grateful that occasionally, for special reasons, the Egyptians built settlements in desert terrain, for these are the only such sites to have been extensively excavated: the city of Akhenaten at Amarna, the town of Kahun, close to the entrance to the Faiyum basin, and the workmen's villages at Amarna and Deir el-Medina. Although there are good reasons for believing that these are not representative of settlements as a whole, they provide our only source of information in this area and for this reason will be referred to frequently in this book. They do not, however, fill the vast lacunae in our knowledge of settlements, and we are left knowing virtually nothing about the villages and towns where the ancient Egyptians lived their daily lives and the houses they inhabited. Since a major part of a woman's responsibility lay in the running of the house, this loss is especially grievous in any study of women.

Textual material presents a different set of problems which derive from the purposes for which the Egyptians composed their texts. First, only a tiny proportion of the population, perhaps one per cent, was literate. This group formed the scribal bureaucracy that ran the country; the rest of the population was illiterate and therefore incapable of producing textual material. Further, it is unclear whether women of the scribal class also were literate, and if so, whether all or only some of them acquired the skills of reading and writing. Certainly, in the present state of our knowledge, there is no text that can be unequivocally shown to have been penned by a woman. Therefore surviving texts have an in-built bias in that they were produced by a small elite group, predominantly if not wholly male, that was not representative of the Egyptian population as a whole.

Although writing was fundamental to Egyptian civilisation, it remained limited to specific types of use, whose purposes must be understood before texts can be properly interpreted. Monumental texts written in hieroglyphs on temple and tomb walls were usually composed according to traditional models. Their contents were made to conform to the Egyptian world-view and ideals, and so cannot be read at face value. Thus the so-called autobiographies of officials are in the main stereotypic. Their purpose is to confirm that the subject lived his life in accordance with accepted standards. Once we know this, we can expect to learn something of what these standards were but little of the life of the individual official. It is also a significant fact that similar auto-biographies were not written for women. This lack means that we have no comparable record of accepted standards of behaviour for women in society.

Non-monumental texts usually written in hieratic, or later demotic, script on papyrus or ostraka provide important information on the functioning of temple and government institutions, on legal matters, and economic affairs, but we have to remember that the selection of texts that we have is due to the chance of survival, and many more have been lost. The majority of private economic and legal documents come from the atypical workmen's village at Deir el-Medina dating to the New Kingdom. There is a dearth of comparable material from other periods and places. Very often documents survive incomplete making them difficult to understand, and we usually lack the context that would have been clear when the document was written. The same is true of the letters that have survived. They tend to be concise and assume the recipient's personal knowledge of a situation, so that the modern reader is left in the dark about their meaning.

The Egyptians did not develop a tradition of expressing personal opinions or of self-examination in their writing. Letters do not comment on political or other events. They do not give accounts of the writer's daily life, descriptions of travels, or observations of what is going on around. Nothing like a personal notebook or diary has ever been found. Neither men nor women jotted down their thoughts or a record of events at the end of the day before lying down to sleep. Thus we seldom encounter individual personality in Egypt because the Egyptians do not seem to have been concerned with perpetuating themselves as they actually were, but only as they conformed to society's ideals.

In many ways, representational material presents similar problems to written texts. It was commissioned mostly by the male scribal elite, and executed, as far as we know, by male artists. The aim in temple and funerary art was to represent the ideal, and like monumental texts, it cannot be taken at face value. Seldom did Egyptian artists simply sketch life around them as they saw it. Each piece of art was made for a particular purpose which must be understood before it can be used as evidence.

If the source material carries in-built biases, so also do the presuppositions of modern Egyptologists. However objective scholars try to be in their approach, they carry with them sets of assumptions embedded in their immediate cultural outlook, of which they may well be unaware. A book on women written before the women's movement of recent years was bound to take a different approach and ask different questions from a book written today. When the accepted ideal for a woman was that of a model wife and mother who did not go out to work or take part in public life, it is no wonder that scholars failed to notice the absence of women in public life in ancient Egypt. If in writing about women they tended to concentrate on dress, makeup and jewellery, despite the fact that all these were also worn by men, it was because those scholars were the product of a society that associated such things with women and regarded a male interest in them as unhealthy.

Another area where modern prejudice seems to have come into play relates to the issue of father-daughter marriages in the royal family. This has aroused great passions among those scholars who wish to deny that the marriages existed as real unions. However, these strenuous objections seem to arise from a modern bias based on ingrained notions of incest in our society. Consummated brother-sister marriage also breaks modern incest taboos, but its presence in the royal family of ancient Egypt has had to be accepted because of the overwhelming evidence for it. Father-daughter marriage, on the other hand, not only violates our society's definition of incest, but it also cuts across generations and raises the stereotypic image of a lascivious old man forcing himself on an innocent young girl. Many scholars, then, prefer to believe that king's daughters who are also king's wives received the title to mark the fact that they sometimes substituted for the actual king's wife in ritual functions. The marriage can then be regarded as a fiction to give rank to the king's daughters, and the distasteful idea of a consummated marriage between father and daughter can be avoided. The problem with this line of reasoning is that it is based on today's prejudices and not on evidence from ancient Egypt. We have no idea how Egyptians would have regarded sexual relationships between kings and their daughters.

Another area where ancient sources and modern scholars combine to form an opportunity for error is in the unevenness of the material, providing an inducement for scholars to read evidence backwards and forwards in time, sometimes over centuries. The history of Egypt from the First Dynasty to the conquest of Alexander in 332 BC spans nearly three millennia, and during this time Egyptian society, and the position of women within it, was not unchanging. Surviving sources, however, are not constant over this time span and different kinds of material become more or less prominent at different periods; in general, there is more evidence surviving from later than from earlier periods. This is certainly the case with material relating to the study of women. Much of it comes from the New Kingdom or later, and it is dangerous, although tempting, to read it backwards to supplement a dearth from earlier times. In addition, because the Egyptians so often did not record the sort of things we want to know, we are forced to piece together many of our hypotheses from a fragment of evidence here and a few scattered ambiguous facts there. With so little material, it is essential to avoid the temptation to extrapolate from the particular to the general, a practice which can only too easily introduce error. It is also important not to gloss over lacunae. Researching into ancient Egypt is like trying to repair a tapestry with gaping holes where much of the design is lost. From what is left some idea of the pattern may be gained, but where too much has gone to be recovered it is no good just pulling together the remaining threads to cover the hole as though nothing were missing. One can fill in a new design from one's imagination, but only at the risk of going far beyond the original. In the same way, however tempting it may be for scholars to present a coherent account of women in ancient Egypt, they must acknowledge the gaps and not try to patch them up, either by pulling together the few known facts into a story that ignores all deficiencies in the evidence or by imaginative infilling which may produce an interesting account but which has no firm basis in reality. Because of this imbalance of material over time, the present book is arranged along thematic lines rather than taking a strict chronological approach. Since so much of the available evidence comes from the New Kingdom, the text will concentrate on this period. Earlier material, however, will be introduced where it exists, as will more recent evidence from the Third Intermediate and Late Periods.

Before attempting to understand the place of women in society, it is necessary to know something about the social structure of Egypt. In the Egyptian world–view, the organisation of society was hierarchical. At the top was the divine world, itself strictly ordered but clearly ranking above humankind. The king, at the pinnacle of human society, shared certain attributes with the gods and stood as mediator between the divine and human spheres. Members of his family who, by association with the king, shared some of his separateness formed a close-knit group at the top of society. Next came the elite scribal class, consisting of the one per cent or so of the population who formed the male ruling bureaucracy of Egypt together with their family members. This tiny group was responsible for most of our source material concerning ancient Egypt. Below these were artists and craftsmen, and minor professionals who were probably illiterate. From the evidence at Deir el-Medina, it is clear that some artists were literate and that the dividing line between scribe and artist was not always clear-cut. The vast majority of the population was presumably of the peasant class, working the land to produce a surplus to feed the non-food-producing elements of society. It is likely that this vast class of peasants, to which most of the population belonged, was itself hierarchically structured. However, we know very little about this group, since its members – being illiterate – have left no records of their own. At the very bottom were slaves, including foreign captives, who could be bought and sold. The little that can be said about the lower classes has to be gleaned from the sources pertaining to the elite, who usually had no interest in recording information about their inferiors.

Thus it can be seen that any study of Egyptian society is basically a study of the elite scribal group. It follows that a study of women in ancient Egypt must almost wholly concentrate on women of this elite class, together with the women of the royal family about whom a certain amount of material survives.

Above the human world stood the divine, inhabited by male and female deities. As a construct of the human mind, the divine world is bound in some way to reflect the workings of the human world. However, the interaction between divine and human spheres was always extremely complex, for while the human originated the divine, the human world in turn modelled itself on its own construct, so that the two worlds came to reflect and interact with each other. In the Egyptian view of the universe, both the divine and the human worlds had come into being at the time of the creation, before which there was only undifferentiated matter. The act of creation took place when this matter was separated into the myriad different forms that make up the created world. In one of the major creation myths, associated with the religious centre of Heliopolis, the creator god, who was self-generated, began the process of creation by producing through masturbation the first pair of male and female deities, Shu (air) and Tefnut (moisture). Their interaction produced another pair, Geb (earth) and Nut (sky), who in their turn produced Isis and Osiris, and Nephthys and Seth. Thus the creation of the universe was begun by the interaction of the male and female principles embodied in pairs of deities. The creator god must have contained both male and female potential which then separated out into the first divine couple. Later the female aspect of the god came to be distinguished as a goddess called 'the god's hand', regarded as the instrument of masturbation. By the Eighteenth Dynasty she was identified with Hathor, the goddess of sexuality. Other myths were also used to give expression to the miracle of creation, and it is interesting that in these too the creator god, although logically combining male and female, was usually conceptualised as male.

The interactions of the male and female principles not only set the workings of the universe in motion, but were also a means of perpetual cosmic renewal. This is embodied in the concept of Kamutef 'the bull of his mother', in which the setting sun impregnates the sky goddess and is born of her again in the morning. Thus she is both the god's consort and his mother, while the god is both father and son. In this way a self-perpetuating cycle of successive generations is set up like a loop tape, by which age can be transformed into youth, and the universe constantly renewed.

The female principle was embodied in the goddesses worshipped by the Egyptians. The study of these deities is complex because even goddesses with distinct identities often merge into one another, sharing attributes, insignia, epithets, and functions. One of the major female deities was Isis, sister and consort of the god of the dead, Osiris. When Osiris was murdered by his brother Seth, Isis mourned him and searched throughout Egypt for his body. When she eventually found it, she used her great magical skills to restore Osiris to life and to conceive a son by him who would grow up to avenge his father. Isis gave birth to her child Horus in the marsh of Khemmis in the Delta where she kept him hidden from the destructive plotting of Seth and from other dangers that threatened the child, through the strength of her magic. Isis became the embodiment of motherhood and many images survive from about 1000 BC onwards showing her with her infant son. In magical spells she is frequently invoked for the protection of children. She was also an important funerary goddess, bringing the hope that she would resurrect the deceased as she had resurrected Osiris.

If Isis was the ideal wife and mother, the goddess Hathor was the embodiment of female sexuality, love, music and dance, and inebriation. She was a bringer of fertility and protected women in childbirth. Because of her close connection with fertility and childbirth, she was also a funerary goddess concerned with rebirth into the afterlife. But Hathor was not always benevolent. Together with other goddesses like Tefnut, Mut and Sakhmet, she could be identified with the angry goddess, the daughter and eye of Ra who, in a rage, left Egypt and had to be pacified and brought back by a male god. When Ra wished to destroy mankind, he sent Hathor as his eye to carry out the slaughter. Later the god changed his mind and tried to halt the destruction, but the goddess had become out of control, and only by using a trick to get her drunk could Ra make her stop.

Hathor and goddesses associated or identified with her were perceived as having a dual nature. On the one hand they were beneficent, bringing fertility and new life; on the other hand they were dangerous, bringing destruction in their wake. In their cults, part of the ritual was aimed towards pacifying their perilous side, and the sistrum, the rattle sacred to Hathor, was shaken to achieve this end. In fact, the essence of divine being, whether manifested in male or female deities, could be dangerous to humans who approached it, and the use of the sistrum as a means of control spread into other divine cults.

The duality manifested in goddesses was also reflected in the Egyptian view of human nature, where women were seen as incorporating a good and a bad side. They were honourable if they met the standards of society, but there was always the danger that they would break the rules, in which case they were dishonourable and to be condemned. Men, too, had to conform, but for them the rules were different. Since society was male-dominated, the norms were set by men for the benefit of men. For instance, these insisted on the faithfulness of married women to their male partners, but not the other way round, which was of advantage to men because only then could they be sure that they were the fathers of their wives' offspring. By contrast, women had no doubt of their motherhood, and therefore had less to gain by the arrangement.

CHAPTER ONE

Royal women and queenship

The king and kingship

Royal women in ancient Egypt derived their importance from their relationship to the king, who was always, apart from a very few exceptions, male. According to tradition, Egypt had been ruled by successive male gods after the creation, but later, in 'historical' times, human kings governed the country. However, the office of kingship remained divine, and its holder, by the very fact of occupying a divine office, was set apart from other humans and took on aspects of divinity. This transformation was effected by rituals performed at the time of a king's accession. Much of royal iconography reflects this event and provides for its continual renewal.

The office of kingship was essential to the very existence of the state of Egypt.[1] The king stood between the divine and human worlds, acting as the point of contact and mediator. In theory, he performed the rituals in the temples which were necessary to keep the universe functioning. He received the gift of life from the gods and in turn dispensed it to his subjects. In reality, temple rituals throughout the land were carried out by priests, but temple decoration always showed the king and not priests interacting directly with deities.

Just as the king was responsible to the divine world, so he was responsible for the human. He embodied the state and was ultimately liable for the government of the country through the elite scribal bureaucracy. When the world was created, the creator god had established the correct order of things, known in Egyptian as *maat*. The authority of the king sprang from the belief that he governed in accordance with *maat*.

Since kingship was intended to pass from father to son, kings married and fathered families in order to provide their successor. Within the king's immediate circle, therefore, we find a number of royal women: the king's mother, wives, and daughters. Because of the impersonal nature of the source material, we know little about these women as individuals, but we can learn something of their importance and the various roles that they played. The surviving evidence, which spans nearly three millennia from the First to the Thirty-First Dynasties, shows a number of changes over time relating to their titles and insignia and to the contexts in which the women were represented. It

1   Queen Ahmose, pregnant with Hatshepsut, is led to the birthroom. She wears the vulture headdress.

is unclear how far these represent basic changes in the way royal women were regarded, and how far they simply reflect different and developing ways of portraying the same fundamental truths. Most of what I say in this chapter will draw on evidence from the Eighteenth and Nineteenth Dynasties.

The divinity of queenship

From early times the status of royal women was defined by reference to the king through the titles 'king's mother', 'king's wife', 'king's daughter' and later also 'king's principal wife' and 'king's sister'. The question must be asked: if the king was to a certain extent divine, how did this affect the women closely associated with him? Or to put a slightly different question: if kingship was divine, was there also a concept of divine queenship?[2]

One way to approach this question is to look at the insignia worn by queens. By 'queen' I refer specifically to the 'king's mother' and 'king's principal wife'. King's daughters may have been potential queens, but they do not share the common iconography and titularies of king's mothers and principal wives.

One of the oldest items of queenly insignia is the vulture headdress, a close-fitting cap formed from the body of a vulture with the two wings of the bird spread against the sides of the wearer's head, while the head of the vulture juts forward from the wearer's forehead (fig. 1). The uraeus (royal cobra) could be substituted for the vulture head (fig. 2). The headdress is known from the Old Kingdom. It was originally worn by the vulture goddess Nekhbet, protectress of Upper Egypt, when she appeared in human rather than vulture form. Nekhbet was paired with Wadjyt, the cobra goddess of Lower Egypt, and by analogy, when Wadjyt appeared in human form she adopted the vulture headdress of Nekhbet, only substituting a uraeus for the vulture head. Later the vulture headdress became used by other goddesses too. From the Fifth Dynasty it was also depicted as an item of queenly insignia, and from then on it was worn by queens throughout pharaonic history. Since it originated as a divine crown and continued to be used by female deities, the fact that it was also transferred to queens suggests that it may have marked a divine aspect of queenship.

In addition to substituting the uraeus for the vulture head when they wore the vulture headdress, queens could also wear the uraeus alone (fig. 3), although this does not seem to have become common until the Middle Kingdom. The uraeus had wide associations, of which one of the most basic was with the cobra goddess Wadjyt mentioned above. Like the vulture headdress, the uraeus was also taken over by other goddesses. The uraeus was also associated with the sun god Ra, and with the goddess Hathor as the eye of Ra, which through its fierce aggression protected the king and the gods against their enemies. In addition, the uraeus was the most characteristic mark of the king. Thus the use of the uraeus by the queen may have carried a range of meanings. It could have derived partly through her connection with the king and thus be a mark of her 'royalty'. But it could also have carried references to Wadjyt and other female deities on the one hand, and to solar mythology on the other, linking the queen with Hathor as the daughter and eye of Ra. From the late Eighteenth Dynasty, the uraeus might be decorated with the cow horns and solar disk of Hathor (fig. 4), thus strengthening the Hathoric connection.

In the Eighteenth Dynasty, queens began to wear two uraei side by side, a combination usually called the double uraeus (figs. 5, 12). Evidence suggests that it referred to the two goddesses Nekhbet and Wadjyt, and thus to Upper and Lower Egypt, and this is confirmed by the fact that one snake sometimes wears the white crown of Upper Egypt and the other the red crown of Lower Egypt. Like the single uraeus, the double uraeus also possessed a solar connection through identification with the eyes of Ra, and the two snakes were often decorated with the Hathoric horns and sun disk instead of the two crowns. The double uraeus was not limited to queens but was worn by goddesses too. From the later Eighteenth Dynasty on, increasingly elaborate combinations developed between the vulture headdress, the vulture head, and the single or double uraeus (fig. 6). This probably reflected a general stylistic elaboration in iconographic elements; the range of meaning represented by the insignia probably stayed much the same.

From the Thirteenth Dynasty onwards, queens appear wearing a pair of straight falcon plumes mounted on a circular support resting on the head (fig. 5). The origin of the queen's double feathers is unclear. They were not worn by goddesses at that time, but similar feathers were characteristic of male falcon gods, and of the male fertility god Min and the male Theban god Amun. In the *Book of the Dead* dating from the New Kingdom, the double feathers are identified with the double uraeus. They are also mentioned in connection with Ra, and an Eighteenth Dynasty sun hymn identifies them with the eyes of Ra. Although the associations of the feathers are with male deities, their solar connections, especially with the double uraeus and eyes of Ra, bring them into the same sphere of reference as the uraeus and double uraeus worn by the queen. In addition, the goddess Hathor wears a pair of curved ostrich feathers. While these were always carefully distinguished inconographically from the double falcon feathers worn by male gods and queens, the Egyptian term 'double feathers' (*shuty*) was applied to both types of paired feathers. The Egyptians may thus have seen a connection between Hathor's ostrich feathers and the queen's falcon ones, since their names were the same. This is made more plausible by the fact that in the reign of Amenhotep III of the Eighteenth Dynasty, queens began to wear Hathor's cow horns and sun disk in combination with the double falcon feathers (fig. 7), just as Hathor frequently combined them with her paired ostrich feathers.

From the Old Kingdom onwards, there are representations in which a queen holds the *ankh* sign (the sign of life; fig. 5). This is not, of course, a special mark of the queen, and the *ankh* is more commonly held by deities and kings. It is, by

2 Block showing part of a scene in which Hatshepsut, wearing the insignia of a queen, offers to a deity. She is followed by a female figure almost certainly to be identified as her daughter Neferura.

contrast, only very occasionally held by private people.[3] When the queen carries an *ankh*, it is usually in contexts where she is in some way associated or identified with a goddess, or where she is shown in relation to private people to whom she was superior, rather than to deities who were superior to her, or in cult or funerary contexts where she is represented as dead. The *ankh* may have been used to place the bearer outside the human sphere.

To sum up, the items of queenly insignia just discussed are all items with a divine origin that were transferred to a royal context to become attributes of queenship. Their use shows that just as kingship was divine, there must have been a notion of divine queenship extending back to the Old Kingdom, which continued to be a vital part of royal ideology throughout the ages.

The 'heiress' theory

For over a century scholars have been reiterating the belief that the right to the throne of ancient Egypt was transmitted through the female line of the royal family in direct descent from one 'heiress' to the next. Thus, any king, whether or not he was the son of his predecessor, had to legitimise his claim to the throne by marriage with the 'heiress', who would be the daughter of the previous king and his 'heiress' queen. This meant that in most cases a king had to marry his sister or half-sister. Although the right to the throne, according to this hypothesis, descended through the female line, the office of kingship was not exercised by the 'heiress' but by the man she married.

If this theory were correct, each king would have had to marry a woman of royal birth, and it should be possible to trace a line of royal women in direct descent from one another. A study of the situation in the Eighteenth Dynasty, the period in connection with which this theory is most often cited, shows that such a line of descent simply did not exist.[4] Women of royal birth can be identified by the use of the title 'king's daughter', since there is no evidence in the Eighteenth Dynasty of women who are known to have had non-royal parents being given this title. This rules out the possibility that the title was sometimes awarded to enhance the status of non-royal women. Among the queens of the Eighteenth Dynasty, some bear the title 'king's daughter' while others do not. Although filiation is rarely given for queens, in cases where we

3   The 'Donation' Stela of king Ahmose showing the king and his queen Ahmose Nefertari with their son before the god Amun-Ra.

find queens filiated to non-royal parents, those queens are not attested with the title 'king's daughter'. Thus we can undoubtedly distinguish between queens of royal and non-royal birth, and it becomes clear that there was no line of 'heiresses' in unbroken descent. By way of refutation, it is enough to point out that the principal wives of Thutmose III, Amenhotep II and Amenhotep III were all of non-royal origins.

There is no doubt, however, that some kings did marry their sisters or half-sisters and had children by them, and the 'heiress' theory was developed partly in an attempt to explain a form of marriage which scholars regarded as incestuous. In fact, there is nothing within Egyptian texts to suggest that there was such a thing as an 'heiress'. The mythological basis for kingship that had developed to underpin the king's authority is not predicated on legitimisation through an 'heiress'. Instead we must look for the explanation of brother-sister marriage elsewhere. Such marriages seem to have been rare among non-royal Egyptians, but as we have already seen in the Introduction, they occur among deities. At the time of creation, the creator god produced a pair of offspring who in turn produced a second divine couple and so on, the most famous being Osiris and his sister-consort Isis. So at the time of creation, choice of partner was perforce limited to brother or sister. By marrying his sister, the king set himself apart from his subjects who did not normally marry their sisters. By imitating the gods, he stressed the divine side of kingship.

The origins of king's wives of non-royal birth

Nothing in the surviving evidence gives us a hint as to how the king chose the woman who was to be his principal wife. Nor is there anything to show that when a king chose a principal wife of non-royal birth, it was because he had no surviving sister to marry. By the New Kingdom, Egyptian kings were polygamous. They may well have been so earlier, but this is disputed by some scholars. However, in the Thirteenth Dynasty we find for the first time the title 'king's principal wife' in addition to the simple 'king's wife', suggesting that one woman is now being singled out from a number of wives. In the Eighteenth Dynasty, we have seen that king's principal wives divided into those who were of royal birth and those who had been born to non-royal parents. In the case of the latter women we know extremely little about their origins, often only recognising them by their lack of the title 'king's daughter'. However, Satioh, the first principal wife of Thutmose III, is filiated on a monument to a woman who was a royal nurse. She had almost certainly been concerned with the upbringing of Thutmose III, as she has the additional title 'one who raised the god', the term 'god' referring to the king. The same king's second principal wife can be deduced to have been the daughter of a woman who held the priestly title of 'adoratrice of the god'. Finally, the parents of Amenhotep III's consort Tiy stand out by the frequency of their mention in certain royal texts and by the discovery of their tomb in the Valley of the Kings. Tiy's father Yuya had titles connecting him with the chariotry and can be presumed to have had a career in the army. It is not clear whether his wife Tjuyu held her various high-ranking titles before the marriage of her daughter to the king or as a direct result of it.

Unfortunately, this information does not help us understand how these queens were selected, although one can conjecture that Thutmose III may have known the daughter of his nurse from childhood. It does, however, lead us to ask what effect such a choice of queen had on the families from whom these women came. Again this is hard to answer because we have no monuments belonging to officials where they claim a relationship with a queen or indeed with any other royal woman. We do, however, know that queen Tiy had a brother called Anen, because an inscription in the tomb of Tiy's parents, Yuya and Tjuyu, names Anen as the son of Tjuyu. Now Anen has left a number of monuments of his own, from which we know he was second priest of Amun at Thebes, second only in the priestly hierarchy to the chief priest himself. It is tempting to see Anen's elevation to high office as a result of his connection with the king through his sister. On none of his monuments, however, does he mention his relationship to queen Tiy, which suggests that it was not done for officials to claim such relationships. This does not mean to say that these links to the king were not important to an official's career or perhaps to the fortunes of whole families. Behind the official record of one king smoothly succeeding his predecessor, there may have been much manoeuvring to get a female relative accepted as a sexual partner for the king (and above all named as 'king's principal wife') and to have her son named as heir.

There is an instructive model to be found in China during the Western Han (206 BC–AD 8). Like the Egyptian king, the Chinese emperor stood at the head of the government which was run by a bureaucracy staffed by men who had received a formal education. Officials were promoted by the emperor within the system to the highest offices and were totally dependent on the emperor for their positions. However, in the struggle among the various educated families, whose members were thus eligible for office, there was no surer way to achieve and consolidate power than to have a close relative proclaimed empress, although to have a sister or a daughter as a favourite concubine could also be quite efficacious. The family of an empress and its clients were usually able to monopolise the best offices, but if the empress died or was disgraced, the downfall of her relations usually followed swiftly as their enemies lost no time in demolishing them, while the faction of the new empress rose to power. In fact, an innocent empress ran the risk of being falsely denounced for ill conduct simply to cause the destruction of her family. Often the emperor, for all his supreme position, was incapable of controlling these machinations.[5] It is possible that in Egypt, too, male officials related to queens and other king's wives hoped to exploit this relationship in terms of influence with the king, and to obtain investiture in high office. If a king's mother and his principal wife were both of non-royal birth, it is even possible that the interests of the king's maternal relations might come into conflict with those of his principal wife's family. In fact, one practical advantage of brother-sister marriage on the part of the king would have been to avoid encouraging the ambitions of official families, although this is unlikely to have been the origin of the practice.

Father-daughter marriage

In addition to kings who married their sisters, there were some who married their daughters. Amenhotep III's daughter Satamun is well-attested as 'king's wife' and even 'king's principal wife'. She is known to have been the daughter of the king and of his principal wife Tiy, and sometimes all three of them are named together. Kings did not normally have more than one principal wife at a time, but Satamun is sometimes given this title although we know her mother was still alive. It is noteworthy, however, that where her name appears alongside that of her mother, she is called only 'king's wife', whereas the title 'king's principal wife' is reserved for occasions when her mother's name is not present.

The evidence for the existence of father-daughter marriages in the reign of the succeeding king, Akhenaten, is hotly disputed.[6] Two of the king's daughters, Meretaten and Ankhesenpaaten, appear as the mothers of king's daughters called Meretaten junior and Ankhesenpaaten junior respectively. A third daughter, Meketaten, probably died in childbirth. Unfortunately the paternity of the children is nowhere stated. It is tempting to assume that the title 'king's daughter' must mean that they are daughters of a king and thus Akhenaten, but there is some evidence that the daughter of a king's son could also be called 'king's daughter'.[7] Akhenaten, therefore, would not have to be the father of the junior princesses, although whether he had sons old enough to have fathered these children is a moot point. However, none of the three princesses who seem to have borne children have the title 'king's wife'. Later, towards the end of her father's reign, Meretaten became 'king's principal wife', but this was well after the birth of Meretaten junior. There are too many gaps in our sources to determine whether or not Akhenaten fathered his daughters' children.[8]

In the next dynasty, three daughters of Ramses II, Bint-Anath, Meritamun and Nebettawy, became king's principal wives.[9] Bint-Anath in particular is well-attested on monuments and, like Satamun, sometimes appears alongside her mother, the king's then principal wife Asetnefret. In Bint-Anath's tomb, one scene shows her followed by the figure of a king's daughter. Since Bint-Anath is known to have been her father's consort by the middle of his reign, it is unlikely that anyone other than Ramses could have been the accepted father of this child, for he would surely have allowed no other male access to his wives. After her father's death at the end of his sixty-four year reign, Bint-Anath was almost certainly too old to bear children by the next king, her brother Merenptah. The existence of Bint-Anath's daughter makes it harder to argue that the title of 'king's wife' or 'king's principal wife' was only given as a ranking title to king's daughters who substituted in the role for their mothers and were thus not involved in a consummated marriage.

Diplomatic marriages of the king

In addition to marrying women of Egyptian origins, some kings of the Eighteenth and Nineteenth Dynasties also married foreign princesses in order to cement diplomatic alliances.[10] Earlier this century a tomb belonging to three wives of Thutmose III was illicitly plundered and the contents put on the market.[11] The names of the women (Menhet, Mertit, and Menway) are non-Egyptian and point to origins for the women somewhere in Syria-Palestine. Thus, they could have been daughters of Syrian rulers married for diplomatic reasons to the king of Egypt. It is curious that they were buried in the same tomb with similar sets of funerary equipment, but it is possible that they died at the same time, perhaps as the result of an epidemic in the palace. All three of them bear the title 'king's wife', but there is no filiation that would give a clue to their origins.

Egyptian diplomatic marriages seem to have been of two types. In one the father of the bride was of equal status with the king of Egypt, and the two rulers addressed each other as 'brother'; in the other, the father of the bride was a vassal of the Egyptian king whom he addressed as 'my lord, my god, my sungod'. The annals of Thutmose III record that in year 24 of his reign after a military campaign in the area, tribute from the land of Retjenu included 'the daughter of a chief, together with her ornaments of gold and lapis lazuli of her land, and the retainers belonging to her, male and female slaves, thirty of them'.[12] The word for chief (*mer*) was the one normally used by Egyptians to refer to foreign rulers, so it seems likely that the daughter of a defeated ruler was being sent to Egypt as a sign of submission on the part of her father.

Much of our knowledge of diplomatic marriages comes from the so-called Amarna letters. These consist of some of the correspondence between Amenhotep III and his son Akhenaten on the one hand and Near Eastern rulers on the other. They are not written in Egyptian script on papyrus, but in cuneiform on clay tablets, mostly in the international diplomatic language of Akkadian but occasionally in some other language. In one of these letters an Egyptian king wrote to a Syrian ruler: 'Send your daughter to the king, your lord, and as presents send twenty healthy slaves, silver chariots, and healthy horses.'[13] The ruler presumably had to comply or be regarded as defying Egypt. Another foreign ruler writes to the king: 'And see, I have sent my daughter to the court, to the king, my lord, my god, my sungod'.[14] Thus a number of foreign women, daughters of rulers, could have arrived in Egypt as a sign of their fathers' submission to Egypt and as guarantors of the fathers' loyalty.

During the time of the Amarna correspondence, Egypt was one of the great powers of the ancient Near East, controlling vast territories to her south in the

4 Scene in the tomb of Kheruef showing Amenhotep III accompanied by queen Tiy at the *sed*-festival.

gold-producing lands of Nubia, and to her north in Palestine and the southern part of Syria. She stood on an equal footing with the kingdoms of Babylon in Mesopotamia and of Mitanni situated in the great northern bend of the Euphrates, and she made treaties and marriage alliances with both of them. Egypt and Mitanni had been at war for decades, but peace was made in the reign of Thutmose IV, and one of the Amarna letters tells us that the Egyptian king married a daughter of Artatama, king of Mitanni.[15] When Thutmose died, his son Amenhotep III reconfirmed the alliance by marrying Gilukhepa, the daughter of the next Mitannian king, Shuttarna. Amenhotep ruled for thirty-eight years, and some time towards the end of his reign, Shuttarna died and was succeeded by Tushratta. Immediately Amenhotep wrote to the new king asking for his daughter in marriage. Exactly the same thing happened in Amenhotep's marriage relations with Babylon. In the first part of his reign, he married the daughter of Kurigalzu II of Babylon and then later he requested the daughter of Kurigalzu's successor, Kadashman Enlil I. It seems as though these marriage alliances were made not between two states but between two individual rulers, so that when one ruler died, the connection had to be re-established through another marriage. This may explain why, when Amenhotep III died, his son Akhenaten married Tadukhepa, the Mitannian princess who had come to Egypt two years before as the wife of Amenhotep III.

Akhenaten, in addition, renewed the alliance with Babylon by marrying the daughter of Burnaburiash II, Kadashman Enlil's successor. Amenhotep III had also made a marriage alliance with Tarkhundaradu, ruler of the state of Arzawa in Anatolia, but there is no surviving evidence to show whether it was renewed under Akhenaten.

Between the reigns of Akhenaten and Ramses II we hear little of diplomatic marriages between Egyptian kings and foreign princesses. This is not to say that they did not occur, for it may only be that documentation is lacking. Hittite texts do, in fact, tell us that a queen of Egypt, (usually identified with Ankhesenamun, the widow of Tutankhamun) wrote to the Hittite king asking for one of his sons as her husband. The son was eventually dispatched to Egypt, but was murdered *en route* and never arrived.[16]

In the reign of Ramses II, we learn of marriages to a daughter of the king of Babylon and a daughter of a North Syrian ruler. Ramses' most famous diplomatic marriages, however, were to two Hittite princesses. One of these took place in year 34 of his reign in order to seal the peace made between Ramses and Hattusilis, king of the Hittites, after decades of hostilities. When the other marriage occurred is unknown, although it was clearly later in the reign than the first. It is possible that the first princess had died, and the alliance had to be reconfirmed by a new marriage.[17]

Although we know little about the forms of marriage within Egyptian society, we can glean from different texts a surprisingly homogeneous account of what validated a diplomatic marriage. Three things seem to have been necessary: the bride's father had to send a rich dowry with his daughter; the prospective husband had to return an equally rich bride price; and oil was poured on the bride's head, presumably in a ritual anointing that marked the actual marriage ceremony.

During the reign of Amenhotep III, Egypt was probably the most powerful state in the Near East. In answer to a request for an Egyptian bride from a Babylonian king, Amenhotep makes it quite clear that 'from old, the daughter of an Egyptian king has not been given in marriage to anyone'.[18] In a form of one-upmanship, the kings of Egypt maintained their superiority by accepting the daughters of foreign rulers as wives but refusing to give the rulers their own daughters in return. After the end of the New Kingdom, an Egyptian king, probably Satamun of the Twenty-First Dynasty, gave a daughter in marriage to King Solomon of Israel, but Egypt by then was no longer the great international power that it had been.

Much of our knowledge concerning diplomatic marriages comes from non-Egyptian sources like Hittite texts, and like the Amarna letters, which are non-Egyptian in that they accord with Near Eastern diplomatic conventions rather than with the Egyptian world-view. When references to similar marriages occur in Egyptian sources, they are represented in a totally different way. What were in fact negotiated marriages between rulers of equal status are

5 Scene in the tomb of Kheruef showing Amenhotep III accompanied by queen Tiy seated in a kiosk giving audience to the tomb owner.

described in terms of presentation of tribute.[19] In the first decade of his reign Amenhotep III issued a series of commemorative scarabs with texts recording various of his achievements. Included in these was his marriage to Gilukhepa, the Mitannian princess: 'Year 10 under the majesty of . . . the king of Upper and Lower Egypt, lord of ritual, Nebmaatra chosen of Ra, son of Ra, Amenhotep ruler of Thebes, given life, and the king's principal wife Tiy, may she live . . . The wonders which were brought to his majesty, life, prosperity, health: the daughter of Shuttarna, the king of Naharin (Mitanni), Gilukhepa, and the chief women of her entourage, three hundred and seventeen women.'[20] Here there is no negotiation or exchange of bride price and dowry, nor even any mention of marriage. Gilukhepa was 'brought' and the verb 'to bring' (*ini*) was frequently used in ancient Egyptian with the meaning of bringing booty or tribute. In Egypt, then, Amenhotep's marriage with Gilukhepa was expressed as though she were an item of tribute or booty brought from Mitanni to the king of Egypt.

This formulation is made even clearer in the Egyptian sources concerning the two Hittite marriages of Ramses II. According to these, the first marriage took place because Egyptian armies had ravaged the land of Hatti where the Hittites lived. 'Now after they saw their land in this miserable state under the great power of the lord of the Two Lands, then the great prince of Hatti said to his soldiers and his courtiers: "Now see this! Our land is devastated . . . Let us strip ourselves of all our possessions, and with my oldest daughter in front of them, let us carry peace offerings to the Good God [i.e. the king of Egypt], that he may give us peace, that we may live" . . . Then he caused his oldest daughter to be brought, the costly tribute before her consisting of gold and silver, many great ores, innumerable horses, cattle, sheep and goats...' Eventually this great procession reached Egypt and the daughter of the Hittite king 'was led into the presence of his majesty, with the very great tribute behind her . . . She was given the name Maathorneferura, may she live . . . and caused to reside in the palace of the king's house.' The second marriage is described in a similar style except that the princess is called the 'other daughter' of the Hittite king.[21]

We can contrast these accounts with a letter written by Ramses to the Hittite queen, Pudukhepa: 'See, the great king, the king of Hatti, my brother, has written to me, saying: "Have people come to pour good, fine oil upon the head of my daughter, and let her be brought into the house of the great king, the king of Egypt".'[22] To the Egyptians, Egypt was the centre of the world and all foreigners were theoretically subject to her. Any goods coming into Egypt, whether as gifts or trade, were represented on the monuments as tribute signifying submission to the king of Egypt. Clearly, meaningful diplomatic relations could not have been sustained with foreign states if Egyptian kings had insisted on conducting them according to these premises. In reality, in their dealings with foreign rulers, they adopted the diplomatic forms that had long been established in the ancient Near East, but at home, they cast events into a form that fitted into their own ideological framework.

For the most part diplomatic negotiations were conducted by male ambassadors between male kings except for the occasional participation of a royal woman, like the Hittite queen Pudukhepa to whom Ramses II wrote, and Ramses' queen Nefertari who sent greetings of her own to Pudukhepa. On the whole, though, women had little active part to play in diplomatic negotiations; they were important only in that they provided through marriage the means to cement international alliances. But what happened to all these foreign women once they arrived in Egypt, having left behind everything with which they were familiar and come to a country with an unknown language and strange customs? The answer is that we have very little idea. The three wives of Thutmose III, Mertit, Menway and Menhet, received an honourable Egyptian-style burial, but of their life before that we know nothing. Kadashman Enlil of Babylon wrote an extraordinary letter to Amenhotep III questioning the fate of his sister who had been sent to Egypt years before. While the letter no longer survives, Amenhotep quoted some of it in his reply. The Babylonian king had written: 'Indeed, you want my daughter to be a bride for you even while my sister, whom my father gave you, is there with you, although no one has seen her now or knows whether she is alive or dead.'[23] Amenhotep replies that none of the people sent by Kadashman Enlil to Egypt had ever known the princess, so how would they be able to recognise her? He suggests that someone who did know her should be sent to speak with her, which implies that she was still alive. The impression given is that the Babylonian princess had become a fairly obscure figure.

By contrast, when Ramses II married the first Hittite princess she was given an Egyptian name, Maathorneferura, and made 'king's principal wife'. As far as we know, no other foreign princess achieved this. It is possible that the Hittite king had insisted on this rank as part of the marriage agreement. When the Hittite king Shuppiluliumash had earlier given his daughter in marriage to one of the kings of Mitanni, part of the contract ran: 'You shall not bring my daughter into the position of a second wife. In Mitanni she shall rule as queen.'[24] Perhaps Hattusilis made the same stipulation to Ramses II.

It is clear, however, that the case of Maathorneferura was an exception, and that we shall never know much about these foreign wives of Egyptian kings. In fact, we have no idea how many such marriages any one king might enter into. Two of Ramses II's foreign wives are known purely from a chance reference in a Hittite source and go unmentioned in Egyptian texts. We cannot, then, rule out the possibility that he and other kings made diplomatic marriages of which no record survives. While Egypt was at the height of her imperial power, there must have been many minor rulers who saw an advantage in having an alliance with her, while others may have been compelled to send daughters as part of the tribute Egypt demanded. What did the king do with all these women? In addition to the royal brides there were the women who made up their entourages. Gilukhepa, for instance, brought more than three hundred with her. Further, subject rulers sometimes sent batches of non-royal women as gifts to the king as part of their tribute. Abdikheba of Jerusalem records in one Amarna letter: 'I gave 21 maidens ... as a gift for the king my lord', while another city ruler writes: 'Indeed, I have paid very close heed to the word of the king, my lord, and, indeed, I have given 500 cattle and 20 maidens'.[25]

All these women had to be housed, clothed and fed. While some may have had sexual relations with the king, many may never even have seen him. It is probable that rather than being allowed to sit idle, they were put to productive work. We know that Maathorneferura lived in a palace at Miwer, modern Medinet el-Ghurab in the Faiyum. Documents suggest that the establishment was involved in the production of cloth and that many of the personnel were foreigners.[26] Spinning and weaving had been one craft in which women had worked since the Old Kingdom, and it seems likely that some of this influx of women was channelled into textile production. Others may have been assigned household duties within the various palaces that the king had throughout Egypt.

The lot of many of these women may not have been pleasant. In a strange society, far from their families, perhaps not proficient in the language, they would have had no natural protector against exploitation and abuse. A minor ruler subject to Egypt could hardly question the king's treatment of his daughter or sister. So long as powerful rulers sent greetings and gifts to their daughters and their ambassadors enquired after the women, they would have had to be well-treated or risk an international incident. However, once outside concern for their well-being was lost, their position was potentially vulnerable. In fact, such women were little more than commodities to be traded for peace and an alliance. They had no say in their fate, and yet they became important cogs in the workings of the international diplomatic system: while the system was run by men, the women were needed to make it work.

Royal children and the succession

Since kings had a plurality of wives, we might expect them to have had a large number of children. In fact there is little sign of this until the reign of Ramses II, when that king departed from previous custom and depicted long processions of his children in various temples throughout Egypt and Nubia. In addition, royal sons appear in their father's battle scenes, taking part in campaigns and bringing in prisoners. In keeping with earlier traditions, a few of the king's daughters are shown with him on royal monuments. Altogether more than a hundred children are associated with Ramses II.[27] Most of them are known only from the processions, and we have no idea who their mothers were. The royal daughters who appear elsewhere with the king are children either of Nefertari, Ramses' first principal wife, or of Asetnefret, his second. In addition to the children who survived long enough to be attested on monuments, there must have been others who were stillborn or died in infancy. Clearly, two women could not have produced so many children between them. We know that Ramses was also married to his sister Henutmira, three of his daughters, two Hittite princesses, a Syrian princess and a Babylonian one, and it is likely that there were still more royal wives whose names are today totally unknown. It is strange that while secondary royal wives must have been given burials, as in the case of Mertit, Menhet and Menway in the reign of Thutmose III, we have hardly any evidence for them.

In the Eighteenth Dynasty, we know that kings made multiple marriages but, in contrast to the children of Ramses II, very few royal offspring for each king are known. In general they are not shown in temples or on royal monuments. Most are known from private monuments belonging to their nurses, tutors, or other officials, and from some funerary objects. Some king's daughters are better known because they married the king, their brother, and became his principal wife. A few princesses who are not attested as principal wife appear with the king in ritual scenes. The best known is Neferura, who is depicted with her mother Hatshepsut after she had claimed the titles of king. Two daughters of Thutmose III accompany their father in a temple offering scene, and the daughters of Amenhotep III are shown with that king in various *sed* festival scenes relating to his ritual renewal in the kingship.

A unique series of royal children of the Eighteenth Dynasty is known from mummy labels found in a Theban tomb, which were written in the Twenty-

6   Colossal statue
of Amenhotep III
and queen Tiy.
The queen wears a
vulture headdress
with a vulture
head between two
uraei.

First Dynasty at the time of their owners' reburial after their original tombs
had been plundered.[28] Most are totally unknown from elsewhere, a circum-
stance which underlines the paucity of our information about royal offspring.
It is likely that many royal children have left no record of their existence.

When a royal child was born, its sex would immediately determine the
child's place in life. A son was a potential heir to the throne who needed to be
given an upbringing appropriate to a possible future king. A daughter had no
kingly expectations because Egyptian tradition did not accept female kings;
that a woman very occasionally succeeded in gaining the throne did not mean
that this was a normal option for royal daughters. Daughters were, however,
potential queens, and with the king's mother and king's principal wife they
formed a triad of mother, consort and daughter which was a reflection of a
similar triad combined within the person of the goddess Hathor in her relationship with the sun god Ra. It was this close connection between the royal
women that allowed king's daughters occasionally to appear with their fathers
in ritual scenes where normally one would expect the king's mother or wife.

King's sons, by contrast, had no ritual role during the reigns of their fathers
and are unattested from the reigns of their brothers. This is because although

every son was a potential heir, there was in the mythology of kingship only one heir. Egyptian kingship was deeply rooted in the myth of Osiris and his son, Horus, in which Horus claims the kingship as the son of Osiris; the living king of Egypt was identified as Horus and his dead predecessor as Osiris. So on this level, the throne always passed from Osiris to Horus, and this was the official view perpetuated on monuments, where we see only an endless succession of kings with no place for other king's sons who failed to win the throne. In the myth of the divine birth of the king, the god Amun-Ra impregnates the king's mother and so fathers the king. Of course, no one would know that this had happened until a king had ascended the throne, when it followed that he was the one fathered by the god. Here, too, there was no ritual role for a multiplicity of sons.

Officially, there was little scope for women to play a part in the succession to the throne. However, we should not confuse the official framework within which the mechanics of the succession functioned with the ability of an individual to affect the working of the system unofficially. A powerful king's mother, king's consort, or even king's favourite might have found a way to influence the choice of heir. There is also evidence that royal women sometimes went outside lawful processes and conspired to alter the legitimate succession.

The best-known of such cases, recorded in hieratic on a papyrus now in the Egyptian Museum in Turin, occurred in the reign of Ramses III.[29] The document is concerned with the trial of a group of people caught out in a plot 'to stir up enmity in order to make rebellion against their lord [i.e. the king].' The conspiracy seems to have been hatched between a royal woman called Tiy, her son, other palace women, and a small group of palace officials. Others, mainly with duties in the 'harim', were drawn into the plot. In addition, some outside the palace, including a commander of the army and an overseer of priests of Sekhmet, became involved; a captain of archers of Nubia is specifically mentioned as having been brought into the plot by his sister, who was in the 'harim'. Although it is never explicitly stated, we can deduce that the aim of the conspiracy was to assassinate Ramses III and put Tiy's son on the throne instead of the rightful heir. If this move had been successful, Tiy would have gained the position of king's mother, and all the supporters of the plot would presumably have been well-rewarded by a grateful king. In the event, the unfortunate prince had to commit suicide. Some of the other plotters were also allowed to take their own lives, but for most of them we are simply told for each one that the examining officials 'caused his punishment to overtake him'. Nothing in the document mentions a trial for Tiy or the other palace women, nor what their punishment was.

From the Middle Kingdom there comes evidence of an attempt on the life of Amenemhat I, founder of the Twelfth Dynasty; scholars dispute whether it was successful or not. An account of the affair is given in a text known as the

'*Teaching of Amenemhat I*'. The document was actually written in the reign of his successor Senusret I, but it is cast in the form of an address from the dead Amenemhat I to his son. In his teaching, Amenemhat warns Senusret against treachery from all quarters, and goes on to describe the attack on his life: 'It was after supper, when night had fallen, and I had spent an hour of happiness. I was asleep upon my bed having become weary, and my heart had begun to follow sleep . . . As I came to, I awoke to fighting, and I found it was an attack of the bodyguard . . . Had any woman previously raised troops? Is tumult raised in the residence? . . .'[30] The attack clearly came from within the palace and the question 'Had any woman previously raised troops?' suggests that the conspiracy may have involved one or more of the royal women.

In the Old Kingdom, the autobiography of an official includes information that he presided over the secret trial of a queen of Pepy I.[31] While we are never told what her crime was, it was plainly serious, and she may have been caught conspiring against the king. We cannot, however, rule out other possibilities, such as adultery.

The institution of the 'harim'

Important queens had their own establishments, endowed with estates, and administered by male officials. A favourite wife might also be given estates in her own name. Most royal women, however, were housed in one of several 'harims' situated in Memphis, Thebes, and Medinet el-Ghurab located at the entrance to the Faiyum.[32] Each 'harim' was an independent institution on a level with the households of the king, of his mother, and of his principal wife. The establishments were endowed with lands and cattle, and administered by a network of male officials. Fragmentary administrative documents record amounts of grain, oil and fish delivered as provisions to the 'harim' at Medinet el-Ghurab. Other texts suggest that the women were involved in producing textiles, so that they would contribute to, and perhaps even cover, the cost of their upkeep.

The 'harim' at Medinet el-Ghurab was founded in the reign of Thutmose III. It was not an adjunct to a palace of the king, but was an independent establishment, where royal women and their attendants were housed. We have already seen that the Hittite queen of Ramses II, Maathorneferura, became a resident here. It is not clear whether the king would visit periodically, or whether it was where he sent surplus women or those of whom he was tired. It can be assumed that the royal children were brought up in the various 'harims', and the tomb of a Ramesside prince, who had died in his twenties, was found in one of the large cemeteries near Medinet el-Ghurab, which provided the final resting places of the inhabitants.

Documents also record an institution called the 'household of the royal children'. It is unclear whether this was a part of the 'harim', or comprised a separate administrative unit of its own. Nothing is known of the lives of the

7   Statuette of queen Tiy wearing the double feathers together with the horns and disk.

majority of royal offspring. Did they live in the 'harim' or 'the household of the royal children' until they died? Were they allowed to marry, and if so, who might their partners have been? Evidence exists showing that some of Ramses II's sons married and produced children during their father's lifetime. It is extraordinary that despite the vast number of Ramses' children, within two generations of his death, there was a crisis in the succession and the dynasty ended after the brief rule of a woman.

The ritual role of the king's mother and king's principal wife

Of all the royal women, the most important were the king's mother and king's principal wife. Although we can say little about them as individuals, we have already seen that the evidence suggests that these women held a position that was to some extent divine. Ritually, they were the most important of the royal women, and they were singled out from the rest by their insignia, titles, and the contexts in which they were depicted. Because there is virtually no distinction made between the two women, they can both be referred to as queens.

Queens most frequently appear in scenes in temples or on royal stelae, following the king who performs a ritual action. Since the presence of the king in temple scenes does not refer to specific occasions, the presence of a queen is unlikely to refer to a particular event either. However, it demonstrates that queens could be depicted in a ritual context, which may reflect a real ritual role. Normally queens are inactive in these scenes, but they may offer to a deity or shake a sistrum. It is possible that a queen actually took part in some rituals when the king performed them in the temple himself, which was probably rarely.

Scenes showing the divine birth of the king are of a different character from other temple scenes. First, they claim to represent a specific occasion when the king's mother conceived the king through impregnation by the god Amun-Ra. In fact, their reality lies on a mythological not a mundane level. Second, the queen achieves direct contact with the gods without the mediation of the king, which rarely happens elsewhere. Two complete birth cycles survive from the Eighteenth Dynasty together with fragments of others from later periods.[33] In them the king's mother is visited by the god Amun-Ra, who is said to take on the form of her royal husband, and she conceives and later gives birth to the heir to the throne. The whole birth cycle can only be depicted retrospectively, since no one knew for certain until he came to the throne who the next king would be. Once the king was crowned, it followed that his mother had been visited by the god and that the king was the son of Amun-Ra. This meant that every king's mother had been on one occasion the earthly consort of the god Amun-Ra, and this may have been one reason for her importance.

Several king's mothers in the Eighteenth Dynasty were not the principal wives of their royal husbands, but in the reigns of their sons they were given, in addition to the title 'king's mother', that of 'king's principal wife'. This, together with their identical use of other titles and insignia, suggests that the two roles were somehow identified. This can perhaps be explained by analogy with the divine Kamutef myth in which the sun god impregnated the sky goddess every night and was born of her again in the morning, thereby perpetually renewing himself. The sky goddess is thus both mother and consort to the god. In royal mythology, the king hoped to achieve renewal through a similar model, in which mother and wife had to be conceptualised as identical. In reality, the role was split into two parts and played by separate women, but ritually the women were identified as one entity. Ideally, every principal wife should have become king's mother, but in practice this did not happen, so instead any king's mother who had not been the principal wife of the previous king was given the title in the reign of her son.

FURTHER READING

K. A. Kitchen, *Pharaoh Triumphant: The Life and Times of Ramses II*, Warminster, 1978, chapter 6.

A. Schulman, 'Diplomatic marriage in the Egyptian New Kingdom', *Journal of Near Eastern Studies* 38 (1979), 177–93.

L. Troy, *Patterns of Queenship in Ancient Egyptian Myth and History*, Uppsala, 1986.

CHAPTER TWO

Queens, power, and the assumption of kingship

It is clear that the position of queen, like that of king, was rooted in mythology and the divine world. Although women occupying the position of queen were human, they were to some extent removed from the mortal sphere and given divine aspects. The notion of queenship was complementary to that of kingship, and the interconnection of the two meant that one could not exist without the other. Thus queens were very important ritually, but how much actual power would a queen have been able to exercise? It is impossible to answer this fully, but we can gain some idea. The question needs to be posed on two levels: how much power was vested in the actual position of king's mother or king's principal wife, and how much power could a strong-willed individual additionally acquire? We know that queens were given their own estates and that they also had male officials such as stewards in their service. A queen might thus have enjoyed not only a certain amount of economic independence but also the service of men loyal to her and her interests. The combination may have had the potential, at least, to provide a power base for an ambitious queen. However, Egyptian monuments only record the ideal and omit what does not fit the official model, which had no interest in individual personalities. Thus, we can never expect to find evidence of the careers of individual queens and their possible manipulation of power. Nor do the monuments yield a pattern suggesting that power was vested in queens on a regular basis. This notwithstanding, it is possible to say something more about a few queens.

Ahhotep II

When King Ahmose, founder of the Eighteenth Dynasty, came to the throne, the northern part of Egypt was still occupied by the foreign Hyksos rulers, while Nubia to the south was controlled by a ruler who was allied with the Hyksos. During his reign, Ahmose conquered Nubia, suppressed two uprisings, and drove the Hyksos out of Egypt. It must have been a time of tension and difficulties for the Theban ruler, and there is evidence that the king's mother Ahhotep played a crucial role in these stirring events. Ahmose later set up a great stela at Karnak in which he included a passage praising Ahhotep as 'one who cares for Egypt. She has looked after her [i.e. Egypt's] soldiers; she has guarded her; she has brought back her fugitives, and collected together

8   Stela of Thutmose II showing the king followed by queen Ahmose, widow of Thutmose I, and his own queen, Hatshepsut.

her deserters; she has pacified Upper Egypt, and expelled her rebels.'[1] Although far less precise than we would like, the passage breaks free of the stereotypic phrases usually applied to queens, suggesting that it is rooted in actual events. When Ahmose had succeeded the previous king, Kamose, he may have been still young, since it seems to have been some years before he continued the drive begun by Kamose against the Hyksos. It is possible that the events described took place at a time when Ahhotep was queen regent for the young king. Whatever the case, and the Egyptian record is not precise enough for us to be sure, it is clear that Ahhotep was a queen who exercised real power.

Ahmose Nefertari

Ahmose's principal wife, Ahmose Nefertari, seems to have been no less important than his mother, although no surviving text speaks of her in such terms as Ahmose spoke of Ahhotep.[2] Ahmose Nefertari was Ahmose's sister or half-sister and the mother of his successor, Amenhotep I. During his reign, Ahmose bestowed on her the title 'god's wife of Amun' (Chapter Eight). This event is known from a stela which was set up in the temple of Amun at Karnak (fig. 3). It records what is basically a legal document establishing the office together with an endowment of goods and lands on Ahmose Nefertari and her heirs in perpetuity. The office was a priestly one giving the bearer an important position in the cult of the god Amun at Thebes.

Other evidence from later in the reign suggests that the queen was involved in some way in the building projects of her husband. Her name appears alongside that of Ahmose above texts recording the reopening of the limestone quarries across the river from Memphis in year 22 of the king's reign. Her name is also found in the alabaster quarries near Assiut. When Ahmose decided to erect a cenotaph at Abydos for the mother of his father and the mother of his mother, Tetisheri, he left a stela recording the decision which describes how he sought the approval of Ahmose Nefertari for his plans. Such participation for a queen is unique in the records, and it may reflect Ahmose Nefertari's interest in the religious building projects of the reign.

We know that Ahmose Nefertari not only outlived her husband but also her son Amenhotep I, surviving into the reign of his successor, Thutmose I. Although it is most likely that Thutmose was not related to Ahmose Nefertari, it is clear that the queen was still highly honoured in his reign. Her figure is included in the scene on a stela dating to year 1 of Thutmose I on which the king promulgated his official titulary, and he set up a statue of her in the temple of Karnak. We do not know when Ahmose Nefertari died, but a fragment of a private stela, unfortunately preserving neither a date nor a king's name, actually mentions the queen's death: 'when the god's wife Ahmose Nefertari, justified with the great god, lord of the west, flew to heaven.'[3]

A number of ritual offerings dedicated by Ahmose Nefertari have been found in temples at Karnak, Deir el-Bahri, Abydos, and Serabit el-Khadim in Sinai. Other queens and also kings dedicated similar objects but, chronologically and numerically, Ahmose Nefertari heads the list and perhaps set the trend. The evidence leaves no doubt as to Ahmose Nefertari's involvement in cult, through concern with the buildings that housed it, through participation in its performance, and through the dedication of ritual objects. Much of this may have been in her capacity as god's wife, which Ahmose Nefertari seems to have regarded as equally important as her position as queen. Quite frequently, queens used only one title before their name instead of a longer titulary. The title selected was a significant one, usually 'king's wife', 'king's principal wife', or 'king's mother'. Ahmose Nefertari had the right to these, but rarely used them as sole titles. Instead she most frequently selected the title 'god's wife'.

Ahmose Nefertari's importance did not end with her death. Together with her son Amenhotep I, she was deified and worshipped by the workmen of Deir el-Medina as their patron (fig. 47). Her cult lasted there throughout the New Kingdom, testifying to the extraordinary status of this queen. Indeed, both during her lifetime and after her death, she overshadowed her son's principal wife and sister, Meritamun, who is not well attested. Although Meritamun had the title 'god's wife', the next important holder of the office after Ahmose

9 Part of a temple scene showing Hatshepsut as king together with Thutmose III. The two figures are virtually identical.

Nefertari was Hatshepsut, daughter of Thutmose I, and it is possible that Meritamun died before Ahmose Nefertari. While Thutmose I was clearly the chosen and legitimate successor of Amenhotep I, his mother Seniseneb is not called 'king's wife'. This can only mean that Thutmose was not the son of a king, and that he was chosen as heir by Amenhotep because the latter had no living sons. Hatshepsut was thus no blood relation of Ahmose Nefertari, unless Thutmose belonged to a junior branch of the royal family.

Hatshepsut

We know little of Hatshepsut during the reigns of her father, Thutmose I, and of her half-brother and husband, Thutmose II. She appears on a stela of Thutmose II as his principal wife and as god's wife (fig. 8), but she only seems to have come to prominence after the death of Thutmose II. The biography of an official of this time explicitly states that Thutmose II 'went up to heaven and was united with the gods. His son arose on his throne as king of the Two Lands and ruled on the seat of the one who begot him. His sister, the god's wife, Hatshepsut, controlled the affairs of the land.'[4] Since Thutmose III had a reign of nearly fifty-four years' duration, it is likely that he came to the throne as a boy and that Hatshepsut acted as regent for him. Thutmose was not the son of Hatshepsut, who is only attested with one daughter Neferura, but of a woman called Aset who was a minor wife of Thutmose II.

With the accession of Thutmose III, Hatshepsut suddenly comes into prominence on the material. At this time she continued to use the insignia and titulary of a king's principal wife, but like Ahmose Nefertari, when she used a title alone before her name, she almost always preferred that of god's wife. In other ways, though, she departed from queenly precedents. She is shown in scenes that are drawn from kingly iconography and uses titles modelled on those of kings. Where officials used titles or phrases that would usually have contained a reference to the king, they substituted a reference to Hatshepsut as 'god's wife' or 'mistress of the Two Lands', the latter clearly modelled on the king's title 'lord of the Two Lands'. While she was still regent, Hatshepsut had a pair of obelisks quarried and set up at Karnak, an act which took over a kingly prerogative. She was also depicted in a building at Karnak in scenes offering directly to the gods (fig. 2), something that is normally done only by kings. Thus as regent of Egypt, Hatshepsut reinforced her authority by drawing on kingly iconography, titulature, and actions.

At some point in Thutmose III's reign, and not later than year 7, Hatshepsut abandoned the titles and insignia of a queen. From then on, she adopted the fivefold titulary of a king, and on the monuments at least, if not in life, she appeared in the male costume of a king (fig. 9). To support her legitimacy as

10   The god Amun-Ra with queen Ahmose at the conception of Hatshepsut.

ruler, she set up texts which claimed that she had been chosen by her father as his successor and presented by him to the court and to all the gods of Egypt. She also had the myth of her divine birth depicted in her mortuary temple at Thebes, in which the god Amun-Ra is shown with her mother queen Ahmose (fig. 10) followed by the birth of Hatshepsut as king.[5]

It was once supposed that Hatshepsut had taken the throne because she regarded herself as the last representative of the pure dynastic line descended through the royal 'heiresses', while Thutmose II and Thutmose III were merely sons of non-royal concubines. However, we now know this cannot be so, as there was no line of 'heiress' queens. We can never be sure why Hatshepsut defied tradition and became king, nor why the male bureaucracy tolerated this aberration, but we can suggest some hypotheses. First, Hatshepsut probably possessed a strong character and made the most of the power that had accrued to her as regent. On a practical level, we can imagine that when she became regent, she carefully chose the officials who were to serve her. The most famous of these was Senenmut who, among numerous offices, held the positions of steward to the queen and tutor to her daughter (fig. 11).[6] Once these officials had taken office under her, their fortunes would be to some extent linked to hers. Many of them may have worried about what would happen to them when the young Thutmose III took control of the government for himself. Would he want to replace them with his own appointments?

We can be sure that Hatshepsut was meant to hand over control to the young king when he was old enough to rule for himself. However if, like many regents, she had come to enjoy the exercise of power, she probably found the prospect of giving it up unpleasant. But with Thutmose III growing older every year, she could hardly prolong the regency indefinitely. Murdering the young king would not help her much, since he was her means to power. There was, however, in ancient Egypt, a system whereby two kings might rule at the same time. Originally, it was instituted so that an ageing king might associate his heir with him on the throne in order to accomplish a smooth transfer of power from one ruler to the next. Hatshepsut was able to make use of this institution of coregency. She was crowned king with a full royal titulary without having to oust Thutmose III from the throne. He remained king throughout her period of rule, and the regnal dates used during their joint reign are his. Although he was represented less often than Hatshepsut at this time, he was shown with her in temple scenes (fig. 9), and a number of officials used the names of both kings on their monuments. Hatshepsut, however, was undoubtedly the dominant partner.

In the past Hatshepsut has often been seen as a pacifist in the midst of her warlike male relatives, but Donald Redford has shown that the picture is not so clear-cut, and that military campaigns were conducted during her reign.[7] In her mortuary temple at Thebes, however, one achievement which she chose to commemorate prominently was a trading mission to the land of Punt, a country situated on the coast of Africa and reached by the Red Sea. Its purpose was to bring back products of the region like panthers and panther skins, ostrich feathers and eggs, ivory, tropical woods, gold, and above all incense which was lavishly used in the cults of the gods in Egyptian temples.

When Hatshepsut became king, she had to give up the office of 'god's wife', and she handed it on to her daughter by Thutmose II, Neferura. Of all the king's daughters of the Eighteenth Dynasty, Neferura stands out by the large number of her attestations. While she is not certainly mentioned in the reign of her father, she is in evidence by the time of her mother's regency for Thutmose III. Most attestations, however, date from her mother's reign, when Neferura was shown in temple scenes following Hatshepsut who, as king, offered to a deity. The large number of scarabs that bear the name of Neferura far exceeds those belonging to other king's daughters and to many queens. While a few of the scarabs use the title 'king's daughter', or 'king's daughter, king's sister', most name Neferura as 'god's wife', showing that this office was as important for her as it had been for her mother and Ahmose Nefertari.

What should we make of Neferura's prominence? Her appearance in offering scenes with the king is not unknown for a king's daughter, but it is rare. On the other hand, scenes of this type are the ones in which queens are most frequently shown. I would suggest that Neferura's appearance here was vital to

11   Statue of Senenmut holding Neferura, the daughter of Hatshepsut and Thutmose II.

12   Head from a statue of queen Tiy.

Hatshepsut. As a female king, Hatshepsut could not have a 'king's principal wife', but in certain rituals, it was necessary for a king's mother or king's principal wife to be present, or, much less commonly, a king's daughter. Since her mother was by now dead, Hatshepsut needed her daughter to fill this role. What her eventual plans for Neferura were are unclear. Could she have meant her daughter to succeed her as king on her death, or did she intend Neferura to marry Thutmose III? That Neferura did not do so during her mother's lifetime seems clear, because she is never attested as 'king's wife'.

Unfortunately, we do not know what happened at the end of Hatshepsut's reign. By year 22 Thutmose III was ruling alone, but whether Hatshepsut had died naturally or been forcibly removed is not the sort of thing that Egyptian sources would record. When Neferura died is also uncertain. At one time it was thought that it was during her mother's reign, and there is evidence that her figure was in some cases removed from scenes in Hatshepsut's mortuary temple at Deir el-Bahri during her mother's lifetime. However, a stela of Thutmose III dating to the beginning of his sole reign may have originally depicted the figure of Neferura.[8] The identifying name has been changed to that of Satioh who was Thutmose's first principal wife, but the only title on the stela is 'god's wife'. As we have seen, this was Neferura's most important title, but it was one which was never borne by Satioh. If the stela originally showed

Neferura, we can hypothesise that she died and her name was replaced by that of Satioh.

How then should we see this remarkable episode in which Hatshepsut occupied the throne of Egypt as king for more than a decade? She was not the first or last woman to do so; a queen called Nitiqret may have ruled as king at the end of the Sixth Dynasty,[9] Nefrusobk was the last king of the Twelfth Dynasty, and Tausret the last of the Nineteenth. There is, however, a difference between these women and Hatshepsut. They all ruled at the end of a dynasty for a few years only, as if they were the last resort of families that had come to the end of their fortunes. Hatshepsut, by contrast, took power in the middle of a flourishing dynasty and ruled for over ten years, and possibly for nearly twenty. She enjoyed a prosperous reign as attested by her building activities, as in the temple of Amun at Karnak and her mortuary temple on the west bank at Thebes. She had to have the strength of character to break with the traditions of kingship which demanded that the king be male, and a forceful enough personality to win the support of key male officials. We can also assume that she had a love of power and the ability to exercise it. Since there was no provision for a female king within Egyptian ideology, she had to adapt to a male gender role, appearing on her monuments in male costume with the figure of a

13 (*left*) Stela from a household altar at Amarna showing Akhenaten, Nefertiti and three of their children beneath the disk and rays of the Aten.

14 (*right*) Fragment of relief showing the head and upper torso of Nefertiti. She wears the double feathers, horns and disk, and the uraeus.

man. We have no idea how she dressed in real life. In texts, her scribes were less sure how to cope with the situation. Sometimes they used masculine pronouns and grammatical forms to refer to her, and sometimes feminine ones. Traditionally the king was identified with the male god Horus, but Hatshepsut often calls herself the female Horus, which would appear to be a contradiction in terms. There was thus tension between Hatshepsut's biological sex and the male gender role of king. It is clear that a woman did not easily occupy the Egyptian throne, and indeed in nearly three millennia, only four out of two to three hundred kings were female. A woman as ruler was plainly not a normal option in ancient Egypt.

There remains the question as to why Thutmose III tolerated the situation for so long, and why in the later part of his reign he removed Hatshepsut's names and figures from her monuments, frequently changing them into his own or those of earlier kings. If Thutmose was too young at first to protest, it is impossible to believe that he was later too meek to assert his rights. If he was eight or nine when his father died, he would have been thirty when he came into his sole rule. Immediately he showed his mettle as a military commander, and went on to enlarge Egypt's possessions in Syria-Palestine with year after year of brilliant campaigning. Was this same man unable to stand up to Hatshepsut? Two possible answers spring to mind. First, that he accepted the coregency and worked willingly with his coruler, content to wait until she died in order to rule on his own. Second, that he was by no means content, that he did take action, and that his assumption of sole rule was a result of the assassination of Hatshepsut.

The obliteration of Hatshepsut's names and figures on her monuments has sometimes been explained as an expression of his hatred for her. But there is compelling evidence that the removal did not take place immediately at the beginning of his sole reign, and that it should be dated to his later years.[10] It would be odd if Thutmose waited so long to take revenge. On the other hand, if the destruction was motivated not by hatred but by a desire to expunge the memory of a woman who had improperly ascended the throne, the gap is less important. Indeed it could be explained by assuming that Hatshepsut had died naturally and that Thutmose felt no resentment against her. He might then have been reluctant to mutilate her monuments; but as time passed by, political expediency might have won over sentiment, and he might finally have agreed that all traces of the unnatural female king should be erased, since they did not conform with *maat*, the natural order of the world. It may be significant that the name and figure of Hatshepsut as queen were not attacked.

Tiy

The queens of the mid-Eighteenth Dynasty attested during the sole rule of Thutmose III and the reigns of his successors Amenhotep II and Thutmose IV are shadowy and poorly documented. It is not until the reign of Amenhotep III that we meet another outstanding queen. Sometime early in his reign, Amenhotep issued a commemorative scarab with a text that runs: '... King of Upper and Lower Egypt, Nebmaatra, son of Ra Amenhotep ruler of Thebes, given life, and the king's principal wife Tiy, may she live. The name of her father is Yuya, and the name of her mother is Tjuyu; she is the wife of a mighty king whose southern boundary is at Karoy [in Upper Nubia], and whose northern is at Naharin [Mitanni].'[11] In this way we are introduced to the king's principal wife Tiy, who was born to non-royal parents and mother of the king's heir who would rule as the heretic king Akhenaten. Tiy held the position of principal wife throughout Amenhotep's reign, and appears in scenes with the king at the celebration of his *sed* festivals to renew his kingship (fig. 4), as well as in audience scenes in private tombs (fig. 5). She is shown on an equal scale with the king in a colossal seated statue originally from Amenhotep's mortuary temple at Thebes (fig. 6). Once she is depicted in a private tomb scene sitting on a throne, on the arm of which she appears in the form of a sphinx trampling enemies, a device taken straight from kingly iconography (fig. 5). Her name appears alongside Amenhotep's or alone on cosmetic objects and countless scarabs. It is in this reign that the queen first adopts the horns and disk of Hathor as part of her insignia (fig. 7). It was also a time of increased emphasis on the solar and divine aspects of kingship, when Amenhotep III established a cult to a deified form of himself. We have already seen that there was a solar, Hathoric aspect to queenship, and the prominence of Tiy and other royal women in Amenhotep's reign may have been related to the stress on the divinity of kingship, leading to a corresponding emphasis on the divine side of queenship. Once again the evidence is lacking to pass judgment on Tiy as a person, although her distinctive image in statuary and relief, where she is shown with pouting lips and downturned mouth, might suggest that she was a woman of some character (fig. 12).

Nefertiti

Prominent though Tiy might seem to have been in the reign of Amenhotep III, her position was in general consonant with what we know about other Eighteenth Dynasty queens. Her successor Nefertiti, the principal wife of Akhenaten, was a different matter. No other queen was ever shown so frequently on the monuments, in temples, tombs, and statuary.[12] Her husband Akhenaten was originally called Amenhotep, but after a few years on the throne he changed his name to Akhenaten to honour his special god Aten, who was imminent in the sun's disk. Akhenaten ceased to worship the traditional gods of Egypt, and instead raised temples to the Aten at Karnak, traditionally the cult centre of the god Amun. Finally, he abandoned the established cities of Egypt which were all closely associated with particular deities, and built a new capital city dedicated to the Aten on a previously unsettled desert site in Middle Egypt. He called it Akhetaten, 'the horizon of the Aten'; today it is better known as Amarna.

Already in the temples at Karnak, Nefertiti's figure appeared frequently, and in one building she was depicted offering directly to the Aten without the presence of the king. Her importance in the Aten religion is also shown by her

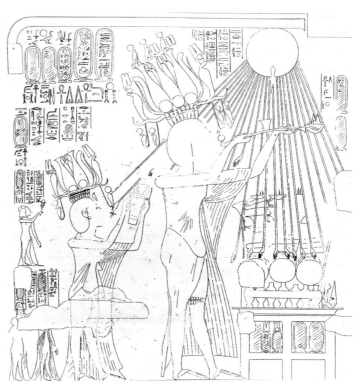

15 Scene showing Nefertiti wearing the same type of crown as Akhenaten.

16   Scene showing Nefertiti smiting enemies.

appearance on stelae from household altars seated with Akhenaten below the disk of the Aten (fig. 13). These stelae were the focus of domestic cult, and it is clear that the royal couple and the Aten together formed a triad that was worshipped, echoing the triads of deities that had been common in traditional religion. Other evidence shows that private people could address prayers directly to the queen. Thus, Nefertiti played a fundamental role in the Aten cult, filling the gap left by the proscription of traditional goddesses.

At first, Nefertiti wore insignia common to queens in general, including the double feathers, the horns and disk, the uraeus and the double uraeus (fig. 14), all of which had solar significance. She did not, however, wear the vulture headdress, which was perhaps unsuited to the Aten theology. Later in the reign, Nefertiti most commonly wore the tall blue crown made famous by her bust now in Berlin. This crown was unique to Nefertiti (fig. 13). In addition, Nefertiti sometimes wore kingly crowns (fig. 15). She was also occasionally shown smiting enemies in a type of scene borrowed directly from kingly iconography (fig. 16). It has been suggested that Nefertiti eventually took the titles of king as Akhenaten's coregent in the last years of his reign.[13] The events at the end of the Amarna period are, however, still hotly disputed by scholars.[14]

Despite Nefertiti's prominence and important ritual role during the reign of Akhenaten, she was not the king's only wife. Traces of another woman have been found on some monuments and on various items of funerary equipment under changed inscriptions[15]. Her stereotypic titulary can be pieced together to run: 'Wife and greatly beloved of the king of Upper and Lower Egypt living on truth, lord of the Two Lands Neferkheperura Waenra the perfect child of the living Aten who is living for ever Kiya.' Unlike all other known wives of kings Kiya is not given the title 'king's wife', and unlike any king's wife who is not a principal wife, she was depicted on monuments with the king. However, in the second half of his reign, her titles and name were erased and those of Akhenaten's daughters Meretaten and Ankhesenpaaten substituted. Unfortunately, there is no parallel to help us understand Kiya's position at court, nor is there any evidence of her fate, although it is extraordinary that items of funerary equipment made for her, including a coffin and canopic jars, were reused for other burials. This leaves us wondering whether she did not receive the proper burial planned for her.

In addition to Kiya, Akhenaten was also married to Mitannian and Babylonian princesses, but they never appear on his monuments. It is possible that he had other wives of whom we know nothing. But it was Nefertiti who achieved a prominence and ubiquity on the monuments that was never again attained by any other queen.

Conclusion

While we may suspect that women like Ahmose Nefertari, Hatshepsut, Tiy and Nefertiti were strong-minded individuals, Egyptian sources will never provide us with the insight into their characters that we would like. When all is said and done, we know more about the positions that they occupied than about the type of people they were. What we learn is that kingship itself was not an office open to women on normal terms, and that the role of the royal women was to complement the divine aspect of kingship through divine queenship. On an ideological level, the queen represented the female principle of the universe through which the male king could renew himself. On a practical level, the royal women provided potential heirs to the throne. Both the king's mother and the king's principal wife had important ritual roles to play, and it is possible that these offered potential power to the holder. Other wives had no ritual role, but might have wielded influence if they attracted the king's favour. Sometimes royal women went outside the legitimate framework of power and tried to influence events by assassination in order to bring a prince to the throne who was not the official heir.

Kingship was essential to the Egyptians' view of their world. Society was organised around the king, who formed the point of contact between the divine and human spheres. He also provided the only form of government that had any validity in Egypt. Integral to the functioning of the kingship were the female kin of the ruler, and the Egyptian concept of kingship can only be properly comprehended if the complementary notion of queenship and the rule of the royal women is also understood.

FURTHER READING

C. Aldred, *Akhenaten King of Egypt*, London, 1988.

P. Dorman, *The Monuments of Senenmut*, London, 1988.

M. Gitton, *L'épouse du dieu Ahmès Néfertary*, 2nd ed., 1981, Paris.

D. Redford, *Akhenaten The Heretic King*, Princeton, 1984.

G. Robins, 'The god's wife of Amun in the 18th Dynasty in Egypt', in: A. Cameron and A. Kuhrt (eds.) *Images of Women in Antiquity*, London and Canberra, 1983.

CHAPTER THREE

Marriage

Defining marriage in ancient Egypt

Private monuments show that one important level of social organisation in Egypt was through family groups, and that these groups centred around the concept of a man, a woman, and their children. This is confirmed by a register of the inhabitants of the workmen's village at Deir el-Medina, dating to the New Kingdom, which lists the occupants house by house.[1] Although the document is very fragmentary, enough is preserved to show that the owner of each house is given together with filiation to his parents. This is followed, if he is married, by the name of his 'wife' and her filiation. Finally the names of his children, if any, are listed together with their filiation. I have, as is customary, used the term 'wife' to translate the Egyptian word *hemet*, thus presupposing the existence of marriage. However, defining marriage in ancient Egypt has presented scholars with a number of problems. There is no mention in our sources of any legal or religious ceremony to formalise a marriage. In fact, 'the sole significant act seems to have been the cohabitation, and, in particular, the entry of one party, usually the woman, into the household of the other.'[2] This is seen in some of the Egyptian terms which we take to mean 'to marry', such as 'to establish a household', 'to enter a household', and later 'to live together'. Conversely 'divorce' is expressed in terms meaning 'expulsion' or 'departure'. Another expression signifying marriage simply means 'to take (somebody) as wife'. The equivalent expression 'to take a husband' is not found until the second half of the sixth century BC, when it occurs in a particular type of document, not attested earlier, concerning divorce. This does not necessarily mean that the expression did not exist earlier. It could be that since most formal documents and texts are written from the point of view of the man, there may have been a few occasions to use the phrase in writing until the late advent of divorce documents.

A tiny number of texts records the authority of a third party in sanctioning a marriage. The first, inscribed on a statue belonging to the king's hairdresser Sabastet and dating to year 27 of Thutmose III of the Eighteenth Dynasty, runs: '(As for) the slave belonging to me called Ameniuy, I captured him with my strong arm when I was following the ruler ... I have given to him the daughter of my sister Nebetta as wife, her name being Takemet.'[3] In a long papyrus from

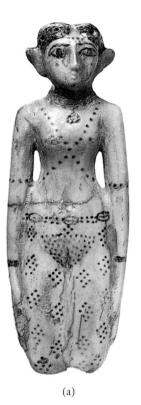

17 Fertility figurines:
(a) Middle Kingdom (b) 18th
Dynasty, dedicated as a votive
offering to the goddess Hathor
(c) New Kingdom.

(a)

(b)

(c)

18   Fertility figurine with a child carried on the left hip and a text requesting a child.

later in the New Kingdom, we learn that a widow called Rennefer brought up three children born to a slave girl whom her husband Nebnefer had purchased. Since the couple's marriage was childless, it is possible that the girl had been bought specifically to provide offspring and that these children were fathered by Nebnefer. In any case, Rennefer tells us that 'the stablemaster Padiu entered my house and he took Taiemniut their [the children's] elder sister to wife, he being my relative and my younger brother. I accepted him for her and he is with her at this day.'[4]

A third occurrence is found in a much later document dating to the Twenty-Seventh Dynasty but describing events which had taken place in the Twenty-Sixth Dynasty.[5] Psamtek I had appointed a man called Padiaset as priest of Amun-Ra at Teuzoi in the Faiyum. In year 14 of that king, a priest of Amun-Ra at Thebes called Horwedja asked Padiaset for an appointment at Teuzoi on the grounds that his father had been a priest there. In addition, he asked for Padiaset's daughter Nitemhat as his wife. Padiaset's reply was that 'Her time has not yet come; become a priest of Amunrasonter and I shall give her to you.'[6] The next year Horwedja brought the evidence showing that his father had indeed been a priest at Teuzoi and 'Padiaset arranged for Horwedja . . . to be made a priest of Amun of Teuzoi and he gave him Nitemhat, his daughter, as a wife.'[7]

The first two texts deal with unusual situations. Sabastet mentions his wife, his sister, and his sister's daughter, but no children of his own. It is possible that he is childless and has adopted Ameniuy as his son, bringing him into the family by marrying him to his sister's daughter. Whether Nebetta had any say in the disposal of her daughter is not recorded, but the marriage was probably an economically advantageous one because the text continues: 'She [Takemet] has shared with [my] wife and sister also. When he [Ameniuy] goes out he is not destitute.' In other words, wealth is being kept within the family, and the whole arrangement may be a way for Sabastet to obtain an heir and also provide for his sister, perhaps a widow, and her daughter.

In the second case, we again find an economic arrangement behind the marriage, for we learn that Rennefer adopted the three children and Padiu as her heirs. The text may imply that even if Rennefer did not arrange the marriage, she had to approve it, and this might be because she had authority over the disposal in marriage of the children. However, we do not know if she would have had the authority to prevent such a match had she wished. Her approval may not have been necessary to enable the marriage to go ahead, but had she refused to regard Padiu as a suitable husband, she might not have included him, or even his wife, as one of her heirs. On the other hand, the children were not free until she manumitted them, so she may well have had authority to arrange their marriages, and the situation would not then represent what was customary between free couples.

The third case, however, is clearly cast in the form of a father giving his daughter to a man as his wife. It is possible that Horwedja was a relative from a Theban branch of Padiaset's family, which might explain the latter's willingness to obtain a job for him.[8] Padiaset might well have thought that a relative to whom he stood in position of patron would make a good 'son-in-law'. However, the text tells us that Horwedja saw Padiaset's daughter when he was invited to Padiaset's house, and that he then asked for her in marriage. Young as the daughter was, it is possible that she and Horwedja decided at that point that they wished to marry. Asking the permission of her father might then be either a vital part of the proceedings, or a mere fiction. In the latter case, it would be similar to a father in England today giving his daughter away in church; just as that reflects a time when the father really had authority to dispose of his daughter in marriage, so the Egyptian case might be a pointer to a father's authority in this matter existing at one time. If, on the other hand, the arrangement was in fact made between the two men, we have no idea whether Nitemhat was consulted or could have vetoed it. Thus we see that what appears to be a clear-cut case of a father arranging the marriage of his daughter cannot be taken wholly at face value.

Returning to the New Kingdom, we find that two further texts, both from Deir el-Medina, suggest the involvement of the father in his daughter's marriage arrangements. In one papyrus a man states that 'I brought a bundle to the house of Payom, and I married his daughter',[9] while an ostrakon gives a 'list of all objects which Usekhnemte gave to his father(-in-law?) when he made Aset [his] wife'.[10] If indeed in the second case father-in-law rather than father is to be understood, and the Egyptian word for 'father' includes the meaning of father-in-law,[11] it is possible that in both cases a father is involved in the marriage arrangements of his daughter, and that the prospective husband was supposed to make a present to him. However, even if this is the correct interpretation, we still do not know whether it could be agreed between the couple first, after which the man approached the father.

In the so-called marriage contracts known first from the seventh century BC and continuing in use through the Late Period into Ptolemaic Egypt, we find mention of a gift made by a husband to his wife called the *shep en sehemet*, which one scholar suggests was originally payment to the father of the woman, so that one can translate the Egyptian phrase as 'price or compensation for (marrying) a woman'.[12] These contracts, drawn up by the man, do not, in spite of their misleading name in English, have anything to do with the legal establishment of marriage. They need not even be drawn up at the time a couple come together, for in some of them the man and woman concerned already have children. The documents are, in fact, economic in force and are concerned with the disposition of property and the economic rights of the spouses, especially in the event of the man repudiating his wife: 'I have taken you as a wife. I have given you (sum of "money" listed here) as your *shep en sehemet*. If I repudiate you as a wife, be it that I hate you, be it that I want another woman as a wife instead of you, I shall give you (a sum of "money" is here listed) apart from (sum of "money" listed) which I have given you as your *shep en sehemet* ... And I give you ⅓ (part) of all and everything which will be between you and me from this day onwards.'[13] These documents usually go on to confirm that any children who have been born or who will be born will be the man's heirs, and to promise to return the value of what the woman has brought with her to his house, whether he repudiates her or she leaves of her own free will.

It is tempting to read the situation we find in the 'marriage contracts' back into earlier periods, regarding the documents as recording what had previously been unwritten custom. However, without confirmation, this is a dangerous exercise that should be avoided. For a start, how far back should one take it? The end of the New Kingdom already lies some four hundred years before the first 'marriage contract' was written, and its beginning is five hundred years earlier still. It would be folly to assume that there had been no changes. Thus we have to admit that we know remarkably little about the forms of Egyptian marriage for most of pharaonic history. To make matters even more difficult there is, in addition, a lack of understanding on our part concerning Egyptian terminology referring to a 'wife'.

The word *hi* 'husband' is rarely found on monuments, because these usually belong to a male owner who, therefore, is never named as 'husband'. It sometimes occurs, however, when a member of his family is called, for example, 'the husband of his daughter'. The equivalent term for 'wife' is *hemet*, known from the Old Kingdom onwards. It was used almost exclusively on monuments up to the middle of the Eighteenth Dynasty, but was then largely replaced by the word *senet*, which is the usual term for 'sister' or any other female collateral. *Hemet*, however, continued to be used with the meaning of 'wife' in hieratic records where *senet* never seems to have that meaning. In these documents alongside *hemet*, we find far less commonly women who are called *hebsut*, a term which has sometimes been translated 'concubine'. In fact, we have little idea of what distinction in meaning, if any, the two words had.[14] There are a few New Kingdom examples of women who are referred to both as a man's *hebsut* and as his *hemet*. In one papyrus a priest wants to settle some property on his second wife Inksunedjem.[15] This involves a court hearing with the children of his first marriage in order to confirm that the property their father is settling on his second wife is his to dispose of. In the course of the document Inksunedjem is referred to both as *hebsut* and as *hemet*. In another papyrus a woman says: 'I am one of four wives' (*hemet*), but elsewhere she is referred to as the *hebsut* of the goldsmith Ramose.[16] In another document we find a woman called Nesmut who is referred to both as the *hebsut* and as the *hemet* of the trumpeter Perpatjau.[17] In addition, in hieratic documents women who are *hemet* and those who are *hebsut* both use the ubiquitous title *ankhet en niut* which seems to signify a 'married' woman.

Hebsut is already used in the Middle Kingdom. The most famous example is in the Heqanakht letters written by the head of a family, Heqanakht, who is away from home, to his dependants. One of the matters he is concerned with is the treatment of a woman called Iutenheb who is resented by the other members of the family, although Heqanakht clearly values her. At one point Heqanakht writes 'See! This is my *hebsut* and it is known what should be done for a man's *hebsut*. See! Whoever will do for her the like of what I have done – indeed, would any of you be patient if his *hemet* had been denounced to him?'[18] In other words, here too a *hebsut* is also a *hemet*, but if that is the case, why make a distinction? William Ward has suggested that, since in several cases it can be shown that a woman called *hebsut* was not the first wife of her husband, the word signifies a subsequent wife married after the death or divorce of previous wives.[19] This would fit in with the problems in Heqanakht's family, if the rest of the family resented the introduction of a new wife into the household of their father, a situation that can be paralleled in many other cultures including modern western society.

The main problem with this interpretation is the relative infrequency with which the term appears. Considering the risk of death to women in childbirth and the frequency of divorce, many wives will have been subsequent to a first wife, yet few are called *hebsut*. Indeed, this term rarely appears on the monuments, where cases of multiple marriage, whether consecutive or concurrent, are recognised by the presence of more than one woman called *hemet*. The answer to this problem might be that because the term *hebsut* was rarely used in monumental contexts, women who in non-monumental contexts might have been called *hebsut*, would appear in tombs and on stelae and statues as *hemet* or, from the mid-Eighteenth Dynasty onwards, *senet*. This split between terms used on monumental and non-monumental material can also be found in two of the commonest women's titles found in the New Kingdom: *ankhet en niut*, usually translated 'citizeness' and *nebet per* 'mistress of the house'. The former occurs in hieratic documents but rarely on monumental material, while the situation is reversed with the latter.

We may tentatively, then, accept Ward's suggestion that *hebsut* indicates a wife subsequent to the first wife of a man. While Ward is clearly thinking in terms of serial monogamy, there is no evidence to show that if, a man did have two concurrent wives, the second could not also be called *hebsut*. Thus, when the *hebsut* Mutemheb says: 'I am one of four wives (*hemet*), two being dead and another (still) alive',[20] we do not know whether her husband is divorced from 'the other' or whether he is married to both at once. Whatever the case, a *hebsut* is clearly also a *hemet*, and the term 'concubine' should be avoided as a translation, since it carries connotations that are almost certainly inapplicable to ancient Egyptian society.

Documents dating to the New Kingdom from the workmen's village at Deir el-Medina present a further problem relating to marriage. In the same type of documents where women are called *hebsut*, some women are said to be 'wife of', while others are said to be 'with' a particular man. Again the distinction, if any, is not clear, but it would be dangerous to assume that the second means 'living with' without being married, that is without the women being *hemet*, since marriage seems to come into being when a man and a woman set up house together. It is difficult, therefore, to see what the difference could be, unless it lay in the expectations of how long the marriage would last, or whether a formal economic agreement had been entered into. However, in the *Adoption Papyrus*, Padiu took Taiemniut as his *hemet* and was then said to be 'with her'. Further, women who are 'wife of' and those who are 'with' can both be referred to as 'married woman' (*hemet tjay*), and it was considered disgraceful for another man to have intercourse with them, suggesting that there may in fact be little difference in the meaning between the two phrases. This is confirmed in a case where a woman said in a hieratic document to be 'with' a man is called on a stela in hieroglyphs 'his wife, mistress of the house'.

Divorce

While we may not fully understand the Egyptian concept of marriage, there is enough evidence to show that something akin to divorce was not uncommon, whereby couples who had been living together separated. It is unclear what all the possible grounds for this may have been, but infidelity on the part of the woman and infertility would surely have been high on the list. From about 500 BC onwards, there is evidence that women could initiate the divorce,[21] in which case infidelity on the part of the man might also have been a cause. It is unclear whether male infertility, as compared to impotency, was understood, so in a case of infertility the woman may always have been blamed. In the 'marriage contracts' referred to above, dislike of one's wife or the wish to marry another woman are cited as possible reasons for divorce. Much earlier, a man points out in a letter to his dead wife that he married her 'when I was a young man. I was with you when I was carrying out all sorts of offices. I was with you and I did not divorce you. I did not cause your heart to grieve. I did it when I was a youth and when I was carrying out all sorts of important offices for Pharaoh, life, prosperity, health, without divorcing you, saying "She has (always) been

19   The goddess Taweret, protectress of pregnant women and women in childbirth. She carries a knife and rests her paw on a *sa* sign.

with <me>" – so said I!'[22] In other words, as men climbed the bureaucratic ladder, it was probably not unknown for them to divorce the wives of their youth and remarry a woman more appropriate or advantageous to their higher rank.

Just as marriage had no legal or state-religious sanction, neither did divorce, although a court may have been involved as witness to the end of a marriage. Remarriage after divorce was possible for both parties, and indeed may well have been the purpose of the divorce.

Multiple marriages

Such remarriage would mean that it would have been possible to have had more than one marriage partner in a lifetime. This possibility would have been made even more common by the fairly low life expectancy in ancient Egypt and, for women, by the risk of death in childbirth. Many monuments from all periods produce evidence for multiple marriages. From the New Kingdom we even find the occasional example of women labelled 'his former wife'.[23] These women are unlikely to have been divorced, because divorced women seem not to have been shown on their husband's monuments. It is more likely that the 'former wives' died, and that their husbands remarried. This is probably also the case where the owner of a tomb chapel or other monument appears with several wives, wishing to perpetuate the memory of all of them, living and dead, although it is unclear how to distinguish today between consecutive and concurrent marriages. It is usually said that most Egyptians were monogamous but that there was no proscription against multiple marriages for men. The control is thought rather to have been economic, in that a man could usually not afford to support more than one wife. It has been pointed out that the various suggested cases of polygamy all stem from the upper echelons of the elite class, implying that a man had to be wealthy before contemplating taking more than one wife;[24] but, as we have seen, there is very little surviving documentation concerning the non-elite classes, so this argument tends to be circular.

In fact, one would need to weigh the productive capabilities of a wife against the cost of her upkeep before categorically stating that men could not afford more than one wife. For instance, during the Old and Middle Kingdoms, textile manufacture was conducted entirely by women, and they continued to play a large part in it in the New Kingdom. Women appear to have been responsible for the cloth used by their families, and to have been able to trade any surplus they produced. Thus, theoretically wives could have contributed materially to the family income by producing textiles, so making it economically viable for a man to have more than one wife. Further, if wives in peasant families provided agricultural labour (a matter about which the records are silent), again it might pay to have a family unit with several wives who, together with their progeny, would also form a free workforce in the fields. Only if wives were totally unproductive and had to be fully supported out of their husband's income would they become an impossible expense except to the very wealthy. Then a multiplicity of such wives could become a status symbol.

Even if we can never know about the majority of the population, we can look at the situation in the workmen's village at Deir el-Medina dating to the New Kingdom, the one community about which we know a fair amount. Unfortunately, although divorce and remarriage are not uncommon, there is no definitive evidence concerning concurrent marriages. In fact, the physical layout of the houses does not seem designed to accommodate a man and more than one wife, and the register of the villagers listed house by house does not, on surviving portions at least, name more than one wife per household. However, in a papyrus of the Twentieth Dynasty relating to an official investigation into tomb robbery at Thebes, a list of women involved is given which includes:

> The citizeness Herer, the wife of the watchman Paaemtawemet (of) the treasury of Pharaoh.
> The citizeness Tanefery, his other wife, making two.[25]

It is, of course, possible that the husband is divorced from the first wife, but it is strange that both women are identified by their relationship to Paaemtawemet. In another papyrus also relating to the tomb robberies and already referred to above, one woman says: 'I am one of four wives, two being dead and another still alive.' Again it could be argued that these are consecutive wives, two having terminated their marriages by dying and the third by divorce, but as it stands the statement is ambiguous and might mean that at one point there were four women married to one man at the same time. Some centuries later the 'marriage contracts' of the Late Period do not so much as suggest the possibility that the husband might take a second wife without divorcing the first, and indeed they are very much concerned with the consequences of the woman being divorced by the man.

It seems possible that among the elite at least, the taking of more than one wife at a time may have occurred but was not particularly common; we know nothing about the non-elite. In addition, married men may often have had sexual relations with female servants or other women in the household who were their social inferiors. For instance, in some Eighteenth Dynasty tomb chapels there seem to be children born to mothers other than the owner's wife, suggesting that the head of the house might have had access to other women.[26] In one text, a son specifically says he did not have intercourse with the female servants of his father,[27] suggesting that such personnel were vulnerable to this type of behaviour, a situation that could be paralleled in legally monogamous Christian Europe, as in Richardson's novel *Pamela*. We do not know, however, whether such relationships would be frowned upon in ancient Egypt or not. The man may be denying that he had intercourse with his father's servants not

20 (*left*) Alabaster vessel in the form of a pregnant woman.

21 (*right*) Gold amulet in the form of the god Bes.

because it was wrong to have intercourse with servants, but because in the father's household this was the father's prerogative not to be usurped by the son.

There is no evidence from monuments or from elsewhere of the concept of illegitimacy in children. While this might not show up on the monuments, which tend to reflect the male ideal of society, if it existed one might expect to find reference to it in other documents, especially among the community at Deir el-Medina. We know of a woman who conceived a child by one man while she was the *hemet* of another.[28] Unfortunately the document is more concerned with the behaviour of the man, which was condemned even by his own father, and we never discover what happened to the woman and her child. If we turn to monumental material, we have already seen that in some Eighteenth Dynasty tomb chapels children occasionally appear who seem to have been born to women other than the owner's wife. The fact that these children are included in tomb scenes suggests that there was no stigma attached to their origins and that they did not violate the image of ideal family life perpetuated in the tomb chapel. What their economic and social position in life would have been is unknown. Whether all offspring, irrespective of their mother's identity, shared automatically in their father's estate, or whether a man had to make special arrangements for any children not born to his wife if he wanted to provide for them, is not recorded on the material we possess. It would seem obvious that such children would have no claim on their father's wife's estate, although they presumably had inheritance rights from their own mothers. It has been suggested that one reason filiation is often given to the mother and not to the father is to make a person's maternity and inheritance rights clear in just such a situation.[29]

The number of cases where there is reason to suspect that a child is not the offspring of the man's wife is limited. Nevertheless, on a family monument where a man's children are just labelled 'his son/daughter', this could disguise children who were born to a woman other than the wife. Further, on some monuments, we find grouped with family members other figures who are neither identified by a kinship term nor by a title showing a function within the family. Sometimes they are filiated to women who also have no identification and are otherwise unknown. These people could simply be members of the household who are included with the family on the monument, but they could be further offspring of the monument's owner.

If it was possible for men to have more than one wife at a time, there is no evidence at all that a woman could have several husbands concurrently. However, there was no stigma attached to the remarriage of divorced or widowed women, so that women too might have more than one spouse in a lifetime. For instance, at Deir el-Medina in the Twentieth Dynasty, a woman called Naunakht married a man named Kenherkhepeshef. When he died in his sixties, Naunakht was left a childless widow. She subsequently remarried and had eight children, which suggests that she had been considerably younger than her first husband. Economically the marriage had been advantageous for her and she had inherited property from her husband when he died.[30]

Adultery

While married men might have sexual relations with women other than their own wives, married women were not supposed to have affairs with other men.[31] If we have understood it properly, one text from Deir el-Medina which concerns a dispute that was taken to the local court, contains the statement: '. . . (a) wife (*hemet*) is (a) wife. She should not make love. She should not have sexual intercourse.'[32] Obviously, we must understand that this means with someone other than her husband. Thus although marriage does not seem to have had a legal or state-religious basis, there was clearly social recognition of couples who set up house together which included the expectation that the woman would be sexually faithful to the man. This is understandable since the purpose of marriage was to have children, and the man would want to be sure he was their father, especially since children born of the union had legal rights of inheritance in the father's property. They also had rights in the mother's property but maternity, unlike paternity, was never in doubt. It is not surprising, then, that infidelity on the part of a wife is deplored in the texts and that men are criticised for having affairs with married women. By contrast, complaints about young men consorting with 'prostitutes' are as much to do with time wasted away from scribal studies as with any moral or social censure.

There are a few New Kingdom texts which are concerned with complaints levelled against individuals who are charged with acting illegally or immorally, especially in connection with their official duties. Included among these accusations is the charge of engaging in sexual intercourse with married women. A legal case at Deir-el-Medina opens with the accusation: 'You copulated with a married woman in the-place-of-carrying-torches.'[33] While the text is hard to follow, the rest of the case seems to be concerned with 'the honesty, or otherwise, of the transport of some fats.'[34] The accusation that the man had intercourse with a married woman is clearly meant to give him a bad character and throw doubt on his trustworthiness in other matters. Another complaint from Deir el-Medina was made against an unpopular chief work-man Paneb who seems to have been a very nasty character.[35] Along with various accusations of irregularities in the conduct of his official position, he too is accused of having sex with married women: 'Paneb had intercourse with the citeziness Tuy, when she was the wife of the workman Qenna. He had intercourse with the citeziness Hunero, when she was with Pendua. He had intercourse with the citeziness Hunero, when she was with Hesysunebef . . . And when he had had intercourse with Hunero, he had intercourse with Webkhet, her daughter. And Aapehty, his son, had intercourse with Webkhet as well.'[36] The fact that Paneb and his son also had sexual relations with Hunero's daughter, although she does not as yet appear to be married, seems to be presented as another sexual irregularity, although what aspect of this rather unsavoury affair was being condemned is unclear. Possibly to have intercourse with a mother and then her daughter was in some sense 'incestuous', as it may also have been for both father and son to have sex with the same woman. But perhaps the accusation does not rest on such formal grounds. The matter of Webkhet may simply have been thrown in to clinch the extraordinary depravity of Paneb.

More interesting would be to know what happened to these women. In most cases there is no way of finding out, but we do know more in the case of Hunero, wife of Hesysunebef. By sheer chance we have an ostrakon dating to year 2 of the reign of Setnakht that records the fact that Hesysunebef divorced her; perhaps this was the result of her infidelity with Paneb.[37] In addition, the ostrakon provides the information that for three years after the divorce, some-one, who unfortunately remains unnamed, gave Hunero a small amount of grain each month. After that we do not know what happened to her. The daughter Webkhet later married despite her earlier sexual adventures.[38] It must be added that it is unclear whether the women were willing partners in these affairs or whether the accusations are ones of rape.

Clearly, this disapproval of men having sex with married women ran deep in Egyptian society. In the 'negative confession' in chapter 125 of the *Book of the Dead* we find that the dead man had to declare 'I have not copulated with a

married woman', or 'I have not copulated with the wife of another.'[39] In the
Eighteenth Dynasty *Instruction of Any* the author warns the male reader:

> Beware of a woman who is a stranger,
> One not known in her town;
> Don't stare at her when she goes by,
> Do not know her carnally.
> A deep water whose course is unknown,
> Such is a woman away from her husband.
> 'I am pretty' she tells you daily,
> When she has no witnesses;
> She is ready to ensnare you,
> A great deadly crime when it is heard.[40]

The danger here seems to be based on the assumption that a woman will have a
husband, so that any man foolish enough to succumb to her will be having an
affair with a married woman which will bring reprisals. An older text, the
Instructions of Ptahhotep, probably dating from the Middle Kingdom,[41] contains another warning:

> If you want to make friendship last
> in a house you enter,
> whether as lord, or brother, or friend,
> in any place you enter,
> beware of approaching the women!
> The place where this is done cannot be good;
> there can be no cleverness in revealing this.
> A thousand men are turned away from their good:
> a little moment, the likeness of a dream,
> and death is reached by knowing them.
> It is a vile thing, conceived by an enemy;
> one emerges from doing it
> with a heart (already) rejecting it.
> As for him who ails through lusting after them, no plan of his
>   can (ever) succeed.[42]

This implication that death may be meted out to the man involved can also be
found in literary stories. In the New Kingdom *Tale of Two Brothers*, the older
brother's immediate reaction when he was misled into thinking that his
younger brother had attempted to seduce his wife was to try and kill him. When
he discovered that the whole event had occurred the other way around and in
fact his wife had tried to seduce his younger brother, then 'he killed his wife
(and) cast her to the dogs.'[43] In a Middle Kingdom story, a magician who
caught his wife with another man killed both parties.[44] In real life, however, the
end result, as we have seen, was most likely to have been divorce. In some of the

'marriage contracts' from the Late Period, there is a clause which stipulates that a wife would lose her financial rights in divorce because of 'the great sin which is found in a wife',[45] which can only mean infidelity.

At Deir el-Medina, when a man called Merysekhmet was caught in bed with the *hemet* of another workman, the workman complained to the court and eventually Merysekhmet swore not to speak to her again.[46] However, he broke his oath and made the woman pregnant. His own father took him to court this time and he was made to swear another oath that he would not go near her. Whether this was any more effective and what happened to the woman, her child, and her husband, remains unknown, but clearly there was no question of punishment by death for Merysekhmet who, one may add, came from a higher social stratum at Deir el-Medina than the woman's husband. This probably explains why, when the husband first complained of Merysekhmet's behaviour to the court, he was the one to be beaten. It was only because one of the chief workmen spoke out on his behalf against such injustice that the court was persuaded to take action against Merysekhmet at all.[47]

There is an interesting letter from Deir el-Medina dating to the Twentieth Dynasty. The sender is unknown and the text difficult to understand, but it seems to concern a married man who has been having an affair with another woman for eight months. Local indignation is running high, and a crowd gets together to go and beat up the woman and her household. Their complaint is that 'eight full months until today he is sleeping with that woman, though he is not (the?) husband ... If he were (the) husband, would he (then) not have sworn his oath concerning your woman?'[48] In other words, the problem seems to be that the man has taken up with another woman without divorcing his wife. The vengeful crowd, however, is held back by an unnamed steward who proceeds to send a message to the woman: 'As regards Nesamenemipet, why did you receive him repeatedly ... If the heart of that man is after you, let [him] enter the court together with his wife and let [him] swear an oath and return to your house ...'[49] If he does not follow the advice, the steward will not another time restrain the people from coming to beat her up. The steward's advice seems to be that if Nesamenemipet really wants the woman he is having an affair with, he must divorce his wife before moving in with the other woman. Since marriage and divorce were not legally sanctioned the part to be played by the court may seem puzzling. However, there may be two reasons why the court was involved. The oath the husband was supposed to swear may simply have been to the effect that he was divorcing his wife and that she was thus free to remarry. The court would have been witness to this to prevent the husband or anyone else trying to claim that she was still married. Second, it might have been a matter of making a settlement concerning property as a result of the termination of their marriage, and again the court would have been witness to what was decided. The woman with whom the husband was involved would appear herself to have been unmarried at this time or surely her husband would

22 Ostrakon showing a mother suckling her new-born baby in the special birth bower.

have been mentioned as an added complication. The aspect of the man's behaviour that gave rise to such censure was not, then, that he was having an affair with a married woman but that he was guilty of an irregularity in being married to one woman and having a long-term affair with another. As far as public opinion was concerned, the matter could have been settled, if we understand the text correctly, simply by the man divorcing his wife and marrying his lover. Perhaps part of the indignation was aroused by the wife's difficult situation. In the eyes of society she was still technically the wife of Nesamenemipet. This meant that economically her affairs and property were still tied up with his and that she was not free to remarry. Indeed, if she had tried to set up a household with another man, she might have lost some of her financial rights in any settlement on the grounds of infidelity.

Men and women without spouses

To be married was no doubt regarded as the natural state for both adult men and women. Nevertheless, there is some evidence that men occasionally went through life without marrying and as far as we know without offspring.[50] A fragmentary late Middle Kingdom narrative has left us with an account of a homosexual affair between king Neferkara of the Old Kingdom and his general Sasenet 'in whose [entire house] there was no wife.'[51] Homosexuality is apparently advised against in the *Instructions of Ptahhotep*, and in the New Kingdom *Book of the Dead*, one of the statements in the 'Negative Confession' is perhaps to be understood as 'I have not practised homosexuality.' The problem with homosexuality was that it did not conform to the Egyptian ideal of family life based on the concept of fertility, while in a funerary connection, the sterile nature of the relationship could have hindered rebirth into the next world.

There is even less evidence for unmarried women than for unmarried men,

23 Apotropaic wand for the protection of mothers and young children.

24 Scene from the tomb of Qenamun showing the tomb owner's mother, who was the nurse of Amenhotep II, with the king seated on her lap.

although it is unlikely that every woman found a marriage partner. Widows, as we shall see, were considered a disadvantaged group in society, along with orphans, the hungry, and the naked. We know little of what happened to divorced women. Some may have remarried, others returned to their father's house or joined the households of other relatives. The 'marriage contracts' of the Late Period were clearly designed to ensure that a divorced wife was not left destitute. Whether this was drawing on an established tradition or was a new institution is unclear. A Twentieth Dynasty ostrakon from Deir el-Medina may record a father's attempt to make a man swear that he will not abandon his (the father's) daughter on pain of receiving a hundred strokes and forfeiting all property the couple have acquired together.[52] Unfortunately, the word here translated as 'abandon' has also been understood as meaning 'ill treat' which would change the sense of the text. In any event we do not have the background to the case, so it is hard to draw conclusions from it. There is no evidence of what society's views might have been on homosexuality between women, but one can imagine that if a woman entered into such a relationship to the exclusion of bearing children, it would have been condemned in the same way as male homosexuality.

Choice of marriage partner

Little is said in the sources about where one might look for a marriage partner. Although full brother-sister marriage seems to have been confined to the royal family, close kin marriages were probably not uncommon in the New Kingdom.[53] It has also been suggested that when a man remarried after the death of his first wife, his second wife was sometimes the sister of the first.[54] One reason for such close kin marriages may have arisen from the division of inheritance between male and female offspring. Reuniting different branches of the family through marriage would help prevent the disintegration of family property. Unfortunately we are hampered in research into these matters because in most cases there is not enough information to trace the progenitors of both husband and wife back for more than one, or at the most two, generations.

FURTHER READING

Schafik Allam, 'Quelques aspects du mariage dans l'Égypte ancienne' *Journal of Egyptian Archaeology* 67 (1981), 116–35.

Schafik Allam, *Some Pages from Everyday Life in Ancient Egypt*, Giza, 1986.

C. Eyre, 'Crime and adultery in ancient Egypt' *Journal of Egyptian Archaeology* 70 (1984), 92–105.

P. Pestman, *Marriage and Matrimonial Property in Ancient Egypt*, Leiden, 1961.

CHAPTER FOUR

Fertility, pregnancy and childbirth

Fertility, childlessness, and adoption

The purpose of marriage, first and foremost, was to produce children and perpetuate the family. The author of the New Kingdom *Instruction of Any* advises his male readers:

> Take a wife while you are young,
> That she make a son for you;
> She should bear for you while you are youthful.
> It is proper to make people.
> Happy the man whose people are many,
> He is saluted on account of his progeny.[1]

Similarly two older *Instructions* advise: 'When you prosper, found your household, Take a hearty wife, a son will be born you',[2] and 'When you prosper and found your house, And love your wife with ardor . . . Gladden her heart as long as you live, She is a fertile field for her lord.'[3] Thus fertility was of prime importance, and infertility can be conjectured as a possible reason for divorce. In the magico-medical papyri there are tests for determining whether a woman is fertile or not, entitled 'to tell a woman who will give birth from one who will not'.[4]

Although we know less about houses than temples and tombs, evidence from sites such as Deir el-Medina and Amarna shows that houses would have had a domestic shrine. Here would be worshipped household deities like Bes and Taweret, and also the goddess Hathor, all of whom were linked with fertility and childbirth. Also connected with these shrines were small female figurines that are shown virtually naked, often with the pubic triangle marked in. Sometimes they wear a necklace, a girdle round the hips, and an elaborate hair arrangement. They occur in a variety of types and are known from the early Middle Kingdom through the New Kingdom and beyond, and have been found at settlement sites, tombs, and temples (fig. 17). Originally scholars called them 'concubine figures' and speculated that they were put into tombs to stimulate and gratify the sexual desires of the male tomb owner, but this explanation ignored their presence in women's burials, in temples, and in houses. It has now been shown that these objects related to fertility and birth,

25   Stela showing Ankhreni receiving offerings from his brother who is followed by 'his nurse Sithey'.

in life and in death.[5] Their presence in tombs is explained by the fact that the deceased, male or female, hoped to be reborn into the afterlife, so that these figurines were applicable to adult and child burials of both sexes. In life, their role in domestic cult related to the continuity of the family in this world, while in temples they were presented as votive offerings. Since the majority of surviving figures found in temple contexts come from Hathor shrines, this clearly links them to sexuality and fertility. One can only conjecture why they were offered as there are no texts to tell us, but it seems likely that they were presented by people wishing for a child.

In addition to petitioning the gods for favours, the Egyptians believed that the dead were able to have an influence on the lives of the living for good or ill, and a number of letters are addressed to the dead with complaints about the dead person's actions, or with pleas for help in some situation. Just such a letter was written in a hieratic hand of the First Intermediate Period on a red pottery vessel seemingly from a son to his dead father and presumably presented at the dead father's tomb. It asks the father to take action against two female servants, perhaps deceased, whom the writer seems to think responsible for the barrenness of his wife, so that she can bear him a son. As an afterthought the writer adds a request for another son to be born to his sister.[6]

In another case, dating to the Middle Kingdom, it is a daughter who seems to be asking for help. A statuette, clearly similar to a fertility figurine, carries a child on its left hip (fig. 18). It has an inscription on its right thigh which runs: 'May a birth be granted to your daughter Seh.'[7] The form of the hieroglyphs puts the piece into a funerary context, and one can imagine the barren woman Seh placing the little figure at her father's tomb, not to stimulate his own rebirth but in the hope that he could help her to conceive the child she so desperately wanted.

In the New Kingdom we meet a couple at Deir el-Medina, the scribe Ramose and his wife, Mutemwia, who are childless. It is perhaps not a coincidence that of all their surviving monuments, the only two the couple commissioned jointly were dedicated to deities of fertility and childbirth. If they were hoping to be granted a child, their prayers seem to have been in vain, since Ramose's successor in his office, Kenherkhepeshef, was not his son.[8] However, he seems to have been adopted by Ramose. The two men jointly dedicated an offering table to Osiris and Hathor, but more importantly, in an inscription on a stone seat, Kenherkhepeshef included the name of 'the king's scribe in the Place of Truth Ramose', and calls himself 'his son who makes his name to live, the scribe Kenherkhepeshef.' Ramose himself had been adopted by the scribe Huy, who calls Ramose 'son' in his tomb.[9] In another case, the chief workman Neferhotep and his wife Webkhet were childless. At one time Neferhotep seemed to be favouring the young Paneb, son of Nefersenut, who became the unsavoury chief workman we have already met over his affairs with married women. Their relationship, however, ended in a quarrel, and Neferhotep transferred his favour to Hesysunebef who was said to have begun life as a slave. Hesysunebef later dedicated a stela to Neferhotep, and he called his son after his benefactor, and his daughter after his benefactor's wife.[10]

In the *Adoption Papyrus* dating to the Eighteenth Dynasty, Nebnefer and his wife are childless, and Nebnefer adopts his wife as his heir to the exclusion of all other relatives. Later the wife, Rennefer, emancipates three children born to a slave woman that she and Nebnefer had purchased. A male relative of Rennefer marries the eldest girl, and he and the three children are adopted by Rennefer as her heirs. The implication is that Nebnefer fathered the three children on the slave.[11]

One answer, then, to childlessness was to adopt. A hard-hitting letter from Deir el-Medina dating to the Twentieth Dynasty throws further light on adoption. It was written to the scribe Nekhemmut and after the usual greeting continues:

> What's the meaning of your getting into such a bad mood as you are in that nobody's speech can enter your ears as a consequence of your inflated ego? You are not a man since you are unable to make your wives pregnant like your fellowmen.
>
> A further matter: You abound in being exceedingly stingy. You give no one anything. As for him who has no children, he adopts an orphan

instead [to] bring him up. It is his responsibility to pour water onto your
hands as one's own eldest son.[12]

However, we know little about the legal aspects of adoption, if any. As with
marriage, an important part would almost certainly be to do with disposition of
property and inheritance. Adopted children would surely also be responsible
for the burial and funerary cults of their adoptive parents. Adoption into a
family would probably have also brought responsibility towards the domestic
altar and cult of the ancestors.

Menstruation and pregnancy

There is little mention of menstruation in surviving documentation. Possible
references to sanitary towels occur in New Kingdom laundry lists.[13] According
to one interpretation of a passage in the Satire of Trades, the washerman
'cleans the clothes of a woman in menstruation',[14] but this has recently been
disputed.[15] In the much later Demotic story of Setne Khaemwaset, the newly
married princess Ahwere says: 'when my time of purification came I made no
more purification.'[16] Since from what follows it is clear that she means she had
become pregnant, we can deduce both that menstruation, at this time at least,
necessitated purification, and that missing an expected period was taken as a
sign of conception. This observation is surely far older than the text.

The necessity for coitus to produce pregnancy was well-known. Ahwere's
announcement comes after she says: 'He slept with me that night and found me

26 Servant woman
suckling a child.

[pleasing. He slept] with me again and again and we loved each other.'[17] Similar references to conception are found in the New Kingdom stories of the Doomed Prince, and Truth and Falsehood. In the first we read: 'There once was a king to whom no son had been born. [After a time his majesty] begged a son for himself from the gods of his domain, and they decreed that one should be born to him. That night he slept with his wife and she [became] pregnant. When she had completed the months of childbearing, a son was born.'[18] In the second story, Truth 'slept with her that night and knew her with the knowledge of a man. And she conceived a son that night.'[19] In the Old Kingdom Pyramid Texts the conception of the god Horus, son of the divine couple Isis and Osiris is described thus: 'Your sister Isis comes to you [Osiris] rejoicing for love of you. You have placed her on your phallus and your seed issues forth into her . . .'[20] Words relating to copulation and impregnation are often determined in the hieroglyphic script by a phallus emitting liquid, here presumably to be understood as semen. If in other myths and mythical narratives biologically impossible accounts of conception occur, it should not be taken to mean that the Egyptians failed to understand the mechanism of conception in reality. Such accounts are found worldwide in myth and folklore in societies which, like the Egyptians, are otherwise plainly cognisant with the facts of life. However, when in the story of Horus and Seth, Seth eats Horus' semen and becomes pregnant,[21] it shows that the connection between semen and pregnancy was clearly recognised.

Although failure to have a period was understood as a possible sign of conception, the ancient Egyptians had also developed a number of tests that could be performed to indicate whether a woman was pregnant or not. These are described in various magico-medical papyri, some of which deal almost exclusively with gynaecology, obstetrics, and childcare, showing how important successful childbearing and rearing was for Egyptian society. These texts, like all medical papyri, remain obscure in many places because of gaps in our lexicographical knowledge, so that the ingredients of many of the prescriptions remain unidentified. It is often difficult to equate with modern terminology the conditions and diseases described, especially since the Egyptians' understanding of illness was very different from ours today; disease was believed to be caused by the malevolence of demons or the dead. Further, lacunae in many of the papyri make the already difficult task of reading the texts even harder.

Tests for pregnancy included taking the pulse, examining the condition of the breasts and the colour of the skin, and observing the effects of urine on the germination of grains of barley and emmer wheat. The last test, if positive, was also supposed to indicate the sex of the expected child. The woman was to urinate on the grains every day. If they sprouted, she was pregnant. If the barley sprouted first, the child would be male, but if the emmer sprouted first, it would be female. If neither sprouted, then she was not pregnant.[22]

Although fertility was of the utmost importance in ancient Egypt, there must have been occasions when pregnancy was unwanted, for some medical texts also contain prescriptions for contraceptives for women.[23] Not all of these would have had much effect in practice, but intravaginal insertions of different substances may in some cases have been effective. For instance, crocodile dung or honey could have served to block the passage of the sperm. One prescription includes ground acacia tips, amongst other ingredients. These contain gum arabic, which has a chemical effect on sperm, and actively retards conception.[24] We shall see later that children might be suckled for up to three years, and this may also have reduced the chances of becoming pregnant. There is no evidence that there were any methods of contraception that could be used by a man.

Pregnancy is rarely depicted in formal art. An exception is found in the cycles of scenes showing the divine birth of the king. Here the king's mother is shown being led by various deities to the birth room. Although the depiction is discreet, the shape of the queen's belly is quite distinct from that found in the normal female image, and clearly signals that she is with child (fig. 1). The only female deity who is regularly shown pregnant is Taweret, the protector of pregnant women (fig. 19). She takes the form of a hippopotamus with the limbs of a lion, the tail of a crocodile, and flat, pendulous human breasts. She stands upright on her hind legs and her obviously swollen belly sticks out in front. In addition, the hieroglyph determining words relating to conception and pregnancy shows a kneeling woman who is clearly pregnant. Otherwise, in formal art, the image of a slender-bodied woman is predominant, despite the fact that between puberty and menopause most Egyptian women probably spent much of their time in one stage or another of pregnancy.

In informal art there is one type of vessel, usually made of calcite (Egyptian alabaster), which is fashioned in the form of a pregnant woman (fig. 20).[25] The figure, which stands or squats, is naked with the hands placed on the abdomen as though rubbing it. In one example, it holds an oil horn, and it is thought that the vessels themselves held oil which would have been used to massage the skin of a pregnant woman, to help prevent the formation of stretch marks and to ease the tight skin over the stomach. Actual oil horns similar to the one carried on the vessel have been found, the majority in female tombs.

Once pregnancy had been achieved, precautions might need to be taken against miscarriage. It is interesting that almost all of the pregnant woman vessels are shown without genitals even though they are naked. Perhaps this was to provide magical protection against miscarriage: if a woman's body is closed up without an opening, she cannot miscarry. One example, however, shows a tampon inserted into the vagina, the purpose of which was perhaps to prevent an escape of blood which might herald a miscarriage. It has been suggested that the so-called Isis-knot often found as a protective amulet originally functioned as just such a tampon for the goddess Isis when she was pregnant with Horus, and Seth was attempting to destroy the child in the

27 Vessel in the form of a lactating woman.

womb.[26] Some of the remedies against miscarriage found in the magico-
medical texts make use of the divine precedent of Isis and Horus to protect the
pregnant woman from bleeding and miscarriage. A spell referring to the divine
scenario was said over certain objects which were then applied to the woman's
posterior or placed in her vulva.[27]

The duration of pregnancy is not specifically mentioned in the magico-
medical texts, but must have been known from experience. In one spell for
speeding up childbirth it is said of Isis that 'her months have been completed
according to the (right) number'.[28] In the New Kingdom *Instruction of Any*, the
writer says: 'when you were born after your months',[29] while in the *Doomed
Prince*, also New Kingdom in date, the hero's mother 'completed the months of
childbearing'.[30] In an earlier Middle Kingdom story, the magician Djedi is able
to answer the question 'when will Rudjedet give birth?' with a date,[31] which
might indicate a calculation based on the duration of pregnancy, or it might
merely be an aspect of Djedi's magical knowledge and ability to foretell the
future.

Childbirth

Little is known about the process of childbirth itself in ancient Egypt. The
hieroglyph determining words relating to birth shows a kneeling woman with
the head and arms of a child appearing beneath her in the process of birth. The
actual delivery is rarely depicted in art, although some Ptolemaic temple
scenes show the birth of a divine child. Usually one goddess stands behind the
mother holding her, and one kneels in front to receive the child. A Middle
Kingdom story records the miraculous birth, as triplets, of the first three kings
of the Fifth Dynasty. The mother Rudjedet is attended at the birth by the four
goddesses, Isis, Nephthys, Meskhenet, and Hekat. Each birth is described in a
similar manner, apart from words spoken by Isis punning on the child's name:
'Isis placed herself before her [Rudjedet], Nephthys behind her, Hekat has-
tened the birth. Isis said: "Don't be so mighty in her womb, you whose name is
'Mighty'. The child slid into her arms . . . They washed him, having cut his
navel cord, and laid him on a pillow of cloth. Then Meskhenet approached him
and said: "A king who will assume the kingship in this whole land".'[32]

As we have seen, a number of magico-medical texts contain sections which
relate to women in childbirth. There are prescriptions or spells concerned with
'separating the child from the womb of the mother',[33] while others are said
specifically to be for speeding up the birth, presumably in the case of a long–
drawn-out labour.[34] The efficacy of these spells often derives from the identification of the woman in labour with one of the goddesses Hathor or Isis:
'Hathor, the Lady of Dendera is < the > one who is giving birth!'[35] One spell is
specifically entitled: 'For speeding up the childbirth of Isis',[36] and describes to
the gods the calamities that will befall if Isis fails to give birth now her time is
come. The implication is that thus threatened the gods will cause her to give

birth, and they are then exhorted to take care of the child-bearing of the human mother in the same way.

While Isis represents the mother *par excellence*, Hathor is the goddess of fertility, sexuality and childbirth. In one unfortunately damaged spell, the speaker is cast as the woman giving birth who invokes Hathor to be present on the joyful occasion: 'Rejoicing, rejoicing in heaven, in heaven! Birth giving is accelerated! Come to me, Hathor, my mistress, in my fine pavilion, in this happy hour.'[37] The purpose of the spell is again to speed the birth and achieve a successful outcome. Many women must have approached childbirth in fear, anticipating long pain and the possibility of death.

Closely associated with Hathor, especially in the Late Period, was the household god Bes (fig. 21). Like her, he was concerned with sexuality and its aftermath, pregnancy and childbirth. He is shown with the squat body and short legs of a dwarf, although his face usually has the mane and ears of a lion. Images of Bes were given to women during childbirth, and are referred to in spells to ease the pain of labour.[38]

Women were often delivered while squatting on two large bricks, and in one text a man, recounting how he was chastised by the goddess Meresger, says: 'I sat on bricks like the woman in labour.'[39] The goddess Meskhenet, whom we met in the story about the delivery of Rudjedet, was a personification of one of these bricks. A spell concerning childbirth in one papyrus invokes Meskhenet and is 'to be spoken over the two bricks . . .'[40] Rudjedet was delivered in a room in her house, but there is some evidence that, at least in the New Kingdom, birth took place, if possible, in a specially built structure erected perhaps in the garden or on the roof of the house.[41] The purpose was probably to isolate the new mother and child from the community, a custom found in other cultures worldwide. These structures have not survived but are known from representations, and it was into such a building that Hathor was invited by the expectant mother in one of the spells quoted above. A number of ostraka from the workmen's village at Deir el-Medina depict the building, while fragments of painted plaster from the same site show that the structure was also included in scenes decorating some of the houses in the village. As shown, the building consists of a matting roof supported by light papyriform columns decorated with convolvulus vines (fig. 22). The mother sits on a stool or a bed. In scenes with a stool, the woman is almost always naked except for a collar and girdle round her hips. Her hairstyle is distinctive in that the hair is tied up on top of her head so that it falls down in bunches all around. She usually suckles a new-born child. She is waited on by one or more young girls who are similarly naked but for collar and girdle. When the mother sits on a bed, she is normally dressed in a fine linen garment with an elaborate enveloping wig and an ointment cone on top of her head. Female servants often carry a mirror and wash the woman's feet. Cosmetic vessels may also be shown. It has been suggested that this is a depiction of the purification ritual that a woman may

28   Model of a weaving workshop from the tomb of Meketra.

have had to undergo after giving birth before rejoining the community.[42] In the story of Rudjedet, we are told that after the birth of her three children she 'cleansed herself in a cleansing of fourteen days'.[43]

These scenes of successful childbirth that decorated the house may have been intended to give protection to mothers and children and to help ensure a happy outcome to the birth. Other fragments of painted plaster both from the workmen's village at Deir el-Medina and from the similar village at Amarna show that rooms were also decorated with figures of the deities Bes and Taweret, whom we have already met.[44] Bes was a protective deity who often carried the hieroglyph *sa* meaning 'protection', and his grotesque appearance was probably apotropaic, to scare off evil demons who might come against the household (fig. 21). His image may also be shown carrying a knife, which was used to ward off any threat to those he guarded. He seems to have been particularly connected with bedroom furniture, and his figure appears on beds, headrests, chairs, mirror handles, and other cosmetic items in both royal and private contexts. We have seen that one aspect of his protective role was to watch over women in childbirth, but he also protected mothers and new-born children after birth. Taweret, with her combination of hippopotamus, lion, and crocodile, also presents a ferocious appearance intended to scare away evil forces. Like Bes, her image often carries the hieroglyph for 'protection', or a knife to drive off demons (fig. 19).

Amulets representing both these deities are widely attested and were surely worn by pregnant women and young mothers to ward off danger (fig. 21). Certainly, pregnancy and childbirth were highly dangerous for women. Apart from the risk of bleeding and miscarriage already mentioned, death in childbirth, as in all pre-modern societies, was an ever-present threat, as evidence from burials shows. Not surprisingly there are spells to try and protect the mother. In one, death is envisaged as harming the woman by having sexual intercourse with her: 'you shall not have intercourse [with this woman] ... You shall not associate with her, you shall not do to her anything bad or evil.'[45] Another spell in the same papyrus provides a test to see whether the birth will go well or badly.[46]

The dangers of infancy

Child mortality was also high, as evidence from both burials and texts shows. In the New Kingdom *Instruction of Any* the author says: 'Do not say, "I am too young to be taken", For you do not know your death. When death comes he steals the infant Who is in his mother's arms, Just like him who reached old age.'[47] A stela from the Late Period belongs to a child who is made to say in the inscription: 'Harm is what befell me When I was but a child! ... I was driven from childhood too early! Turned away from my house as a youngster, Before I had my fill in it! The dark, a child's terror, engulfed me, While the breast was in my mouth!'[48] In one magico-medical papyrus, tests are provided to discover whether a new-born child will live or not. A Nineteenth Dynasty letter was written to a woman in whose care two infants had died.[49] Thus a woman might go through the whole rigorous process of pregnancy and childbirth only to have her child snatched away from her.

In order to avert the risks, a whole range of spells and other magical protection was developed to safeguard the child. One papyrus gives a spell: 'To make a protection for a child on the day of its birth.'[50] Another papyrus, dating to the Second Intermediate Period or early New Kingdom but using material from the Middle Kingdom, contains two books, each written in a different hand, but both with similar subject matter.[51] The first is to do with treating two unidentified childish ailments. The second begins with spells and prescriptions relating to birth, continues with spells against further unidentified infant diseases, followed by a spell for the mother's milk, and ends with spells for the child to protect it against various demons and the dead.

Many of the spells work through the identification of the infant with the Horus child, son of Isis: 'The voice of Ra calls Wepet because the stomach of this [child] whom Isis has born is ill';[52] 'My arms are over this child – the arms of Isis are over him, as she puts her arms over her son Horus';[53] 'You are Horus, you have awoken as Horus. You are the living Horus. I drive out the illness which is in your body and the pain which is in your limbs . . .'[54] The function of many of the spells is to make a protective amulet to hang round the neck of the child. The following example was meant to protect the child against fever:

> Spell for a knot
> for a child, a fledgling:
> Are you hot in the nest?
> Are you burning in the bush?
> Your mother is not with you?
> There is no sister there <to> fan (you)?
> There is no nurse to offer protection?
> Let there be brought to me a pellet of gold,
> Forty beads, a cornelian seal–stone,
> (with) a crocodile and hand (on it),
> to fell, to drive off this Demon of Desire, to warm the limbs,
> to fell these male and female enemies from the West [the dead].
> You shall break out! This is a protection.
> ONE SHALL SAY THIS SPELL OVER THE PELLET OF GOLD,
> THE FORTY BEADS, AND THE CORNELIAN SEAL-STONE,
> (WITH) THE CROCODILE AND THE HAND.
> TO BE STRUNG ON A STRIP OF FINE LINEN;
> MADE INTO AN AMULET;
> PLACED ON THE NECK OF THE CHILD.
> Good.[55]

Actual seal-stones like the one described in this spell have been found. The crocodile is here a protective demon while the hand perhaps represents 'the magician's gestures of power'.[56] The spell is entitled 'for a knot', and in many cases the instructions for making an amulet include tying a particular number of knots: 'One causes the child . . . to eat a cooked mouse. Its bones are placed at his neck in a strip of fine linen and one makes seven knots';[57] 'It is made from a lock of hair with four knots and placed at the neck of the child';[58] 'One says this spell over a seal (with) a hand being made into an amulet, being knotted into seven knots, one knot in the morning, another in the evening until the completion of seven knots'.[59]

In the Middle Kingdom and the Second Intermediate Period a common item associated with mothers and children was a wand decorated with apotropaic figures. The curved wands were usually made from the tusk of a hippopotamus, though other materials were occasionally used. The tusk was split in half so that one side was flat and the other convex; one or both were decorated with figures of fantastic animals, benevolent demons, and apotropaic symbols (fig. 23). The figure of a frog represents Hekat, a goddess associated with childbirth whom we have already met in the story of Rudjedet, while a seated cat probably refers to the sun god Ra. The most common figure is the pregnant hippopotamus goddess, whom we have already met as Taweret although she may not yet have acquired this name in the Middle Kingdom, when she was usually called Ipet. A figure resembling Bes is also frequently found. In two cases there are inscriptions giving the name as Aha, who is known to have been a Middle Kingdom precursor of Bes. These figures are often associated with apotropaic symbols like the *wedjat* eye, or hieroglyphs like *sa* meaning 'protection', and *ankh* meaning 'life'. In addition the figures on many examples carry knives to threaten any evil which attempts to come against mother or child.

The protective nature of the wands is further made explicit by the inscriptions which some of them bear. Several simply say 'protection by night, protection by day'. Others are longer; one runs: 'Cut off the head of the enemy when he enters the chamber of the children whom the lady . . . has borne.'[60] These inscriptions usually name women, who are presumably their owners, and also often given the name of a child. Some of the women are called 'mistress of the house', while others are 'king's daughter', showing that the wands were used in both royal and private contexts.

A study of these objects has shown that their supposed effectiveness was derived from an identification between the child concerned and the young sun god.[61] The wands were presumably placed in the pregnant woman's bedroom or in the nursery after birth, and perhaps used with spells recited for protection. In two tombs, similarly shaped wands are shown carried by nurses, and a secondary use of the objects was a funerary one. The wands could be placed in burials to protect the deceased during the rebirth into the next life by warding off the dangers that threatened at this time.

Also dating to the Middle Kingdom are examples of another form of protection for children, cylindrical charm cases. Sometimes these are solid, but others are hollow and have been found with garnets or balls of copper wire inside. They were designed to be strung and worn round the child's neck, and undoubtedly relate to the amulets over which the spells of the magico-medical papyri were to be spoken. Later, in the New Kingdom, it became customary to write protective spells on pieces of papyrus which were folded up so that they could be placed in small cylindrical cases. These again would be hung round the neck of a child. Called oracular amuletic decrees by modern scholars, the spells take the form of a decree issued by a god, and cover every sort of disaster

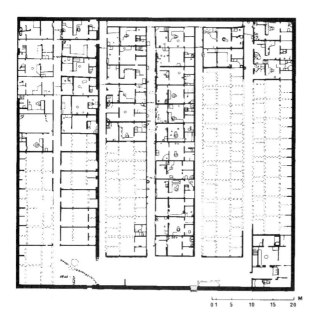

29   Plan of the workmen's village at Amarna.

that might befall the child named in the text. They also look ahead to the future and guarantee the successful production of the next generation: for a male child, 'I shall open the womb of his wives to bear male and female children as seed which has come forth from his body. I shall cause them to live, I shall cause <them> to be healthy, I shall cause them to grow up, I shall cause [them] to become clever...';[62] for a female child, 'We shall (cause) her to conceive <male> and female children. We shall cause her to be healthy. We shall cause those whom she bears to live, we shall cause her to bear with a happy delivery...'[63] In addition, other amulets, like the *wedjat* eye, were probably given to women and children to wear for protection.

Suckling

While texts make clear both the desirability of having children and the dangers of childbirth, there is little said about whether there were any celebrations or ceremonies attending a successful birth, apart from the purification of the woman. In many cultures, the parents are congratulated and gifts are given. In the story of Setne Khaemwaset, pharaoh sends gifts to Ahwere when he learns that she is pregnant, not at the birth of the child.[64] Nor is there any good evidence for celebrations from Deir el-Medina despite a possible reference to gifts given to a father 'at the confinement of his daughter',[65] for, even if understood correctly, this could recount a singular occurrence rather than custom.

From the *Instruction of Any* we learn that a mother might suckle her child for three years. This length of time is not unusual in many societies; one benefit may be that a woman reduces her chances of becoming pregnant while she is lactating, so that she can diminish the rate at which she bears children. While the majority of women probably suckled their own children, wetnurses are attested for royal children and also in elite scribal families. Royal nurses were themselves members of elite families, often the wives or mothers of high officials. Their connection with the king's children brought great prestige to their own families, and may have helped to advance their husbands or later their sons to higher rank. Most often these women can only be recognised by their titles; occasionally they appear in association with their royal charges (fig. 24), but it is very unusual for them to be shown actually suckling a child.[66]

Similarly, wetnurses employed by elite scribal families are rarely shown suckling. They are occasionally depicted in private tomb chapels and on funerary stelae together with members of the family, perhaps in association with the child they nursed (fig. 25). Wetnurses were also employed in the workmen's village at Deir el-Medina. A letter makes mention of a woman, her child, and her nurse,[67] while an account records payment made to a doctor and a wetnurse after a man's wife had given birth to a child.[68] It is unclear whether wetnurses were employed only when a mother's own milk failed or when the mother had died. It might have been considered more prestigious to use a wetnurse rather than feed one's own child, just as in recent times cachet has, in some circles, been attached to bottle-feeding. Certainly, if royal children usually had a wetnurse, this custom might have been copied in elite families as a status symbol. However, the author of the *Instruction of Any*, himself a member of the scribal elite, assumes that a son is suckled by his mother, and another New Kingdom text compares the joy of being a scribe with the joy a mother feels in 'giving birth, when her heart knows no distaste. She is constant in nursing her son; her breast is in his mouth every day'.[69] If suckling reduces the chances of conceiving, women who wanted to conceive again quickly might

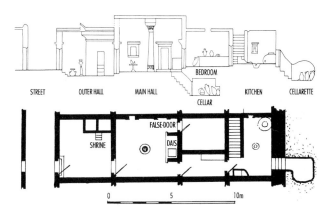

30   Plan and section of a house in the workmen's village at Deir el-Medina.

deliberately use a wetnurse. No doubt, as in other societies, the use of wet-nurses may have varied from period to period, and gone in and out of fashion.

A wetnurse needed to be a woman who had given birth to her own child. Perhaps it had died, or perhaps she was feeding two children at once. Whatever the case, it was important that the milk supply, whether a child was suckled by a nurse or by its own mother, should not dry up. The magico-medical papyri also contain ways to stimulate the production of milk, and include tests to help recognise whether milk is good or bad.

Suckling by human mothers is not a common subject in Egyptian art, although examples, including ostraka from Deir el-Medina (fig. 22) and some fertility figurines, can be found at all periods. The women shown, however, rarely belong to the elite class but are mainly peasants and servants.[70] Some-times a nursing woman is included in subsidiary 'daily life' scenes in private tomb chapels in which the mother suckles her child while continuing to carry out her normal job (fig. 26). The same subject is occasionally represented on a small scale in statuary. Usually the woman is unnamed, showing that a generic type rather than an individual is being depicted. The nursing woman often kneels or squats on the ground, supporting the child against her thigh or raised knee, or she may sit on a seat holding the child on her lap with both its legs hanging down one side. In other examples she stands and carries the child on her left arm while she offers her breast with her right hand.

Mothers' milk was regarded as an efficacious ingredient in some prescrip-tions. For instance, one papyrus recommends: 'tips of papyrus, *sepet* grains, finely ground and mixed with the milk of a woman who has born a boy. A *hin* (about half a litre) of it is given to the child and he will pass a day and night in a healthy sleep.'[71] A number of pottery vessels have been found in the shape of a squatting woman holding a child (fig. 27).[72] The child, however, is not shown being suckled, but the woman sometimes holds her breast with her hand, perhaps squeezing it to express milk. She wears a skirt and a shawl draped over her shoulders to give easy access to her breasts. In addition she wears a distinctive hairstyle which is different from that of the pregnant woman vessel (fig. 20), from that on the mother in the birth pavilion (fig. 22), and from the

31   Market scene on the banks of the Nile in the tomb of Ipy.

32   Tomb model showing a woman grinding grain. The light colour of the skin identifies the sex of the figure.

styles worn by married elite women found in formal art (figs. 57, 77). The main body of hair falls down the back, while two long thin locks hang down in front, one either side of the face. An amulet representing the rising moon is worn round the neck and relates to the production of milk. These vessels range from 11–17 cm in height with a capacity that 'is roughly the amount that one breast produces at one feed'.[73] It is generally surmised by scholars that these vessels were used to hold mothers' milk for medical purposes.

If human mothers are only rarely shown nursing, it is otherwise in the divine sphere, where goddesses are frequently depicted suckling the king or the deceased, as a means of renewal and to aid the passage from one state of being to another. In addition, texts place the king in a filial relationship with a whole range of deities. By the act of suckling, a goddess confirms the king as her son and thus ratifies his divinity.

FURTHER READING

J. Baines, 'Society, morality, and religious practice' in: B. Shafer (ed.) *Religion in Ancient Egypt*, Ithaca, 1991, 164–72 (Magic and divination).

J. Borghouts, *Ancient Egyptian Magical Texts*, Leiden, 1978.

R. Janssen and J. Janssen, *Growing up in Ancient Egypt*, London 1990.

G. Pinch, 'Childbirth and female figurines at Deir el-Medina and el-Amarna' *Orientalia* 52 (1983), 405–14.

G. Pinch, *Votive offerings to Hathor*, Oxford, 1993.

CHAPTER FIVE

The family and the household

The house and home

One of the commonest titles on the monuments for elite women from at least the beginning of the Twelfth Dynasty is that of 'mistress of the house' (*nebet per*). It seems to have indicated a married woman although this cannot be proved absolutely. Taken at face value, it implies that the bearer was in charge of running the household, and this is supported by a passage in the New Kingdom *Instruction of Any*: 'Do not control your wife in her house, When you know she is efficient; Don't say to her: "Where is it? Get it!" When she has put it in the right place. Let your eye observe in silence, Then you recognise her skill.'[1]

In the Nineteenth Dynasty story of the *Two Brothers*, the two men work in the fields, while the wife of the elder brother (the younger is unmarried) stays in the house. Her husband clearly expects her to be waiting for him at home when he returns in the evening.[2] This gender distinction would fit in with the idealised world of the tomb chapel scenes where women rarely accompany the male owner when he is engaged in activities outside on his estates. Nor is he commonly accompanied by a woman when he goes hunting, and again this has an echo in the story of the *Two Brothers* where we are told that Bata's wife 'sat in his house while he spent the day hunting desert game'.[3] Although the evidence is sparse, we can thus deduce that while men of elite families expected to hold bureaucratic office, to administer estates, and go hunting in the desert, women did not take part in these activities but were, rather, in charge of household affairs for at least part of their time.

Although houses and settlement sites in general are not well-known archaeologically, a few such sites from the Middle and New Kingdoms have been excavated. The Middle Kingdom town of Kahun, which lies close to the entrance to the Faiyum on the edge of the desert, was built to house the personnel responsible for the funerary cult of Senusret II whose pyramid complex was laid out nearby. The Eighteenth Dynasty city of Amarna was a new foundation built by Akhenaten for his god the Aten on a site not previously claimed by any god or goddess. Since all the desirable land along the Nile had long been settled, the city was built on an unoccupied site on the east bank in Middle Egypt where the desert runs almost down to the river. Amarna was

33   Harvesting grapes and trapping and preparing birds for eating.

founded and abandoned within a period of approximately two decades, after which it was reclaimed by the desert. Akhenaten also moved the royal burial site from Thebes to Amarna, and he built a special village to the east of the city, even further into the desert, to house the workmen who were to be responsible for the royal tomb. This village has also been found and excavated. Finally, we have already come across the workmen's village at Deir el-Medina. This was also a government foundation, established near the beginning of the Eighteenth Dynasty in the desert on the west bank at Thebes to house the workmen who built the royal tombs in the Valley of the Kings. The somewhat artificial nature of this village and its counterpart at Amarna is shown, for example, by their distance from the river and the lack of a local water supply; a service had to be laid on by the state to bring water up from the river every day. From these various sites we can gain some idea of what housing was like in ancient Egypt for both the wealthy and the less well off.

The plans recovered for the large houses at Kahun show that the actual living space consisted of a central area of rooms and courtyards, including a garden court entered through a colonnade.[4] In the house there was a central reception room where the roof was supported on four columns and a principal bedroom recognisable by the alcove for the bed, a feature known from other Egyptian houses. This central area was surrounded by groups of other rooms and courts, one of which can be recognised as a granary. During the First Intermediate Period through the first half of the Twelfth Dynasty it was customary for officials to include in their tombs models of various activities that took place on their estates. Granaries for the storage of grain are not uncommon. One of the most extensive set of models comes from the tomb of Meketra at Thebes.[5] If we look at the various 'workshops' shown in the models, we can suggest the sort of activities that might have taken place in the outer areas of the Kahun houses. In addition to the granary, we find a cattle shed, a building where the animals were butchered, a bakery and brewery, a weaving shed (fig. 28), and a carpenter's workshop.

The type of layout that we see at Kahun was still used in the large houses at Amarna which belonged to high officials, but here the elements were more spread out in the spacious grounds of the properties than they had been in the compact town houses at Kahun.[6] A large compound was enclosed by a wall, within which stood the house itself surrounded by other buildings functioning as granaries, animal sheds, a kitchen, and areas for craft production. Evidence has been found which shows that spinning and weaving were carried out somewhere on the premises. In the grounds, there was also a well, a garden with trees where flowers and vegetables may have been grown, and a shrine dedicated to the cult of the king and his family.[7] A porter's lodge stood at the entrance to the compound, and there was a separate small house within the enclosure whose purpose is unknown.

The main house, roughly square in plan, was laid out round a central square living room, which had a low brick dais at one end, where visitors were received.[8] The ceiling was raised on wooden columns and windows were inserted high up on the walls. Other rooms were grouped round the central one and included an outer reception room, storage rooms, and the family quarters in which we can recognise the principal bedroom by its raised alcove at the back where a wooden single bed would have been placed. Beside the bedroom was a small bathroom and lavatory but no drainage. There was also an internal staircase which must have led to the roof, where people would probably have sat, worked, eaten their meals, and slept at appropriate times of the day and year. It is possible that in some of the houses an upper room may have been built over the front of the house which would have somewhat increased the living space.

The housing provided by the state for the workmen at Amarna and Deir el-Medina was built on a rather different plan. The walled villages were laid out along streets running the length of the village enclosure. Rows of houses fronted onto the streets, and each house was rectangular rather than square (fig. 29). At Amarna each house occupied an area of slightly under five metres by ten, and was divided into three unequal parts from front to back.[9] A doorway at one end of the frontage led from the street straight into the front room which measured about five by two or two and a half metres and was often divided by a wall into two parts. The presence of feeding troughs in some houses showed that animals could be kept here.[10] There was often a limestone mortar sunk into the floor for pounding grain with a pestle, and a milling emplacement for grinding the broken grain.[11] Evidence from some houses shows that various types of craft production might take place there, including possibly spinning and weaving, which were certainly carried out somewhere in the houses.[12] Although there is some evidence that the houses were decorated with wall paintings on plaster, little remains. However, fragments of scenes survived in the front rooms of two houses at the time of excavation. One showed a group of dancing Bes figures facing towards a figure of the goddess Taweret. The other depicted a procession of women apparently dancing.[13]

A doorway from the front room led directly into the square living room which was approximately five by five metres. The roof was supported by a central wooden column, and a brick dais, some seven or more centimetres high, ran around one or two sides of the room. It would have been covered with mats on which stools and chairs might be placed. In one house an upturned limestone table was found on the dais.[14] From tomb scenes we can conjecture that people of high status sat on stools or chairs, while others squatted directly on the mats. The usual type of stool found in the village was semicircular, with three legs and a slightly hollowed seat made of stone.[15] At night most of the family may have slept on the dais. One of the commonest features of this room was a hearth made from a large pottery bowl, since in winter in this part of Egypt temperatures can drop to near freezing.[16] There is also evidence that pottery vessels stood in this room,[17] and these may have contained the household's supply of water that had to be specially brought up to the waterless village. At night the room could be lit by lamps, saucers containing oil or fat with a wick, that were placed in niches in the walls about one metre above the ground or else set on a bracket consisting of two pegs driven into the wall.[18]

The rear part of the house was divided into two areas. One, which sometimes had support for shelves and a low dais against the long wall, may have been a bedroom. In one house 'patches of the mud plaster [on the dais] showed traces of wear...It is tempting to see this as a consequence of limestone bed-leg supports having stood here originally.'[19] The other area often contained a staircase with a cupboard beneath it, the stairs running up to the roof. Alternatively the staircase could be in the front room, in which case the layout of the house was somewhat different.[20]

Ovens, necessary for baking bread, were sometimes found in one of the rear rooms, but in many cases there was no oven built into the ground floor. In one house, however, there is evidence that the bread oven, which never reached high temperatures, was on the roof.[21] As in the city itself, use would have been made of the roof to expand available living space, and for instance, spindles

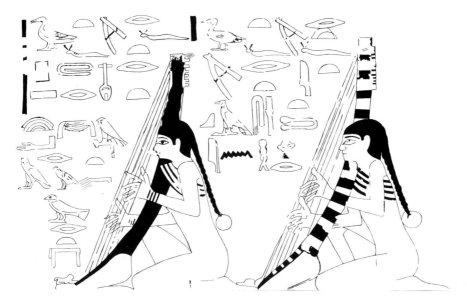

34   Two of the tomb owner's daughters play the harp.

were often found by the excavators on top of debris from the roof suggesting that spinning had sometimes been carried out there. Other evidence suggests that some of the houses possessed a second storey over part of the house.[22] Such an extra room would have increased the rather meagre amount of roofed living space, and possibly provided an area of privacy not possible in the main living room below.

The houses at Deir el-Medina were similar in some ways to those at Amarna, but there were also differences (fig. 30). For a start they were slightly larger, measuring approximately five metres by fifteen instead of ten.[23] A doorway at one end of the façade led into the front room from the street. There was a rectangular raised platform against one wall, surrounded by a low para-pet or a screen reaching to the ceiling, with three to five steps leading up to it. The outside might be decorated with the figure of a deity, often Bes, but sometimes Horus or Isis. The room might also have niches for offerings, stelae, and ancestral busts.

A doorway from the front room led directly into the main room where the ceiling was supported by a wooden pillar in the centre. As at Amarna, a low dais ran along one wall, and a stela or false door was set into the wall. Sometimes a stairway beneath a trap door near the dais led down to a cellar. New-born children who had failed to survive were occasionally buried under the floor.

The back part of the house divided into three areas, two lying side by side transversely and the third situated behind. One of these was the bedroom, entered directly from the main room, while the second lying beside it was really a passage leading from the main room to the kitchen behind. The latter was fitted with grinding equipment, an oven, another cellar in the back wall, and a staircase leading onto the roof.

A letter from a house owner in Deir el-Medina gives us a glimpse of the sort of furniture found in one of these houses. This included two beds, a clothes hamper, two couches for a man, five stools, two footstools, one chest, and a box.[24]

The family in the house

Archaeology has provided us with the physical plans of houses and some evidence of the use of space in them. The problem remains how to relate these findings to the people who actually lived there. Obvious questions are: what size were the families who occupied these houses? Where did they all sleep? Were there areas specific to gender and if so, did these apply equally in large and small houses, or were they a luxury of the wealthy? Unfortunately these questions are extremely difficult to answer, although they clearly have a direct bearing on our understanding of the position of women within the household.

From the New Kingdom *Instruction of Any* we learn that the ideal was for a man to have many children. On stelae of both the Middle and New Kingdoms we find large family groups depicted, and one stela of the Theban Eleventh Dynasty actually tells us that the owner's wife had had twelve children.[25] Documents from the early Middle Kingdom allow us to work out the composition of the household of a small landholder called Heqanakht, which seems to have consisted of more than sixteen people.[26] In addition to Heqanakht himself, there were five men, almost certainly his sons, one of whom had his own family. Then there was Ipi, who was Heqanakht's mother; her maidservant; a woman called Hetepet, who may have been a female relative or a servant; Iutenheb, the wife of Heqanakht; and Senen, a maid who was to be dismissed because of her attitude to Iutenheb. The unidentified women called Nefret and Satweret may also have been female relatives, perhaps even daughters. In addition there was another woman called Hetepet, the daughter of someone called May, and Heti's son Nakht who was a subordinate of Heqanakht, together with his family. These were all people that Heqanakht was responsible for and to whom he gave grain rations. Whether they all lived in one house is unclear.

A Middle Kingdom document from Kahun lists over a number of years the household of a soldier called Hori which later became that of his son Sneferu.[27] At first there was only Hori, his wife Shepset, and their new-born son Sneferu. Then Hori's mother and her five daughters were added. We can surmise that Hori's father had died and that for some reason his widow was without a home and moved into her son's house, together with five daughters who were presumably unmarried at the time. The final entry that we have was made after the death of Hori. Sneferu must have inherited the house and become head of the household. He was not yet married, but had living with him his mother, his father's mother, and three of his father's sisters; the other two had presumably either died or got married. The household thus changed in number over the years from three to nine, and then to six. However, Hori and Shepset appear to have had only one surviving child, while Hori's parents had at least six. This shows that not everybody achieved large families. In this household, except for the death of Hori, the change in size was not due to increase or decrease in the nuclear family. The next alteration would presumably have come if Sneferu had married and had children. Another papyrus from later Middle Kingdom Kahun lists a household of very different composition.[28] It is headed by Khakaura-Sneferu, a priest in the mortuary temple of Senusret II, who appears to have been divorced or widowed as no wife is mentioned. He is listed with one son and one daughter, together with at least twenty-one servants.

Stelae and other material from Deir el-Medina caused one scholar to remark that 'the families of the necropolis workmen were very numerous' (e.g. fig. 50).[29] This is perhaps puzzling when set against the small size of the houses in the village and the information that can be gleaned from a fragmentary house by house register of the inhabitants. Of the thirty households that are still reasonably well-preserved, there is only one couple registered with four children, five couples have three, there are two fathers who each have three children by different mothers, six couples with two children, seven with one child, four with none, and six male householders who are unmarried.[30] While at any given time in the village we might expect to find men who were yet to marry or who were widowed, newly married couples, and couples just starting their families, we might also expect evidence of large, well-established families; yet no household is registered with more than four children. A possible explanation is that older children in the family moved away in their teens. Since only one son could take over his father's job, others may have left to pursue careers elsewhere. Daughters could have left home to get married or possibly to hire themselves out as servants in larger households outside the village. In this way the whole family would never all have lived at home at one time. There is also evidence that many of the workmen had property outside the village and may even have farmed land.[31] Excess family members may have been dispatched to help in this activity, but even young children could have been sent to live with their nurses outside the village. Of course, many children probably did not outlive infancy, so there would have been gaps in age between the surviving members of the family, which would reduce the number of children at home at any one time. However, the offspring shown as adults on the monuments must be assumed to have survived childhood. It is also possible that some families appear larger than they actually were, if some of the members labelled with the kinship terms *sa* and *sat*, traditionally translated 'son' and 'daughter', were actually 'grandchildren' or the spouses of children, since the two terms can also encompass these relationships. In the same way when numerous figures are related to the owner of a monument by the kinship terms *sen* and *senet*, traditionally rendered as 'brother' and 'sister', they may not all be siblings of the owner, but could be other collateral relatives equivalent to 'cousins', 'uncles', 'aunts', 'nephews', 'nieces', and 'in-laws'.[32]

Thus, families occupying a house may not have been as large as they appear on the monuments. It is, indeed, hard to imagine how very big families would have fitted into one of the houses at Amarna or Deir el-Medina, although this may be due to modern Western ideas on privacy. Much of life could have been lived outdoors in the street or on the roof, and at night, the floor would have become sleeping space. Any expectation of privacy might simply not have existed.

The 'mistress of the house'

The various documents listing households show that the Egyptian concept of this unit consisted of a male head, his wife and children, and possibly female relatives, such as mother or grandmother, sisters or aunts. Male relatives apart from sons are not included because they are most likely to establish their own households. It is interesting that other documents indicate that women could own houses, but in the lists, houses or households virtually all belong to men. In what sense, then, is a married woman 'mistress of the house'? Can we make any correlation between the women of the household, particular areas of the house, and the part women played in the household?

We can start by attempting to conjecture something of the life of a 'mistress of the house' married to a high ranking official with a large household. To begin with, if we take the biggest houses at Amarna as a model, for instance the house of the vizier Nakht, there would have been plenty of space within the central living quarters for separate male and female areas, if such gender segregation was customary. Additional rooms to the central reception room might have included a ladies' reception room, so that men and women could have congregated separately. The only evidence we have of social occasions are scenes of banquets in tomb chapels, where from the mid-Eighteenth Dynasty single men and women are often shown grouped separately. Married couples, however, are shown in pairs and not separated according to gender. Unfortunately the scenes give us no idea of the physical location of the groups of men and women, so that they could be in separate rooms or they could simply be seated separately within the same room.

If these scenes are on the whole uninformative, others give us an idea of what went on in large households, showing work in the kitchen, the bakery and brewery, the granary, the butchery, and very rarely within the private rooms of the house itself in such scenes as bedmaking. These belong to the repertory of so-called daily life scenes, in which the tomb owner is shown overseeing activities connected with his private life and official duties. They show us nothing of the role of the 'mistress of the house'. She rarely accompanies the male owner in his activities, but neither is she shown doing her own thing. This is because the vast majority of tomb chapels are owned by men and, although female members of the family may be depicted in funerary scenes and be buried in the tomb, the decoration of the chapel revolves around the male owner. However, no repertory of scenes relating to women was ever developed for the few tomb chapels that do seem to have had a female owner. The prime example is the Twelfth Dynasty tomb of Senet at Thebes.[33] She was the mother of the vizier Intefiqer, who built his tomb in the region of the capital in the north of Egypt. In Senet's tomb chapel it is the figure of her son which is prominent. He is shown hunting in the desert without his mother, and he appears with his wife to receive offerings. It is not surprising that the tomb was originally thought to have belonged to Intefiqer.

Does this mean that all the activities overseen by the tomb owner lay outside the mistress of the house's sphere of responsibility? This is possible, but we need to be careful in equating the idealised male world of the tomb chapel with reality. If women had a role in the latter, it may have been irrelevant in the former. For instance, we know that female servants were involved in baking and that in smaller households the mistress of the house was responsible for producing food. So when tomb scenes show baking and brewing for the household overseen by the tomb owner, we cannot be sure that this reflects actual life. Other considerations may come into play. Bread and beer were the staples of Egyptian life, and thus of the afterlife. It was, therefore, desirable to have a scene showing their manufacture in the tomb chapel. However, in the tomb chapel the male owner held primacy of place, so he might be shown overseeing the baking and brewing because it would go against decorum to yield his

35   Musicians and dancers perform at a banquet.

36 Scene showing agricultural activities on the estate of Nakht, and Nakht and his wife making an offering.

dominant position in the chapel decoration to his wife.

From elsewhere there is evidence that women tended to work more indoors and men outside, so we might not expect to find the high class mistress of the house in the open fields. It is quite possible, however, that she was concerned with some or all of the activities that went on within the household compound, which as we have seen, included not only baking and brewing, and cooking, but also weaving, grain storage, animal husbandry, and possibly craft production.

Duties in the home

In the tomb scenes the actual work is carried out by servants, so one can conjecture that the mistress of the house did not get her hands dirty. Her role was rather to organise and oversee the activities of the servants and to ensure that the household ran smoothly. In the highest ranks of society it is possible that servants enabled the mistress of the house to be released entirely from physical household tasks. Although a fertile mistress of the house probably spent many of her childbearing years pregnant, the employment of wetnurses and nannies would have also freed her from the burden of child-rearing. There could, therefore, have been a group of women with spare time who could not take part in the formal bureaucratic administration of the country which was reserved for men, but who would presumably need to occupy themselves in some way. This may be why, in the Old and Middle Kingdoms, many women from high-ranking families were priestesses of Hathor and, in the New Kingdom, providers of music in temple cults.

Turning to families somewhat lower down the social scale within what can still be called the elite, we can conjecture that the women had a rather different lifestyle. Here the evidence is mainly from the workmen's villages at Amarna and Deir el-Medina, although it must be remembered that these were not typical communities, since they were state foundations that continued to be maintained and serviced by the state. The houses were much smaller than the mansions of high officials, as would be the number of servants employed. Without numerous servants the mistress of the house may have been more closely involved with food preparation. The basic food supply was grain, emmer wheat and barley, which had to be turned into bread and beer. We have seen that the houses at Amarna and Deir el-Medina were fully equipped for bread-making. The grain was broken up in a mortar and then ground into flour. This was then mixed with water, and other ingredients if desired, and baked in the bread oven at the back of the house or on the roof. In models and tomb paintings, grinding grain and baking are one of the few activities usually involving women, so we can probably identify these tasks as ones occupying the women of small households. Because the workmen at Deir el-Medina were government employees with special status they were provided with female slaves, who in fact belonged to the state. Their sole purpose seems to have been to grind grain. Each household was allocated so many days' work from one of these slaves, but the allocation could be sold to another person. While financially beneficial, this transaction left the household having to grind its own grain, a duty which would presumably have fallen to the women, since it was traditionally a woman's job.

In models and tomb scenes showing the brewing of beer in large households, it is mainly male servants who are involved. Although there is less obvious evidence for brewing than for baking in the workmen's villages, one can hardly doubt that beer was prepared there, as it was the staple drink of ancient Egypt. There is little to show whether men remained responsible for its manufacture or whether it fell within the realm of female tasks. In the Middle Kingdom story of the *Eloquent Peasant* the peasant tells his wife to measure out grain and brew beer from it.[34] At Deir el-Medina the men were away from the village for days at a time and beer did not keep, so either some of the male servants employed by the villagers did the brewing, or it fell to the lot of the mistress of the house or a female servant.

We also find in tomb models and scenes from the Old, Middle and New Kingdoms depictions of the preparation and cooking of meat in large households in which the activities are carried out by male servants. There is nothing to show who did the cooking in smaller households.

Evidence of spinning and weaving has come from a number of settlement sites. Textile manufacture is less often depicted in tomb scenes than other activities. A number of Middle Kingdom scenes and models show that the personnel involved were women (fig. 28). Since what is represented is textile production on a large estate, these women are probably servants rather than members of the householder's family. A Middle Kingdom papyrus gives a list of house servants in which the occupations of twenty-nine women are preserved; twenty of them are connected with weaving.[35] One cannot, however, rule out the possibility that the women of the family also took part in textile manufacture. Heqanakht was able to pay for the rent of fields from the sale of cloth probably woven in his household,[36] of which at least ten members were women. While some of these were servants, others belonged to the family. It is possible that they would all have had to be involved to produce the textiles used by this large household, with a surplus to cover the rent of land.

37   Male and female musicians and dancers taking part in temple ritual.

Depictions show that during the Middle Kingdom weaving was done on a horizontal loom (fig. 28). By the mid-Eighteenth Dynasty the upright loom had been introduced, and a tomb scene includes two set up in a large private house being worked by men who are almost certainly servants.[37] How greatly textile production came to involve men is unclear. In the workmen's villages there is evidence of spinning and weaving on upright looms within the houses themselves. While this gives no clue as to the gender of the operators, it is virtually certain that the mistress of the house and other women of the household were involved, given the traditional part played by women in this activity. This is confirmed by various pieces of textual evidence. At Deir el-Medina, one of the charges brought against the unpleasant Paneb was that he ordered 'the workmen to work on the plaited bed of the deputy of the temple of Amun, while their wives wove clothes for him'.[38] In the New Kingdom story of the *Two Brothers*, the wife of Anubis offers to make clothes for Bata if he will lie with her.[39] A New Kingdom administrative document is concerned with the accusation that a woman Irinefret, wife of the overseer of the district, has bought a slave girl with property that did not belong to her.[40] She refutes this by listing all the items she gave for the girl. For many of them she states where she obtained them, but the price also includes '1 wrap of thin cloth, 1 sheet(?) of thin cloth, 1 cloak of thin cloth, 3 loin cloths of fine thin cloth, 1 skirt of fine thin cloth', which she lists without giving any origin. It does not seem too far-fetched to suppose that she wove them herself. We can, therefore, surmise that the mistress of the house was responsible for clothing the household, and might also obtain extra income by selling the surplus.

Business transactions

There is evidence that women, who in some cases can be deduced to be mistresses of the house, were involved in selling produce. When the wife of one of the tomb robbers in the Twentieth Dynasty was asked where she had obtained the wherewithal to buy servants, she claimed: 'I bought them in exchange for produce from my garden.'[41] It must have been plausible that she could have had the produce to sell. Maybe she had a small plot of land somewhere where she grew the goods, perhaps in the first place to supply her family. Another woman who was similarly questioned said she got silver 'in exchange for barley in the year of the hyenas when there was a famine.'[42] Since women could own and farm land, she could have obtained the barley in her own right, or it might have been part of her husband's pay. Alternatively, she could have acquired the grain by selling other products or items in her possession, and kept the grain as an investment against just such a bad year. Market scenes are not common in tomb chapels, but in the Deir el-Medina tomb of Ipy there is a scene on the river bank which shows a boat carrying grain, in exchange for which women sell bread, fish, and vegetables (fig. 31). They may be buying for household needs, but perhaps they are selling perishable surplus goods for

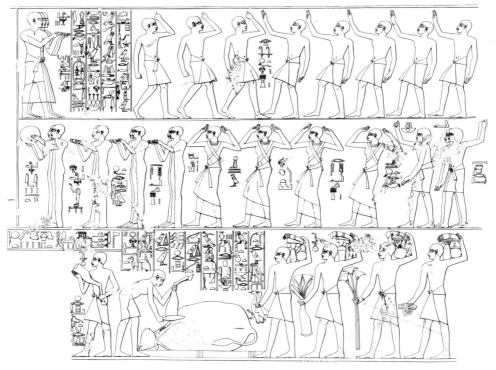

38   Male and female musicians celebrating the raising of the *djed* pillar at the *sed* festival of Amenhotep III.

something more durable, which they could later exchange for silver in time of shortage.

We cannot see households as self-contained and self-sufficient. One of the duties of the mistress of the house may have been to keep the household supplied with all its needs by exchanging what was held in surplus for goods that were in short supply. To facilitate this exchange of goods on a wider scale involving state institutions as well as private households, a system was developed by which male traders (*shuty*) sailed up and down the Nile carrying out transactions.[43] They could be employed by a temple or a private person, and their job was to sell surplus goods and buy whatever their employer needed. The traders were servants not independent agents, and a wealthy merchant class never developed in Egypt. Because their status was not high and they were not owners of tomb chapels and other monuments, we know little about them. In one of the tomb robbery papyri fourteen traders are listed, three of whom were attached to temples and eleven to four private individuals.[44] One household, that of a high-ranking soldier, employed seven, while two other military figures each had one. The other two were in the service of the daughter of an army officer called Aset who was a temple musician. By this system of exchange, households not only supplied all their needs, but perhaps also accumulated wealth. With this they could hire or buy servants, rent or purchase land, help establish the households of their children on marriage, provide offerings at their local shrines and in their own household chapels, and prepare for their own burials. These matters would concern the women as much as the men of the household and, given that women could own property and transact business in their own right (see Chapter Seven), they were probably active within the household in working towards these goals.

Motherhood

Like their high-ranking counterparts at the top of the elite class, most lower-status mistresses of the house would have spent much of their time pregnant. One might suppose that they would be more closely involved with child-rearing because they were less likely to have had wetnurses and nannies available. However, we must be cautious in our assumptions, since wetnurses are mentioned in the material from Deir el-Medina. Of course, we have no way of knowing whether these were a convenience to save the mother trouble, or a necessity because she was unable to feed her own child. What we do know is that the scribe Any in his New Kingdom *Instruction* envisaged mothers taking full care of their children:

> Double the food your mother gave you,
> Support her as she supported you;
> She had a heavy load in you,
> But she did not abandon you.
> When you were born after your months,
> She was yet yoked [to you],
> Her breast in your mouth for three years.
> As you grew and your excrement disgusted,
> She was not disgusted, saying 'What shall I do?'
> When she sent you to school
> And you were taught to write,
> She kept watch over you daily,
> With bread and beer in her house.[45]

Clearly a good scribal mother suckled her child, was responsible for the Egyptian equivalent of changing its nappies, and throughout later childhood looked after its needs. The text specifically deals with a male child who would be sent to school. Girls probably stayed with their mothers until they were married, or perhaps went out as servants to other households. A Middle Kingdom text implies that, at least at that time, some boys might be sent away to school, in which case they would leave their mothers earlier than if they attended a local school.[46]

Ideally mothers were held in great honour. They often appear in scenes on male-owned monuments from the Old Kingdom onwards seated with their sons. In a letter to his dead mother, dating between the Sixth and Eleventh Dynasties, a son reminds her how he tried to please her while she was alive: 'You did say this to your son, "Bring me quails that I may eat them", and this your son brought to you seven quails, and you did eat them.'[47] In the Middle Kingdom *Teaching of Duaf's son Khety* the author first promises: 'I shall make you love writing more than your mother', and later warns: 'Speak not falsehood against your mother; it is the abomination of the officials'. Finally he tells his son: 'Thank god for your father and for your mother, who put you on the path of life.'[48] Thus it is clear that a son should hold his mother in affection and honour, and acknowledge her role in his upbringing as well as that of his father. This fits in with the common epithets found in male autobiographies of the late Old Kingdom and the First Intermediate Period: 'I was one beloved of his father, praised of his mother', acknowledging the importance of both parents.

The lower classes

So far this chapter has looked entirely at households of higher and lower status within the elite class. The evidence is in many ways inadequate and there are consequently large gaps in our understanding of the role of women in these households. In turning to the non-elite classes, the small non-literate professionals and servants of various sorts, and the peasants who made up the majority of the population, we come up against even worse problems. Since these people were illiterate, they were unable to leave any written records, and most of their burials are unknown to us. Thus we can learn nothing of them from material which they themselves produced. We are forced, therefore, to rely on what the elite class has to tell us about them in their textual and representational material.

In the so-called scenes of daily life that occur in tomb chapels, all the activities that the owner is watching are being carried out by members of the non-elite classes, so it looks as though we have a good record of the lives of these people. Unfortunately, the scenes are far from being representative and unbiased. First, they show workshops and estates belonging to the king or to temples, or else the large private estates of high officials, rather than the small holdings of minor officials, soldiers, or peasants. Second, the scenes are very carefully selected to be of benefit to the tomb owner in the afterlife. They either establish the tomb owner's status, or they show the production of goods like food, drink, and textiles which he will need in the next world. The tomb owner is the focal point of these scenes and anything that does not relate to him is omitted. So we see nothing of where the non-elite live, and we learn nothing of their social and family organisation. Further, women appear much less frequently than men, so that they are almost invisible. The figures tend to be generic rather than specific, presenting types, not individuals. Finally, the world of the tomb scenes is an idealised one. Although the strict rules of formal

39   The tomb owner, his mother, and wife performing rites before statues of
Thutmose I and queen Ahmose.

art were relaxed somewhat in depicting subsidiary figures of servants and
peasants, much of the unpleasantness of reality was still avoided. Thus, while
subsidiary figures could be shown aged or with deformities, particularly in the
Old and Middle Kingdoms, these examples form a small minority of such
figures, which, in the Eighteenth Dynasty especially, tend to be youthful and
healthy (e.g. figs. 33, 36). This is unlikely to reflect reality. We shall have
reason to question whether the male-idealised picture of life on a large estate
realistically reflected the division of labour between men and women in the
lower levels of society.

   In the Middle and New Kingdoms, there is a whole genre of literature
written by the elite about the non-scribal professions. Two things stand out
about these accounts: first, these professions are exclusively male, and second,
they are made to sound uniformly unpleasant. The latter is in complete contrast to the tomb scenes showing non-elite life, which are at least neutral in
tone, if not in some cases idyllic. However, the texts have an in-built bias
because they are written for a specific purpose. They are addressed to student
scribes who might be finding the scribal training too much and be tempted to
throw it all in and adopt another career. They are meant to encourage them to
keep their noses to the grindstone by setting out just how awful life is for
everyone else, and how great the rewards are for the scribe. Since women could
not be scribes, the texts are addressed to an entirely male audience. There
would be no point in referring to working women, so we cannot assume that the

professions listed were confined to men only, even though only men are mentioned. It follows that what seem like obvious sources for understanding daily life in ancient Egypt have in fact to be used with extreme caution. In addition to having specific agendas with in-built biases, they have a heavy male orientation which obscures the role of women.

It is not surprising, then, to find that we have no information on the families and households of the majority of the population. Excavation has uncovered little, while the monuments of the elite reveal nothing. We can conjecture that most people lived in mud-brick villages by the river or some other water source, much like today. The men probably worked in the fields, or in one of the humble professions listed in the Middle Kingdom *Teaching of Duaf's son*

40 Dancers and singers in the Old Kingdom tomb of Ti.

Khety as, for instance, potter, gardener, baker, or fisherman.[49] Their wives were probably concerned with food preparation, weaving, and other household tasks, and with childbearing and child-rearing. As today, the women would have had to go down to the river to get water, wash the dishes, and do the laundry. At this level of society servants would be rare and the mistresses of the house must have done the work themselves. There is no evidence to show whether the men in the family helped or not. Women may also have had to work in the fields, perhaps on a regular basis, perhaps only if extra labour was needed.

With regard to size of family, it seems likely that a large number of children would be desirable, just as in higher ranking families and also among the modern peasant population of Egypt. These would provide free agricultural labour, and also ensure that some children would survive to provide for their parents in old age. Infant mortality was certainly high, and therefore the larger the family, the more likely it was that some children would survive to adulthood. Of those that did, the sons probably followed their fathers' employment, while most of the daughters presumably married and raised their own families. However, women did have jobs outside their own homes, especially as servants of one sort or another. We shall see in the next chapter that there was a gender distinction in the sort of work done by men and women, and that women were probably more limited in the occupations open to them.

At the very bottom of society were the male and female slaves who were owned by an institution or an individual.[50] We meet them mainly in documents concerned with their purchase, sale, hire, transmission by inheritance, or manumission. They were presumably housed and fed by their owners. They could have children, and in one recorded case it is likely that these were fathered by the female slave's male owner.

FURTHER READING

A. Badawy, *A History of Egyptian Architecture: The Empire*, Berkeley and Los Angeles, 1968, chapter 2.

T. G. H. James, *The Hekanakhte Papers and other early Middle Kingdom Documents*, New York, 1962.

B. Kemp, *Ancient Egypt: Anatomy of a Civilization*, London and New York, 1989, 149–57, 294–317.

Women outside the home

Women and literacy

If women were responsible for running the household, they were by no means confined to the house. We shall see in Chapter Eight that many high class women had duties in the temples and in Chapter Nine that women could also play a part in the funerary cults of family members. By and large, however, there was a clear-cut distinction between the occupations of men and women which, whatever its origins, was already entrenched in Egyptian society by the Old Kingdom and continued throughout pharaonic Egypt. This was manifested in the formal structure of the state, which was administered through a bureaucracy of literate male officials forming an elite class.

The ambitions of the elite for their sons centred round giving them a proper scribal training and setting their feet on the bureaucratic ladder, the ideal being that the son should inherit the office of his father. By contrast, women were excluded from the official bureaucratic structure.[1] It was boys who were sent to school and encouraged to devote their efforts to becoming scribes. Since women could not join the bureaucracy they had officially no need of the skills of literacy, and therefore no need for formal training in them. This does not necessarily mean that women never learned to read and write, but unfortunately there is no firm evidence one way or the other. There is no document that we know beyond doubt was penned by a woman or was meant to be read directly by a woman. With letters sent to and from women, we must always reckon with the possibility that the letter was written by a male scribe or read out by one to the recipient.

More positive evidence for women's literacy might seem to be the word *seshet*, the feminine form of the male title *sesh* 'scribe' which is found occasionally in the Middle Kingdom.[2] However, this form is taken by some scholars to be merely a shortened form of a female title which has been understood to mean 'painter of her mouth' or 'cosmetician'. This interpretation would seem to be strengthened by the fact that the title is listed with one meaning hairdresser. However, a *seshet* Idwy of the Middle Kingdom owned a scarab seal, which was a matter of some prestige.[3] Such an object was hardly likely to have belonged to a cosmetician, who would have been of low status. The title *seshet* is not found in the Old and New Kingdoms. In the Late Period, a woman

41   A male priest and the god's wife conducting a ritual in the temple of Karnak.

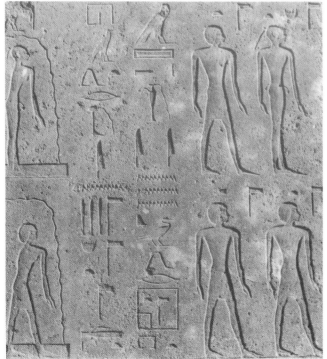

42   The god's wife and male priests being purified in the sacred lake at Karnak and then entering the sanctuary of the god.

in the service of the divine adoratrice and god's wife at Thebes is called *sesh-sehemet*, 'female scribe'.[4]

Whatever the actual meaning of *seshet*, the contrast between its use and that of the masculine form *sesh* is striking. *Sesh* is one of the basic male titles of all periods occurring repeatedly on the monuments. Even if we were to accept all the occurrences of *seshet* as signifying the female equivalent of a male scribe, the number would be pitifully small. In addition, while countless scenes show male scribes at work, there are no depictions at any period of working female scribes. Nor can we prove that these few *seshet* were employed in the state bureaucracy, since they may rather have held a position in a large private or royal household. Two *seshet* are shown among household officials on private stelae, and another appears twice in the burial chamber of the royal woman Aashit at Deir el-Bahri.[5] Clearly, the existence at certain periods of a few women called *seshet* does not destroy the basic gender distinction in the elite class between men who were scribes and could hold government office, and women who in general were not, and did not hold office.

This division reflects the structure of formal government. Outside the bureaucratic world, daughters in literate families could have been taught to read and write, and these skills perpetuated in the female line if literate mothers passed on their knowledge to their daughters. Thus in elite families, while women could never hope to hold office, they might have been able to write letters to each other, keep household and business accounts, and read and copy out literary texts. One Twentieth Dynasty letter tells the recipient: 'And you shall see this daughter of Khonsmose and have her write a letter and send it to me.' Perhaps she really was to pen it herself.[6]

In a few New Kingdom scenes, women are depicted with scribal kits under their chairs, and it has been suggested that the women were commemorating their ability to read and write.[7] Unfortunately in all cases but one, the woman is sitting with her husband or son in such a way that it would cramp the available space to put the kit under the man's chair, and so it may have been moved back to a place under the woman's. This happens in a similar scene when the man's dog is put under the woman's chair.[8] So one cannot be sure that the scribal kit belonged to the woman.

If there was a group of literate women in ancient Egypt, they do not seem to have developed any surviving literary genres unique to themselves, such as a female equivalent to the male *Wisdom Texts* which would have given advice to young women. Of course, we may be putting too much stress on literacy, swayed by the emphasis on reading and writing in modern society. In the Chinese novel *The Story of the Stone* about a literati family of the early Ch'ing dynasty, the daughters of the house are literate and write poetry, but the woman who actually runs the large household and oversees the complexities of income and expenditure has married into the family and is totally illiterate, and keeps all the details of household administration in her head.

The most we can say, then, is that while the ability to read and write was basic to employment in the state bureaucracy, only men could hold bureaucratic office, and women, irrespective of their literacy skills, were excluded. Outside the formal apparatus of government, there is still no unambiguous evidence as to whether women in elite families ever learned to read and write. Certainly the possibility that they did should not be ruled out. We may indeed possess documents penned by women, and simply lack the means of identifying them as such.

Women in society, and their titles

It is hard to write about women in Egyptian society when the structure of that society itself is not fully understood. Undoubtedly it was extremely hierarchical, and the elite class must have comprised many different strata depending on each office holder's position. At the top would be the high officials and

43   The god's wife Amenirdis I, daughter of Kashta.

their families: the vizier, the overseer of the treasury, the first priest of Amun, officials who were part of the central government. Below them would come the officials who served on the staffs in their departments. There would also be officials based in provincial centres whose importance would correspond to the importance of the place in which they held office, but who would presumably rank below officials of the central government. Beneath these would be officials and scribes attached to smaller and less important centres or institutions. Scribes were also employed on private estates, and these were possibly not part of the government bureaucracy at all.

Because so little study has been made of society in general, let alone women in society, I can do no more than present a partial and simplified picture of what was surely a very complex structure. First I shall look at some of the titles attested for women of high elite families in the Old, Middle and New King-doms, and then I shall examine the sorts of occupations in which we find lower class women, including work on the land. Finally I want to consider women as renters or owners of farmland, and women who may have helped with the duties of their husbands' official government position.

For the Middle Kingdom, William Ward was able to distinguish the social status of three groups of title-bearing women based on the ranks of their husbands.[9] The first group consisted of wives of high officials such as the vizier and provincial governors or nomarchs, down to men with the title of 'sole companion' which was the lowest ranking title of the upper hierarchy of officials. The second group were the wives of minor officials below the level of sole companion, and the third group was below that. The titles held by the women in each group were different. In the first group are found women who had the female forms of the prestigious male ranking titles *iry-pat* and *haty-a*, and also the title 'daughter of a *haty-a*'; none of these were particularly common. Much more frequent were 'priestess of Hathor' (*hemet netjer ent Huthor*) and 'sole lady-in-waiting' (*khekeret nesu watet*) which seem to be mar-kers of the highest social status. It is unclear whether a woman gained this status in her own right, or whether it was simply a reflection of the status of her husband; one is not, in fact, mutually exclusive of the other.

In the second group, we find several common women's titles of the Middle Kingdom. One of these was 'citizeness' (*ankhet ent niut*). This continued in use into the New Kingdom and was the most frequent title of women at Deir el-Medina in hieratic documents (but not in hieroglyphic texts) where it would seem to indicate a married woman. Its fundamental significance, especially in the Middle Kingdom, is unclear. Another frequent title is 'lady-in-waiting' (*khekeret nesu*) which is related to 'sole lady-in-waiting' but puts its holder in a lower rank. '*Wab*-priestess' is the feminine counterpart of a *wab*-priest. Fin-ally, 'servant of a ruler' usually marks women married to minor functionaries. The 'ruler' probably refers to a provincial governor rather than the king, so this would not be a position held in the capital. The third group of women contains those who bear titles of minor professions, household servants, and attendants.

In the Old Kingdom women with high status were marked by the use of titles that refer to the king.[10] 'She who is known to the king' is the feminine counterpart of a title used by high officials. 'Noblewoman of the king' is another feminine counterpart of a male title. Both male and female forms of this were first used in the Sixth Dynasty, but the female version continued in use into the Eleventh Dynasty, while the male form died out at the end of the Old Kingdom. Finally the titles 'lady-in-waiting' and 'sole lady-in-waiting' were used from the Fifth Dynasty on.

In addition to these ranking titles, there were female titles in the Old Kingdom which are clearly administrative.[11] Women as stewards were in charge of storehouses and supplies of food and cloth, perhaps as an extension of their responsibility for these items within the family sphere. They also held positions relating to weaving, wigs, singing and dancing, doctors, tenant landholders, and funerary cults. Many of these women seem to have been in the service of other women and may not have been part of the state bureaucracy. Two queens had female stewards, while a princess who was the wife of a high official called Mereruka had not only a female steward, but also a female 'inspector of treasure', 'overseer of ornaments', and 'overseer of cloth'. The one female overseer of doctors known was possibly in charge of female doctors who attended a queen mother. Otherwise doctors were normally male. Women singers and dancers were often supervised by female overseers, but alongside them there were also male overseers. The evidence seems to show that while men could oversee women, women probably did not oversee men. In comparison with male administrative titles, those used by women occur far less frequently and in far less variety. The only high administrative title attested for a woman is that of vizier once in the Sixth Dynasty. It is unclear whether its use was honorary or functional, but the very fact that the example stands alone and causes such surprise underlines the overwhelming absence of women from the administration.

In the Middle Kingdom, women still had a few administrative titles, but they seem to have been fewer and even less common than in the Old Kingdom. We have already discussed the title 'female scribe'. We also find 'keeper of the chamber', 'butler', 'overseer of the kitchen', 'major-domo', and 'sealer'. All these are more commonly found in the masculine form, held by men. They relate to households, and perhaps belong to women in private not government service, possibly responsible to another woman.[12] Henry Fischer, in a study of women's titles in the Old and Middle Kingdoms, concludes that 'it is difficult to avoid the impression that women of the Middle Kingdom were less frequently and significantly engaged in administering people and property than was previously the case – not that their role was ever of great importance except, of course, in the case of mother, wife, or daughters of kings.'[13]

The title 'lady-in-waiting' is also found in the New Kingdom, where it is used by the wives and sometimes the daughters of high officials. For a long time the title was taken to signify a royal concubine. Two scholars have pointed out the unlikelihood of this, since so many of the women were married to high officials.[14] It hardly seems possible that the king would have relinquished his sexual rights over these women and handed them on to his officials as 'royal rejects'. Instead it is now proposed to see the title as signifying some sort of court position. Such an appointment would confer status and be appropriate for the wife of a high official. By the Eighteenth Dynasty the form 'sole lady-in-waiting' was no longer used, leaving 'lady-in-waiting' as the main form, which now carried high status. There is also another form found, 'great lady-in-waiting' (*khekeret nesu weret*).

An important New Kingdom title which related the holder to the king is that of 'wetnurse of the king' (*menat nesu* and variants). These women are mostly known from the monuments of their husbands and sons, who are in the main high-ranking officials. This intimate connection with the royal family, especially with a future king, could bring royal favour to the whole family, and advancement for the male members within the bureaucracy, since as children of the king's wetnurse and thus milk brothers of the king, they were likely to have formed part of the king's intimate circle in his childhood.[15] The position of 'wetnurse of the king' was not an office within the state bureaucracy, yet it was one which carried the potential for influence with the king himself, and therefore was a likely avenue of power. Literacy was unnecessary since the qualification for the position was the ability to produce milk, a biological function that only a woman could fulfil. We do not know how long a royal nurse remained with her charge after it had been weaned.

Occupations of female servants

There are some areas of employment outside the individual's home besides wetnursing in which, throughout Egyptian history, women seem to have been heavily involved: milling and baking, spinning and weaving, and music and dance. In other areas the evidence suggests that they had less involvement: brewing, preparing and cooking meat, craft production, and agricultural activities on large estates. I shall examine representational and textual material to see how far gender effects the division of labour.

We have already seen that in the Old and Middle Kingdoms a few women had administrative titles, and that they were probably in the service of royal women or private households rather than in the state bureaucracy. Their status would depend on that of their employer. Below such titles are a number of what we may conjecture to be titles of female household servants and attendants, including female hairdressers. In the Middle Kingdom there may have been about twenty such titles, though unfortunately we know little of the functions they signify.[16] At least eight women from the Old Kingdom and First Intermediate Period are recorded with the title of 'sealer'. They served women

44   The enthronement of Nitiqret, daughter of Psamtek I. Amun-Ra places his hand on the head of the kneeling god's wife.

in private households. Two more women with the title are known from the Twelfth Dynasty.[17] Sealing was one of the commonest duties of men throughout the bureaucracy, because in the absence of locks and keys seals were used to safeguard property. A sealer carried the authorised seal with which to secure containers and storerooms against unauthorised entry.

Other titles signify a 'wetnurse' or a 'nanny'; women with these titles occasionally appear as part of family groups on monuments. On one Middle Kingdom stela a wetnurse sits opposite the owner,[18] while on another, one stands behind the man who dedicates the stela, holding his arm (fig. 25).[19] In a Middle Kingdom letter the writer says: 'And write me about every matter pertaining to the health and life of the nurse Tima.'[20] Another letter concerned with household matters mentions 'the nurse Yeye'.[21]

When it comes to food preparation, Middle Kingdom titles are more numerous for men than women.[22] The latter are attested once each as 'brewer' and 'miller', both of which are occupations relating to the processing of grain into beer and bread which, as we have already seen, was associated with women. In representations of baking and brewing from the Old through to the New Kingdoms, both men and women are included; in some, women carry out the complete process of breadmaking. Of the individual processes involved, from the Old Kingdom onwards the grinding of grain is much more often depicted being performed by a woman than a man (fig. 32), and it was female slaves that were provided by the government for this purpose at Deir el-Medina. Further, from the reign of Sety I of the Nineteenth Dynasty, administrative documents relating to breadmaking for the royal palace at Memphis list the amount of grain given to twenty-six women for grinding, together with the amount of flour this produced.[23] Thus there seems to have been a tradition that

grinding grain was work normally done by a woman. Women are also frequently shown in other parts of the baking process, fanning the fire and putting
the dough into moulds. However, while various men in the Old and Middle
Kingdoms are identified as 'baker', no example of a woman with this title has
survived. As we have seen, brewing relates closely to the baking process. In the
Middle Kingdom a number of men are known called 'brewer', but only one
woman. In the representations of all periods, more men than women are shown
in tomb scenes and models relating to brewing, although women are by no
means excluded from the process.

In other areas of food preparation the Middle Kingdom evidence also shows
a lack of female titles. There are male 'butchers', 'cooks', and 'confectioners'.[24]
None of these titles is frequent in the textual material, suggesting that it was
not usual to mention such people. Thus, there might be female equivalents
which simply went unrecorded. However, when we come to look at the representational material from the Old, Middle and New Kingdoms we do not find
figures of women performing these activities. Butchery scenes are very
common indeed and show only men. Although many are in a ritual, sacrificial
context, even those relating to a household exclude women. The subsequent
jointing of the slaughtered animal and the preparation of the meat also involves
men only. The same is true of similar scenes showing the preparation of fish
and birds (fig. 33). The slaughter of small animals like goats, sheep, and pigs is
not usually shown, perhaps because their meat lacked prestige compared to
that of cattle, so we do not know whether this too was exclusively carried out by
men. Scenes of cooking show meat either roasted on a hand-held spit over a fire
or boiled in a pot; the cooks are men. In the Middle Kingdom the male title
'cook' is found a few times, but no female form is attested.

Decorated tomb chapels often include scenes of workshops devoted to various crafts such as carpentry, jewellery-making, metal-working, sculpture,
leather-working, and weaving. In all of them except those involving textile
manufacture only male figures are shown. While spinning and weaving are not
depicted in the Old Kingdom, there are scenes of women delivering cloth and
receiving payment. Further, several women are 'overseer of weavers' or 'overseer of the house of weavers'.[25] Since women do not supervise men, this
suggests that the weavers are female, which fits in with the fact that the Old
Kingdom hieroglyph for weaver uses a female figure. In Middle Kingdom
scenes and models, it is women who spin and weave (fig. 28). In a late Middle
Kingdom papyrus listing ninety-five slaves, the ratio of women to men is two
to one.[26] Most of the women whose profession is preserved on the document,
but none of the men, are in the textile industry. The conclusion is that in the
Old and Middle Kingdoms this was one craft in which women predominated.
At this time the horizontal loom was in use. From the beginning of the New
Kingdom we find depictions of upright looms worked by men.[27] Spinning and
weaving are rarely depicted at this period, but one scene in a Ramesside tomb

shows women as well as men in a weaving shed, with one upright loom apparently worked by a woman.[28]

If women were heavily involved in the making of textiles, they were not connected with their laundry. The few representations from the Old, Middle and New Kingdoms show this being carried out by men.[29] The laundry man is included in the list of professions cited in *The Teaching of Duaf's son Khety* precisely because he is male. The laundry service provided by the state for the villagers at Deir el-Medina was staffed by men. *The Tale of the Two Brothers* mentions the 'washermen of Pharaoh'. Professionally it would seem, then, that laundry was done by men.

Music played a large part in temple and funerary ritual, and perhaps also in everyday entertainment. From the Old Kingdom there is plenty of evidence for female musicians and dancers.[30] In Old Kingdom tomb scenes high class women entertain their husbands and fathers with music (fig. 34).[31] There are also scenes showing troupes of dancing, singing and clapping women (fig. 40). Such troupes could be attached to religious institutions, and royal and private households. In the Old Kingdom, it was possible for a woman to be an overseer of one of these troupes, but by the Middle Kingdom this position of authority had passed to men. At first the troupes seem to have consisted exclusively of women, but by the end of the Old Kingdom male singers and musicians could be included. This is reflected in Middle Kingdom titles of musicians, which include both male and female forms. Groups of musical performers are well-known from Eighteenth Dynasty tomb chapels where they appear in banquet scenes to entertain the guests (fig. 35). While they may be all female, there are enough mixed groups to show that men and women could perform together. We shall see in Chapter Eight that musical troupes were also involved in religious ritual and were included among temple personnel.

One of the most important means of travel in ancient Egypt was by boat on the Nile, and we have numerous representations of boats and their crews. Sailors always seem to be men, and among Middle Kingdom titles referring to ships' crews, none are feminine. Women would, of course, travel by boat, but being part of a boat's crew was not a job usually open to them, unless they were 'harim' ladies, dressed in fish nets, commandeered to entertain a bored king.[32]

Work on the land
Egypt was basically an agricultural society, and the majority of the population must have worked in one capacity or another on the land. This is reflected in scenes in tomb chapels of the Old, Middle and New Kingdoms showing the owner's private estates, or royal and temple estates of which the tomb owner had charge. One of the most obvious facts about these scenes is that male figures far outnumber female ones.

In scenes showing the agricultural year from ploughing and sowing to the harvest, women play very little part at all periods. In the Old Kingdom women appear winnowing the grain, and from the Middle Kingdom onwards they follow the male harvesters, collecting the fallen ears of grain in small woven baskets (fig. 36). They are not, however, shown cutting the grain, although sometimes they appear to be bringing refreshment to the male reapers. By contrast, women are depicted taking part in the flax harvest. Whether it is relevant that the flax plant is uprooted rather than cut is unclear. It is possible that there were reasons for not showing women handling sharp blades in the tomb, or perhaps there were ritual reasons for the women not cutting grain. Of course, since women were so closely involved in weaving, this could have led to their participation in the flax harvest, but women were also involved with milling grain and baking.

Although a woman is once shown picking grapes in an Eighteenth Dynasty tomb, viticulture is generally represented as a male occupation. The same is true of animal husbandry and activities in the marshes like bird-trapping and papyrus gathering. The tendency to exclude women from this type of work on estates is echoed by the few Middle Kingdom titles known which relate to these areas: all are male except for one 'winnower', and a couple of female 'gardeners' listed among the ninety-five slaves mentioned above. The latter may have worked in the garden attached to the house. A letter from year 24 of Ramses II gives a list of workers on an estate of Amun in the Delta. Their occupations

45 (*left*) Stela of the god's wife Ankhnesneferibra.

46 (*right*) The god's wife Ankhnesneferibra receiving life from Amun-Ra on a gateway at Karnak.

closely parallel the activities engaged in by workers on estates in the tomb
scenes: cattle herders, goatherds, swineherds, donkey herders, mule(?)
herders, bird wardens, fishermen, fowlers, vintners, salt workers, natron
workers, papyrus gatherers, rope makers, mat makers(?) and cultivators.[33]
They are all quite clearly designated as men, although if the workforce had
included women it would have been easy to indicate this. We know, however,
that there were women attached to temple estates, since there are texts which
mention them. For instance, in a decree of Sety I relating to an estate in Nubia
belonging to the king's temple at Abydos, the text talks of any person belonging
to the temple on this estate 'whether man or woman'. Unfortunately, there is
no information on how the women were employed, whether they worked on the
land, or whether they were involved in producing bread and cloth and other
necessities for the male workforce.

Every Egyptian was probably liable for temporary state labour or corvee
duty.[34] The belief that such a liability would continue into the afterworld led to
the development of the shabti figure to be put in the tomb to take the place of
the deceased if he or she was called up. Presumably in life those who were
wealthy enough could pay for substitute labour; others would have to perform
it themselves. A papyrus from the late Middle Kingdom deals with cases of
people who have fled to escape their term of service.[35] They all seem to have
been allotted to work on state fields. Women as well as men are listed, but
whether they did the same work as the men or whether there was a gender
distinction remains unknown. The document also makes it clear that the
families of the defectors, both male and female members, were held hostage
and perhaps put to work until the escapees were recovered.

This system of punishment seems still to have been in use in the New
Kingdom. In a text trying to persuade an apprentice scribe to be less wild and
concentrate on his studies, his advisor says: 'When I was of your age I spent my
life in the stocks: it was they that tamed my limbs ... I was imprisoned in the
temple whilst my father and mother were in the field as well as (my) brothers
and sisters.'[36] In another text with a similar aim of encouraging apprentice
scribes the writer talks of the drawbacks of being a stablemaster because he has
to toil non-stop lest disaster befall him and his family. One such calamity is
that 'his daughter is in the dyke', and the translator comments that this girl 'is
presumably doing some rough work at the dam.'[37] The whole tenor of the text
makes it clear that such an occupation for a girl lacked status.

There are other indications that women could take part in outdoor work.
First, in a New Kingdom copy of a Middle Kingdom text, women act as beaters
to cause wild birds to rise in the marshes.[38] Although this is not an activity
depicted in tombs, the various marsh scenes all show male workers. Secondly,
two New Kingdom love poems use the image of a girl netting birds.[39] Although
in tomb scenes this is shown only as a male occupation (fig. 33), and the fowlers
listed among the personnel of the estate of Amun were men, the image would

47 Votive stela of Neferhotep adoring the deified Amenhotep I and Ahmose Nefertari.

hardly be effective if it were a mere poetic fiction and not a fact of life. In one poem the girl takes the birds home to her mother, which suggests that the context was not bird-trapping on a large estate, but a small household, catching birds for its own support.

Women were able to own or rent land and farm it, perhaps to provide a livelihood, perhaps as a means of investing surplus wealth. The *Wilbour Papyrus*, dating to the reign of Ramses v, is concerned with grain production on state-owned land that is leased out to tenants.[40] Only about 10 per cent of these are women. The only title they are given is 'citizeness'. The question is whether these women actually worked the land themselves. Tenants might employ a cultivator to do the work, and in two cases the tenant, a scribe, had the land cultivated by a woman. Another document speaks of grain 'from [the house of] the lady Rokha(?) from the farm-land that [she] tilled ....'[41] It is possible that some women were actually involved in working the land.

Women exercising their husbands' authority

If women themselves could not hold state office, they could in some instances participate in the duties arising from that of their husbands. In a Twentieth Dynasty document the scribe of the necropolis Djehutymose reports on his collection of taxes in the form of grain at different places to the south of Thebes, some of which he delivered to the scribe of the necropolis Nesamenemipet and his wife, the musician of Amun, Henuttawy.[42] These were official revenues received by Nesamenemipet in his capacity of scribe of the necropolis. In one of the entries in the document, Henuttawy's name comes before that of Nesamenemipet, while in two others her name only is given as receiving the grain. A letter from Henuttawy to Nesamenemipet is preserved in Geneva about this very matter of grain reception, and certain problems that had arisen.[43] It seems that Nesamenemipet is away and that Henuttawy is deputising for him. She remains outside the official bureaucratic structure, obtaining her authority not in her own right but because she is Nesamenemipet's wife. If Nesamenemipet had lost his job or died, her authority would have ended too.

We see this in another case recorded in a letter sent to a man about his wife's unauthorised entry into an official store from which she had taken various items.[44] Brought before a court and asked why she had opened the store without permission from its keeper, she replied that the keeper was her husband, as though that made it all in order. Unfortunately this met with no sympathy, because her husband had already been moved to another position before she had entered the store. Clearly, any right she may have had to go to the store had ended when her husband ceased to be keeper.

To return to the report of Djehutymose on collecting taxes, we find a second woman who perhaps was also acting on behalf of her husband. Djehutymose received thirty sacks as taxes 'from the hand of the musician of Amun, Mes-

48 Votive stela dedicated by a woman who is shown adoring the ram of Amun-Ra.

hanefer, wife of the Master of the Portable Shrine Herynefer.' These cases may be far from unique, and it may be have been quite customary for women to help their husbands out in their official capacities, while themselves remaining outside the structure of the male bureaucracy.

Conclusion

To sum up, the kind of work a woman did in ancient Egypt not surprisingly depended on her status or the status of her husband. In the Old Kingdom a number of women held administrative positions, probably in private house-holds or in the service of other women. In variety and frequency they are insignificant beside the offices that men could hold. There is no clear evidence that these women ever had authority over male workers. Lower down the social scale a number of gender distinctions occur. Male servants tended to wait on men and female ones on women; men made the bed of the master of the house and women that of his wife; a woman's carrying chair might be carried by women rather than men; dancers performed in separate male and female groups. In the Middle and New Kingdoms, the administrative titles held by women virtually disappeared. A few minor positions for women remained but administration at all levels of society became formally the prerogative of men. Among the personnel employed in large private households and on estates, we find a distinction in the sorts of work done by men and women. While both were employed in the house as servants or in the processes of baking and brewing, most other aspects of food production were male-dominated. Most crafts employed men in their workshops except for the textile industry, which involved mainly women until the New Kingdom when men became part of the workforce, perhaps along with the introduction of the upright loom. Work outside on private and institutional estates was for the most part carried out by men, with only a few areas where women had a part to play.

Women, like men, could be called up for state labour and perhaps put to work on the land. There are scattered pieces of evidence that despite the gender distinctions apparently pertaining on large estates, women did sometimes have to work outside as part of their corvee duty, as a punishment, as a result of hardship, or to cultivate land they owned or rented. Nevertheless, there is enough material to show that there was an ideal division of labour based on gender which limited the types of work a woman could do, but which was much less restrictive with regard to men. It is difficult for us to know how far the ideal was adhered to in practice.

FURTHER READING

J. Baines and C. Eyre, 'Four notes on literacy', *Göttingen Miszellen* 61 (1983), 81–5 (Women and literacy).

H. Fischer, *Egyptian Studies I: Varia*, New York, 1976, 69–79 (Administrative titles of women in the Old and Middle Kingdoms).

H. Fischer, *Egyptian Women of the Old Kingdom and of the Heracleopolitan Period*, New York, 1989.

H. Fischer, 'Women in the Old Kingdom and the Heracleopolitan Period' in: B. Lesko (ed.) *Women's Earliest Records from Ancient Egypt and Western Asia*, Atlanta, 1989, 5–24.

G. Robins, 'Some images of women in New Kingdom art and literature' in: B. Lesko (ed.) *Women's Earliest Records from Ancient Egypt and Western Asia*, Atlanta, 1989, 105–16.

G. Robins, 'While the woman looks on: gender inequality in New Kingdom Egypt' *KMT* 1 no. 3 (1990), 18, 21, 64–5.

D. Sweeney, 'Women's correspondence from Deir el-Medinah' *Acts of the VIth International Congress of Egyptology*, Turin, forthcoming.

W. Ward, *Essays on Feminine Titles of the Middle Kingdom and Related Subjects*, Beirut, 1986.

W. Ward, 'Non-royal women and their occupations in the Middle Kingdom' in: B. Lesko (ed.) *Women's Earliest Records from Ancient Egypt and Western Asia*, Atlanta, 1989, 33–43.

CHAPTER SEVEN

The economic and legal position of women

Ownership of land and property in the Old and Middle Kingdoms
Whether or not all land was in theory owned by the king, the notion of private
ownership of property, that is, land owners could dispose of as they wished,
had already arisen by the early Old Kingdom. Although the evidence from this
period is sparse, we find that women as well as men could own land.[1] In his
biographical inscription a Third Dynasty official called Metjen tells how he
had inherited fifty arouras of land from his mother Nebsenet. An aroura is
about two-thirds of an acre. In the Fifth Dynasty another official, called Tjenti,
refers in a text to two arouras of land which had come to him from his mother.
Other preserved legal documents confirm that wives could inherit from their
husbands, and also show that daughters could inherit from their fathers. These
early texts deal with the upper elite only, and we have no knowledge of whether
men and women of lower status would have had similar rights of ownership.

The number of legal documents concerning property and inheritance from
the Middle Kingdom is somewhat greater, and of these a few concern women.
Towards the end of the Twelfth Dynasty, in year 44 of Amenemhat III, an
official called Ankhreni, the trusted seal-bearer of the director of works, made
a will leaving all his property to his brother Wah who was a priest. This
suggests that Ankhreni had no surviving wife or children. Ankhreni then died,
and Wah duly received his inheritance. In year 2 of the next king, Amenemhat
IV, he made his own will leaving everything to his wife: 'Will made by the priest
... Wah: I am making a will for my wife ... Sheftu called Teti – of everything
that my brother ... Ankhreni gave to me, with all the goods as they should be –
of all that he gave me. She herself shall give (it) to any of her children that she
shall bear me, that she wishes. I am giving her the three Asiatics which my
brother ... Ankhreni gave to me. She herself shall give them to any of her
children that she wishes. As for my tomb, I shall be buried in it, and my wife
also, without letting anyone interfere with it. Now as for the rooms that my
brother ... Ankhreni built for me, my wife shall live there, without letting her
be cast out of it by any person.'[2]

Since Teti does not seem to have had children yet, perhaps this document
was drawn up on her marriage to Wah. If so, Ankhreni would already have been
dead, and Wah would probably not have been young; perhaps he could not

49   Votive stela of the workman Penbuy, his son Amenmose, and his wife Iretnofret.

afford to marry until he had inherited his brother's property. An extra sentence is added to the document in a different hand: 'It is the deputy Geb who shall act as guardian to my son.' This suggests that Teti did bear Wah a child, but that Wah did not expect to live to see it grow up. This may be why in his will he allows his wife to decide how to hand on the inheritance to any children she might bear him.

Another Middle Kingdom will from the end of the Twelfth Dynasty was made by Intef's son Mery, called Keby. In it he hands on his office to his son, annuls a will he had made in favour of the son's mother, who must have been a previous wife, and leaves his house to his yet-to-be-born children by another woman, presumably his new wife.[3] It is interesting that the house is to go to future children and that no provision is made for his wife. Perhaps it is assumed that she will have the use of the house until the children are grown up, and that it will then be their responsibility to look after their mother.

Another later Middle Kingdom document apparently deals with a dispute between a man and his daughter over the ownership of some property.[4] The father intends to make over fifteen slaves in addition to sixty already given to his wife, Senebtysy. His daughter, Tahenwet, however, has brought a lawsuit against him claiming that the property was given to her by her husband, but that her father has given it to his wife. The document seems to comprise a private record of the father's rebuttal of the case, but it is too damaged to understand fully. Perhaps Senebtysy was the father's second wife while Tahenwet was the daughter of the first, which might have led to friction between them. Stephen Quirke suggests that the man involved was the Thirteenth Dynasty vizier Renseneb, which would explain the large number of slaves involved.[5] The case shows that a woman could initiate a lawsuit on her own behalf.

The economic position of women in the New Kingdom

Despite what seems to be abundant source material in the New Kingdom, we know far less than we would like about the workings of the ancient Egyptian economy.[6] There was, however, one essential difference between the economic affairs of men and women of the elite class. The men by definition were scribes and held some sort of government post, for which they received a salary in grain and other commodities since there was no money. By contrast, women were excluded from the bureaucracy and therefore from receiving such income directly. However, an ordinary workman at Deir el-Medina received 4 *khar* (about 300 litres) of emmer wheat for bread and 1½ *khar* of barley for beer a month.[7] It has been reckoned that this could support a family of about ten people, if some of them were small children. Thus a man's government pay was clearly intended to enable him to keep a wife and family. Further, on festival days the workmen were supplied with extra provisions from the temples, and a few texts seem to show that the men passed some of these on to various women. The identity of the women is not made clear, but they were almost certainly family members. Women then were probably expected to be dependent on their husbands for basic support at Deir el-Medina.

Notwithstanding this, women at Deir el-Medina are recorded as engaging in economic transactions on their own account. For instance, a woman was paid 29 *deben* of copper, equivalent to almost 15 *khar* of grain, for some clothes, which she perhaps had woven herself.[8] A *deben* was a unit of weight roughly equivalent to 91 grams. In another business deal a woman purchased items worth 76 *deben*. She made a downpayment of garments and vegetables worth 5 *deben* but owed the rest.[9] The creditor must have believed that she would have been able to pay off this debt within a reasonable time. In another case a woman was able to offer a plot of land to pay for a donkey.[10] One text lists property worth a total of 170 *deben* owed to a woman called Webkhet.[11] We also find a woman who owned rights to a certain number of days' work from ten slaves.[12] This was an ancient form of time sharing: the slaves were owned jointly by a group of people who would each have a right to so many days' work a year. Presumably they could either use these days themselves or sell them to someone else as a way of earning money.

There are also examples of women who were owners of slaves from outside Deir el-Medina. A papyrus from Gurob in Middle Egypt records that a man purchased from a woman and her son seventeen days' work by a female slave

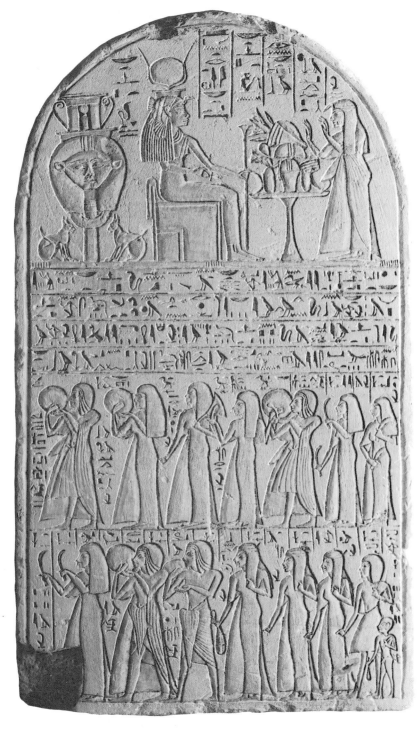

50   Votive stela of the mistress of the house Bukanefptah, wife of the workman Kasa.

called Kheryt and four days by another slave called Henut. Later, the man bought from the woman a further six days' work by Kheryt, the son not being mentioned on this occasion.[13] For the total of twenty-seven days' work the purchaser paid several garments, a bull and sixteen goats. Hiring out slaves could thus provide an extra source of income for a woman, even though the initial capital outlay was considerable. A papyrus from Thebes records the purchase of a slave by a woman for over 400 *deben*.[14] She paid over half the price in clothing worth 223 *deben*, which she had on hand and had perhaps made herself. The rest she paid in goods borrowed from her neighbours. Perhaps she hoped to pay the debt by renting out the slave, or her creditors may have agreed to be paid back in slave days. Unfortunately this is not mentioned in the document, which is less concerned with the transaction as such than with rebutting an accusation that the woman made up the price of the purchase with property not her own.

These cases make it clear that some women were involved in business deals involving goods of high value by comparison with the monthly wage of a Deir el-Medina workman. However, men too carried on private business transactions and at Deir el-Medina, for instance, the workmen made and decorated furniture and funerary goods, hired out their donkeys for profit, and possibly cultivated plots of land outside the village. The records left from the village show that it was men who predominated in the economic affairs there. In a corpus of documents recording financial transactions, collected for a study of the economy of the village,[15] only 18.1 per cent of those which preserve names involve women, and only 10.3 per cent of the people named are women. Either women were not as economically active as men in the sorts of transactions contained in the documents, or most transactions involving women were carried out by men on their behalf.

Outside the workmen's village we have no knowledge of the salaries paid to government employees. High officials like the vizier or overseer of the treasury must have received many times the amount paid to a simple workman. In the *Wilbour Papyrus*, which records the tenure of land in part of Middle Egypt during the reign of Ramses v, the vizier holds twenty arouras of land and the overseer of the treasury 194, but we do not know whether they were granted this land as part of their official income, or whether it was part of their private fortunes. Although the wives of such officials would presumably have shared in their husbands' wealth, we have no idea what sort of income these women might have expected to have in their own right. If, however, they had themselves been born into high official families and had inherited property from their parents, they could have been independently wealthy.

Inheritance in the New Kingdom

During the New Kingdom, as in earlier periods, there is plenty of evidence that women could inherit property. Although only a son could hope to inherit his

father's office, it seems that in normal circumstances all children, both male
and female, inherited goods equally from their parents. Surviving documentation concerning inheritance often deals with disputes between heirs, or with
special circumstances in the division of property. If it had been common for
people to make wills, we would expect more of these documents to have been
found. In most cases property was probably divided among the children of a
man or woman without any dispute, and its disposition would only have been
put into writing when a complication arose. Thus, one law case from Deir
el-Medina concerns the request of a woman that she be given 'her fair share of
the inheritance of her father'.[16] The unusual circumstances that led the twice-
married woman called Naunakht, mentioned in Chapter Three, to make a will,
gives us an insight into the ways she acquired her property, as well as how she
in her turn intended to dispose of it.[17] She had inherited a storeroom from her
father, land and other property from her first husband, and acquired an *oipe* of
emmer wheat together with her husband. An *oipe* is nearly 20 litres. She also
was entitled to a third of the property that she held in common with her second
husband, the other two-thirds being earmarked for the children. In her will
Naunakht makes arrangements for the disposal of all her property, including
the third share from her second marriage, although her husband is not dead.
While her first marriage had been childless, she had borne eight children to her
second husband. However, she considered that some of these offspring were
not looking after her as they should, and so she disinherited these from her
property, thus leaving more for each of the good children. It is explicitly stated
that all the children would share in the two-thirds of the common property that
would come to them from their father. By contrast, Naunakht had absolute
right of disposal over her own property.

Naunakht's will was agreed to before witnesses by her husband and all her
children. It seems that it was wise to get one's children to consent to a disposition of property to prevent later disputes. In one recorded case, a man remarried after the death of his first wife, and wished to settle property on his second.
The children of the first marriage testified that they had been given all the
property due to them, and that the settlement about to be made on the second
wife consisted of property that was their father's to dispose of as he liked.[18]

In the case of Naunakht, she was able to disinherit from her property those
children whom she regarded as unsatisfactory. It is clear that she could not
disinherit them from their father's property, but this has no bearing on
whether he could have, if he had so desired. From elsewhere we know of a man
who disinherited a female relative for neglecting him when he was sick.[19] A
further condition of inheriting property seems to be revealed by documents
recording disputes that hinge on who had been responsible for the deceased's
burial.[20] In one we learn that a woman called Tagemy died and was buried by
one of her sons called Huy without any help from her other children. Apparently this gave Huy the right to his mother's property, but on Huy's death when

51 (*left*) Votive stela showing a man libating and offering to the god Khons, and his wife and her daughters libating and offering to a goddess.

52 (*right*) Votive stela of Iytnefret.

his property should have passed to his son, Huy's siblings tried to gain a share of Tagemy's property on the grounds that Huy had not buried her alone. The son quotes: '"Let the possessions be given to him who buries", says the law of pharaoh', and he cites a precedent: 'See, the landed property of Tanehesy was given to Sawadjyt when she was buried while he gave her his coffin.' We learn from another document that Tanehesy was the mother of Sawadjyt and that he supplied her funerary equipment and buried her 'while his brothers and sisters did not help him.' The workman Nebsemen made for a woman called Iner 'one wooden decorated coffin for her share of the lower storehouse.' Later a dispute arose between the children of Nebsemen and the daughter of Iner over this property. Nebsemen's children claimed it because it was Nebsemen who had buried her.

That the one who was responsible for the burial became the heir also explains the content of an early Eighteenth Dynasty letter: 'Meniupu has come in flight. My father and my mother will support him . . . If he dies, my mother shall bury him, for it is her husband Neni who told her to bury him and to perform the duties of an heir for him.'[21] Once again, carrying out a burial and being an heir are linked. It seems, then, that while sons and daughters had rights of inheritance, not only could they be disinherited by a parent but they could also lose their right to inherit if they failed to take part in the parent's burial.

Nevertheless, women often did inherit property from their parents. At Deir el-Medina, such property might take the form of buildings. Andrea McDowell suggests that this was because the houses in the village were government property that went with the job and could, therefore, only be 'owned' by men.[22] Women might in consequence find themselves homeless on the death of a father or a husband. To compensate, huts or storehouses that were private not government property often went to women. In fact, in a letter to his daughter a father says explicitly: 'If the workman Baki throws you out of the house, I will take action! As for the house, it is what belongs to(?) Pharaoh, life, prosperity, health, but you may dwell in the anteroom to my storehouse because it is I who built it. Nobody in the world shall throw you out of there.'[23]

There is an interesting stela which concerns the second priest Piay, his sister, and mother. Piay cedes all the property of his father, an overseer of granaries, to his sister, including fields, meadows, slaves and trees, while their mother renounces her interest in the property, provided that the daughter looks after her in her old age.[24] Presumably Piay had a good income from his position as second priest, so that he was able to give his sister a considerable independence in this way. Here the family are at a higher social level than the workmen at Deir el-Medina, and more property is at stake.

53   Votive stela of Wennefer dedicated on behalf of his wife.

54 Votive stela of Pay dedicated on behalf of his mother.

Land ownership in the New Kingdom

Although we know far less than we would like about land tenure in general, it is clear from what has already been said that women could own and rent land in their own right. Of the landholders listed in the *Wilbour Papyrus*,[25] between 10 and 11 per cent were women. Most of these held plots of 5 arouras, although some only had 3 and a few had 10 or 20. The 5 aroura plot (about 3⅓ acres) was the commonest size listed in the papyrus, and was held by the majority of stablemasters, herdsmen, and priests listed as landholders. By contrast, soldiers mostly held 3 aroura plots, while the majority of scribes listed held 10 arouras or more. It has been reckoned that 5 arouras would produce enough grain to support five to eight adults, but in fact, some of the grain would be needed to defray other living expenses besides food. However, a 5 aroura plot would provide adequate subsistence for one or two adults and their children. A further estimate suggests that 10 arouras could be cultivated by one man, so that with a plot of 5 arouras, the cultivator would have time to supplement the income obtained by doing something else. For women landholders, one obvious supplement would be the production of textiles.

Large estates

At the other end of the scale were the large family estates of many arouras belonging to the upper elite. Although the descendants of the original owner usually inherited equally, such estates do not seem as a rule to have been split up. Instead, the whole unit would be administered by one of the heirs and the annual income divided among all of them. The heirs did not themselves have to reside on their estate, but could take their share of the income and live where they wanted.

We know something of just such an estate from a long text in the tomb of a man named Mose, dating to the reign of Ramses II.[26] The estate had been in the family for a number of generations and had been the subject of several lawsuits among the heirs, the history of which was recorded by Mose in his tomb. The estate had been given to Mose's ancestor by king Ahmose at the beginning of the Eighteenth Dynasty. By the reign of Horemheb at the end of the dynasty there were six heirs, of whom four were women. The administrator at that time was one of the women who was called Wernero. Her position was subsequently challenged in court by her sister Takharu, who wanted the estate divided up among the heirs. However, the son of Wernero fought this action and won the position of administrator of the whole property, which he held until his death. At that point his wife Nebnefret took over the running of the estate for their son Mose, who was presumably still a minor. The authority of Nebnefret was contested by a man called Khay, whose connection with the family is unclear; he may have been a rank outsider, or he may have been one of the heirs. He used forged documents to support his claim, not only to be administrator but also to own Nebnefret's and Mose's share of the estate. Although the end of the case is lost from his tomb, the very fact that Mose recorded the whole account must be a sign that he was finally able to prove his claim against Khay. This, however, is less important than some of the other facts that can be gleaned from the account. First, it is clear that the administrator of an estate was not automatically a male heir. In fact, one might even ask whether women had more time to devote to the task, since they held no official position. Second, although the women went to court to fight their cases in their own right, it is possible that Khay saw the widowed Nebnefret as easy prey. If she was without adult male support, she may have been vulnerable until her son grew up and was able to take on the case.

Legal actions, crime and punishment

Legal documents of the New Kingdom, many but not all from Deir el-Medina, show that before the law men and women were, in theory, equal. Not only could women inherit, own, and dispose of property in their own right, they could enter into business deals, and they could go to court as plaintiff, defendant, or witness, on an equal footing with men. In contrast to some cultures, a male guardian was not required to act for them. Women were responsible for their own actions and could be taken to court to answer for them, as in the case of Heria of Deir el-Medina who was accused of stealing some tools.[27] She denied this on oath in court, but when her house was searched the tools were found there, together with various items stolen from the temple. It seems that her case was too serious for the village court, so she was sent elsewhere for it to be dealt with. In accounts of court cases, women undergo the same harsh methods of interrogation and penalties as men. When the foreman Hay at Deir el-Medina accused three workmen and a woman of slandering him, they all got the same punishment of a beating, irrespective of gender.[28]

Our knowledge of the court system in ancient Egypt is limited. In the New Kingdom when cases concerned the state, for instance conspiracies against the king, tomb robberies, or thefts from temples, the king would appoint an *ad hoc* court from among his highest officials, who were of course all men. In cases between private individuals, local courts heard the arguments. Most of our evidence for these comes from Deir el-Medina,[29] where the court was made up of officials and workmen from the village. There is only one instance where it is mentioned as including women, who sat along with three workmen. Both the presence of the women and the absence of any officials are unique, suggesting unusual circumstances. It would be dangerous to assume from this one occasion that women usually sat as members of the court.[30] Legal documents, which were often drawn up before the court and produced as evidence, had to be signed by witnesses to validate the contents. While some female witnesses are known, the majority were men.

At Deir el-Medina it was unusual for cases to be brought by the less wealthy against the better off. This may be because the commonest type of lawsuit brought to the court concerned individuals trying to collect debts from others who were either their financial equals or poorer. In a study of the legal system at Deir el-Medina, McDowell has found that 'women are more likely to appear before the court as defendants than as claimants. They stand accused of theft, non-payment, selling a building which perhaps ought not to have been sold, and neglecting a sick relative . . . all except the last perhaps offenses of which a less well off person is more likely to be the perpetrator than the victim. On the whole, however, women appear in relatively few cases either as claimants or defendants, probably because they were involved in few substantial economic transactions.'[31]

With some crimes, the offender's family might be punished also. So the families of escaped corvee labourers were apprehended and put to work. In one royal decree the threatened punishments for male offenders were cutting off the nose and ears and putting the criminal to labour as a cultivator, or impaling. In addition, the offender's wife and children would become slaves. It is not clear whether women ever suffered these more severe punishments of mutilation and impaling and, if they did, whether their families lost their freedom.

Punishing a criminal's family suggests one way in which people became slaves. Other slaves may have been foreign prisoners of war. In extreme financial circumstances people may have sold themselves or family members into slavery. This group must have formed the lowest stratum of society, since slaves unlike servants could be bought and sold. Both men and women could be slaves, and they could be owned by the state, temples, and by private individuals. Several documents attest to the fact that they could be emancipated, in two cases for the express purpose of marrying them into their former owner's family.

The strong and the weak

In any consideration of their legal and economic rights, it must be remembered that women did not form a homogeneous group. While women from elite families had extensive legal rights and could own property and conduct business, other sources suggest that many others found their position insecure. From the Middle Kingdom onwards, the widow in particular appears as one of the disadvantaged of society. The evidence comes from autobiographical texts in which an official recounts how he has led an ideal life, and from the wisdom literature where the author is advising the male reader on how to conduct himself to conform to the social ideal. It is usual for an official to assert that he has fed the hungry, clothed the naked, given to him who had not, and this list of good works includes claims that he was 'the husband of the widow',[32] 'the support of widows',[33] 'a helper for the widow',[34] and one 'who paid attention to the voice of the widow...who anointed the widow who had nothing'.[35] Amenemhat, a Twelfth Dynasty governor of Beni Hasan, describes a time of famine when he contrived to feed all the inhabitants of his province.[36] He specifically states: 'I gave alike to widow and married woman, and I did not prefer the great to the small in all that I gave'. He is at pains to stress that social status did not influence him, and the inference is that a less fair man might have let the widow go hungry.

From the Herakleopolitan Period a royal wisdom text survives addressed to king Merikara concerning the duties of kingship. Among other advice Merikara is told '... don't oppress the widow'.[37] In the New Kingdom *Instructions of Amenemipet* two situations are included in which a man is not to take advantage of a widow: 'Do not be greedy for a cubit of land, Nor encroach on the boundaries of a widow';[38] 'Do not pounce on a widow when you find her in the fields And then fail to be patient with her reply'.[39]

The impression given by the texts is that some widows were very vulnerable, and ranked among the poor and deprived in society. These were not women who were wealthy in their own right or who had strong family support, but those who during life had been dependent on their husbands, and who were left at their spouses' death with little or no means of support. They would be unable to stand up to greedy bullies who might attempt to harass and cheat them. For women such as these, life must have been hard indeed.

55   Votive cloth dedicated by six women to Hathor in her form as a cow.

In a few Middle Kingdom autobiographies we find officials denying that they ever mistreated their inferiors. The same governor from Beni Hasan whom we have already met says: 'There was no citizen's daughter whom I shamed, nor widow whom I oppressed, no farmer whom I drove away, no herdsman whom I turned back. There was no overseer of labourers whose people I seized for labour. There was no pauper in my surroundings, no hungry man in my time.'[40] In a similar text by another governor, we read: 'No daughter of yours was ever enslaved',[41] while a Middle Kingdom official says: '. . . I did not seize a man's daughter, nor did I seize his field'.[42] The inclusion of 'daughters' in these texts suggests that young women also might have been vulnerable to the depredations of the powerful.

It is possible that women in general were often at risk if they moved around too freely without escort. Ramses III is made to say as one of his achievements: 'I enabled the woman of Egypt to go her way, her journeys being extended where she wanted, without any other person assaulting her on the road.'[43] As a corollary one must suppose that women were often in danger of being mugged or perhaps raped if they went out alone, a problem still present in modern society.

Conclusion

What conclusions can we draw, then, from this study of the position of Egyptian women under the law? There has never been a society in which the individual has been completely protected, where high status has not conveyed privilege, and where the less influential have not under the system become personally disadvantaged. In Egypt, taken at face value the sources show that

elite women had legal rights equal to men, and that they could engage in economic transactions on their own behalf in the same way as men. Yet when we set this against women's subordinate positions in other areas of society, we have to ask what sort of equality there was in practice. Undoubtedly women had legal rights, but could they exercise them freely at all times?[44] We have to remember that documents dealing with aspects of property involving women, even from the New Kingdom, are few in number and seem to exist because of the exceptional nature of each situation. Were there other women who were prevented from disposing of their property as they wanted because of family pressure? Were there women cheated by men in positions of authority who did not even bother to bring a case against the perpetrators because they knew they could never hope to win? Even though a woman could conduct a lawsuit on her own behalf, did she have a better chance of success if she had powerful male backing? In other words, was the system impartial, or was it weighted against women? The very fact that members of the court were male makes the latter more probable. Such a bias would be unlikely to show up overtly in our sources, but the much smaller number of women mentioned in legal and economic documents supports the assumptions. The position of disadvantaged persons such as widows suggests that their rights were protected not by law but by the good will of male officials. Women's legal rights clearly did not extend effectively throughout society. They may have required at all levels to be backed up by wealth or by strong family support. Of course, even though the system had an in-built bias in favour of men, their rights, too, would not in practice have extended to the lower classes.

FURTHER READING

Schafik Allam, 'Women as owners of immovables in pharaonic Egypt' in: B. Lesko (ed.) *Women's Earliest Records from Ancient Egypt and Western Asia*, Atlanta, 1989, 123–35.

M. Bierbrier, *The Tomb-Builders of the Pharaohs*, London, 1982, chapter 6.

J. Černý, 'The will of Naunakhte and the related documents', *Journal of Egyptian Archaeology* 31 (1945), 29–53.

A. McDowell, *Jurisdiction in the Workmen's Community of Deir el-Medina*, Leiden, 1990.

56 (*left*) Funerary stela of the *wab*-priest Horemhat. His wife Djab, followed by his daughter Tanetiunet, pours a libation.

CHAPTER EIGHT

Women and temple ritual

Female priestly titles

There is evidence from the Old Kingdom onwards that women in ancient Egypt had a part to play in temple ritual.[1] In the Old Kingdom a large number of high class women were priestesses (*hemet netjer*) of Hathor.[2] *Hemet netjer* is the feminine form of a common male title *hem netjer* which denotes a particular type of priest within the temple hierarchy. Less often women were priestesses of the goddess Neith. Very rarely were they priestesses in the cult of a god, but most usually they were associated with a goddess.

The title 'priestess of Hathor' remained a common one for women into the Middle Kingdom.[3] We have already seen that it marked the bearer as belonging to the upper echelons of society, the husbands of these women being among the highest officials in the land. The male equivalent of this title is rare, although in the Middle Kingdom there were other types of male priests of Hathor. These included overseers of priests, a position which never seems to have been given to a woman.

A few *wabet* priestesses are also known from the Middle Kingdom. This title

57   Female members of the tomb owner's family offer sistra and *menit*-necklaces to the deceased.

58   The rites before the tomb.

is the feminine form of the common male title *wab* priest (from *wab* 'to be pure'), representing a different rank in the priestly hierarchy from *hem netjer*. There had already been women who 'performed *wab* service for Hathor' in the Old Kingdom and received the same payment as male *wab* priests.

It is unclear whether the function of female priests was the same as that of male ones. Since the masculine form '*hem netjer* of Hathor' was very rare, it might appear that the female holders of the title would have to fulfil the same function as that carried out by the *hem netjer* in the cult of other deities. In addition there is evidence that the *hemet netjer* was connected with music-making in the cult.

Outside the cult of Hathor the number of female priestly titles drops to a handful, so that in other cults the temple priesthood was overwhelmingly male. Even in the cult of Hathor, women did not rise to hold positions in the administration but were always under the authority of a man. Nor do we ever find female lector priests. These were the priests who read the ritual from a papyrus roll. The absence of women might be explained by the fact that most of them were unable to read, but it might have been less that they were illiterate than that their literacy was not officially acknowledged.

A few New Kingdom temple scenes show a class of male and female personnel called *henuty* for the men and *henutet* for the women, often translated 'servant'. They are depicted together with the male priests and the god's wife in

59   Scene in the tomb of the workman Inherkha at Deir el-Medina showing the deceased and his family receiving offerings of a shabti-box and a statuette of Osiris.

rituals discussed later in this chapter. The function of these individuals is little understood, and neither *henuty* nor *henutet* appears as a title among individuals of the elite class. It is difficult to say anything about this group of people except that both genders are represented. It is unclear even whether they were some sort of priest or had an entirely different function.

Musicians

By the beginning of the Eighteenth Dynasty at the latest, women no longer held priestly titles. In the Old and Middle Kingdoms, priests were officials who spent part of their time serving in their local cult. By the New Kingdom the priesthood was a full-time occupation in which men made their careers as a branch of the state bureaucracy. Women were thus excluded. The commonest title of the New Kingdom linking women to temple cult was *shemayet*, 'musician'.[4] Male and female musicians were already part of temple personnel in the Middle Kingdom, but *shemayet* was not used on the monuments as a regular title for individual women. In the New Kingdom, by contrast, it was employed as a title by large numbers of elite women, from the wives and daughters of the highest officials to those of the workmen at Deir el-Medina. Except for 'mistress of the house', it must be the commonest title found for women in the Theban tombs. *Shemayet* was normally followed by the name of the deity to whose cult the holder of the title was attached. Unlike the *hemet netjer* in the Old and Middle Kingdoms, the *shemayet* regularly served both male and female deities. At Thebes, where the god Amun had his cult centre, women were most commonly 'musician of Amun'. Sometimes they served in the cult of Amun's consort Mut, or in that of the whole Theban triad, Amun, Mut and their son Khons. In other parts of the country, high-ranking women would be musicians in the cults of their local deities. Wives of priests were frequently musicians in the same cult as their husbands. For instance, a Nineteenth Dynasty man was priest of Amun in the mortuary temple of Ramses II. His wife was not simply 'musician of Amun', as so many Theban women were, but she was specifically 'musician of Amun in the mortuary temple of Ramses II', showing that she served in her husband's temple.

What did a musician do in the cult? In the Eighteenth Dynasty, scenes in tomb chapels and elsewhere only rarely give us an idea. Many women in the families of the elite owners of monuments are given the title 'musician', but in most cases they are shown merely accompanying the owner. They not infrequently carry a loop sistrum, either holding it by the loop at the side of the body or shaking it (figs. 36, 77). A sistrum was a rattle sacred to Hathor used by musicians in divine cult to pacify the goddess and other deities (fig. 37). Exceptionally, one Eighteenth Dynasty tomb scene gives us a glimpse of an actual temple ritual.[5] The owner of the tomb is commemorating his installation as second priest of Amun. The scene shows him going to the temple for the ceremony, and being met by a procession of musicians shaking their sistra, many of whom are also members of his family.

Along with the sistrum musicians often carried a necklace called the *menit*, which consisted of a number of strands strung with small beads that came together into a single strand of large beads at either end (figs. 36, 77). These strands attached to a counterpoise shaped like an upside down keyhole, which fell down the back and held the necklace in place when worn. Like the sistrum, the *menit* was sacred to Hathor who may be shown wearing it, especially in her cow form.

A few Eighteenth Dynasty temple scenes also show women shaking their sistra as part of temple ritual, in the *chapelle rouge* of Hatshepsut, the Festival Temple of Thutmose III at Karnak, and the colonnade of the temple of Luxor decorated in the reign of Tutankhamun. The *chapelle rouge* was a shrine erected by Hatshepsut in the temple of Karnak but dismantled by Thutmose III. The blocks were used as fill in foundations and walls from where they have now been recovered. Two similar scenes show Hatshepsut running before the sacred boat of Amun-Ra.[6] A male harpist sings a hymn to the god, while a number of acrobatic dancers are shown doing back-bends, or dancing energetically with their hair falling over their faces. In one scene, their actions are captioned 'dancing by the dancers'. Other women are not dancing, but shake their sistra with one hand and hold a *menit* necklace in the other; they also sing a hymn. They are labelled 'the musical troupe of the temple' (see section below). Three clapping men sing a hymn about the going forth of the god; they are labelled 'choir' (fig. 37).

A poorly preserved block from the same building shows part of a scene in which three women shaking their sistra lead a procession.[7] They are likewise called 'the musical troupe of the temple'. They are followed by seven priests with shaven heads who carry standards (long poles surmounted by a sacred emblem), and by another figure with a shaven head who is a lector priest. In a lower register there are nine more male figures, probably priests, but the block is very worn here and it is difficult to make out details.

In the tomb of the steward of Tiy, queen of Amenhotep III, a series of scenes shows the celebration of the king's *sed* festival.[8] Included in these is a depiction of the ritual of raising the *djed* pillar. Two registers show singers and dancers present at the rite. In the upper register male dancers are shown together with three clapping and singing men who are labelled as 'musicians'. The lower register shows two women playing tambourines and three pairs of clapping women. They are called 'the musicians who are making music at the time of performing the rituals of erecting the *djed* pillar' (fig. 38).

From the beginning of the Nineteenth Dynasty, tomb chapel decoration starts to change in content, so that scenes sometimes show the tomb owner conducting temple rituals accompanied by male and female members of his family. In Theban Tomb 19 the owner Amenmose, the chief priest of the deified king Amenhotep I, is shown in the leopard skin of an officiating priest

60 Inner coffin of Henutmehit.

censing before the god.[9] There are other male priests present, followed by a group of women including Amenmose's wife shaking sistra, while other women play a flute or a tambourine and one dances with clappers in her hands.

Theban Tomb 31 belongs to Khons, the chief priest in the cult of Thutmose III in the reign of Ramses II. In one scene a priest in a leopard skin censes and libates before Osiris and Anubis.[10] He is followed by the unlabelled figures of a woman, a man, and another woman; the women carry sistra, *menit* necklaces, and flowers. Between the man and second woman is a small male figure identified as 'his son, the second priest of Menkheperre (Thutmose III) Khaemwaset', and following the last unidentified woman is a small female figure carrying a sistrum and *menit* called 'his daughter, the musician of Amun Wiy'. The main figures are probably Khons as officiating priest, his mother, his wife, and a male relative. In another scene in the same tomb we glimpse the ritual in the cult of Thutmose III.[11] A group of women is shown mourning the king, while a musician of Amun and two musicians of Montu shake their sistra.

Theban Tomb 51 also dates from the Nineteenth Dynasty. It belongs to the chief priest of the *ka* of Thutmose I, Userhat. One scene shows Userhat wearing a leopard skin and officiating before a shrine containing images of Thutmose I and his queen.[12] He is followed by his mother and his wife shaking their sistra. Both are called musicians of Amun-Ra (fig. 39).

Evidently in the New Kingdom the title 'musician' carried with it a specific function involving music-making in divine cult. The women who held the title belonged to elite families of all ranks. There were also male musicians, but these usually remain anonymous, and the title 'musician' is not found in the titularies of officials. This suggests that male musicians were not drawn from the same ranks as female ones and lacked the latter's status.

Musical troupes of the temple

From the Old Kingdom we find groups of women called 'musical troupes' (*khener*) attached to religious and secular institutions. For instance, in the tomb of the Fifth Dynasty official Ti, a scene in three registers shows at the top a group of male musicians and below two rows which each consist of five female dancers followed by three clapping women.[13] The captions run: 'dancing by the musical troupe' and 'clapping by the musical troupe' (fig. 40). In a rather obscure late Middle Kingdom letter, which comes from a temple environment, mention is twice made of a 'musical troupe'.[14] For a long time scholars translated *khener* as 'harim', but recently it has been strongly argued that in this context the word should be understood as a troupe of musical performers, hence the translation used in this book.[15] We have already met the 'musical troupe of the temple' on blocks from the *chapelle rouge* of Hatshepsut, where the phrase referred to women who were shaking sistra, suggesting that the musical troupe included women who were *shemayet* (fig. 37). A Middle Kingdom letter suggests that this was also the case at that period. The letter, written to a scribe of the temple, instructs the recipient to have brought a list of people including a '*shemayet* Sattepihu who is in the musical troupe'.[16]

In the New Kingdom these troupes of musicians were in the charge of women with the title 'great one of the troupe of musical performers' (*weret khener*). This position was held by the wives of some of the highest officials, and frequently the wife headed the musical troupe of the cult in which her husband was a high-ranking priest. So a number of 'great ones of the troupe of Amun' were wives of the chief priest of Amun, or in one case, of the third priest. In other cases, we have chief priests of Montu, Thoth, Khons and Amenhotep I, whose wives were in charge of the musical troupes of their respective cults. Elsewhere, the husband was not a chief priest but a high-ranking official. Sobekhotep was the mayor of the Faiyum in the reign of Thutmose IV. The chief god of the region was the crocodile god Sobek, and he was also the overseer of priests of Sobek. His wife Merit was 'great one of the musical troupe of Sobek'. Sobekhotep was the son of a man called Min who was the treasurer of all Egypt, and he himself eventually exercised that office. There is no evidence that his family had any connections with the Faiyum, and Betsy Bryan suggests that it was his wife who came from an important family in the area and that it was through her that Sobekhotep received the office of mayor.[17] Later he inherited his father's office of treasurer and handed on the office of mayor of the Faiyum to his son Paser. Merit was clearly a high-ranking and important woman. In addition to being 'great one of the musical troupe', she was nurse to a daughter of Thutmose IV, who was perhaps brought up in the royal palace at Medinet el-Ghurab situated at the entrance to the Faiyum. She also had the high ranking court title 'great lady-in-waiting'.

There can be no doubt that to be 'great one of the musical troupe' was to be of high rank, and the more important the cult, the higher the status. The holder of the position would have been in charge of the musicians who performed in the deity's cult, perhaps responsible for the training, practice, and rotas of the performers, and for seeing that things went correctly during the ritual. Since men were also often involved in organised music-making the question arises as to whether the 'great one of the musical troupe' had authority over male performers too, or whether they were organised separately.

We know little about how the 'musicians', 'musical troupes' and the 'great ones of the musical troupe' fitted into the overall structure and hierarchy of temple personnel. Were they paid like male priests or were they 'volunteers'? Could there perhaps have been loss of status for women to be paid, and if so, were musicians from the lower ranks of society paid, but not those from the higher? Was it a matter of status for high officials to be able to support their wives, so that they did not need to obtain support from elsewhere, or would this not have been a matter of concern? Did the title 'great one of the musical troupe' bestow authority on a par with the top male ranks of temple hier-archies? Was the 'great one of the musical troupe' ultimately subordinate to the chief priest? What is clear is that in the New Kingdom a distinction was made between the roles of men and women in temple cult. Men were *hem netjer*, *wab*-priests, and lector priests, all headed by the chief priest; women were musicians headed by the 'great one of the musical troupe'. Male singers and musicians usually remained anonymous, and clearly ranked lower than female singers from elite families. The priest who officiated before the deity's statue was a man, but much of the musical accompaniment was provided by women.

God's wife of Amun

Another priestly title for women that occurs occasionally in the Eighteenth Dynasty is 'divine adoratrice' (*duat netjer*). In the reign of Hatshepsut the title was held by the daughter of the chief priest of Amun,[18] and in the reign of Thutmose III by the mother of the king's principal wife.[19] Unfortunately we have little idea of what the title entailed for the holders at this period, but its existence is of interest because in the Third Intermediate Period it became associated with the title 'god's wife of Amun', and the same woman bore both.

We have already come across the title 'god's wife of Amun' in Chapter Two. It was a priestly title borne by some royal women of the Eighteenth Dynasty, most notably Ahmose Nefertari, wife of king Ahmose and mother of Amen-hotep I, Hatshepsut, and her daughter Neferura.[20] The title was bestowed on Ahmose Nefertari in the reign of Ahmose, and was supposed to be handed

61   Part of the *Book of the Dead* belonging to the mistress of the house, musician of Amun, the great one of the musical troupe of Osiris, Anhai, showing the weighing of her heart.

down from heir to heir. Ahmose Nefertari's daughter Meritamun, who married her brother Amenhotep I, held the title, and it then passed to Hatshepsut, daughter of Thutmose I. Its importance is made clear by the fact that Ahmose Nefertari and Hatshepsut often used it as their sole title in preference to 'king's principal wife'. When Hatshepsut became regent for Thutmose III, 'god's wife' remained the title that she favoured, often using it in phrases where one would normally expect a reference to the reigning king. When Hatshepsut herself took the titles of king, she had to give up being god's wife, which was an office incompatible with kingship, and she handed it on to her daughter Neferura. Neferura, too, frequently used 'god's wife' as her sole title. When Thutmose III finally ruled alone, the title almost disappeared. It is attested for his mother Aset, although this use may be posthumous, and at the very end of his reign we find it held by his daughter Meritamun. In the reign of Amenhotep II, it was given to the king's mother Meritra, and in the next reign to Tiaa, mother of Thutmose IV. After that it disappeared from the royal family during the rest of the Eighteenth Dynasty, although an anonymous god's wife is depicted in two scenes in the temple of Amenhotep III at Luxor.

What was the function of the god's wife of Amun? For a long time Egyptologists thought that it marked the royal 'heiress' whom the king had to marry to obtain the throne, and that it referred to the myth of the divine birth of the king when Amun-Ra impregnated the queen in order to produce the next king.

We have already seen that there was no 'heiress' princess. In addition, neither queen Ahmose, the mother of Hatshepsut, nor queen Mutemwia, mother of Amenhotep III, who appear in the birth cycles of these kings, bore the title of god's wife. In fact, god's wife was a priestly office that was not established in the royal family until the reign of Ahmose. Prior to this there are a few examples of non-royal god's wives. Once the title became associated with royal women, it became part of their titularies, and was used even when they were shown carrying and wearing royal insignia. However, there are some scenes where god's wives show none of the insignia of a queen. Instead, they wear a much simpler costume consisting of a short wig, a thin fillet knotted at the back of the head with the loose ends hanging down, and a sheath dress sometimes tied at the waist unlike most such dresses (fig. 41). This costume shows the god's wife dressed as a priestess, taking part in temple ritual. A small building of Amenhotep I, of which only a few blocks now remain, once had scenes showing Ahmose Nefertari functioning as god's wife.[21] More informative are scenes from the dismantled *chapelle rouge* of Hatshepsut which show an anonymous god's wife carrying out the ritual functions of the office. The god's wife may have been Hatshepsut's daughter Neferura, or a substitute if she was still too young to take part in the ritual itself.

Three sets of scenes in the *chapelle rouge* involve the god's wife.[22] In one the god's wife is shown entering the open court of the temple together with another female figure labelled as a *henutet*, a male figure called *henuty*, and another male figure entitled 'many priests'. In the court the god's wife and a male priest face each other holding a firebrand, while in the next scene, only partially preserved, the god's wife turns, perhaps to light a brazier with the brand. Then the god's wife and the priest face each other again. Both hold semicircular fans on long handles. Each fan has an image of a bound captive on its face. The final scene is again only partially preserved, but the god's wife is turned away from the priest presumably to burn the image of the enemy in the lighted brazier (fig. 41). This fits with other evidence for rituals destroying the names or images of Egypt's enemies.

In the second ritual, the gods are called to receive the evening meal. Hatshepsut as king stands before a list of seventeen gods of Karnak, each with a list of offerings below. Both the king and the names of the gods face into the temple. On the other side of the list from Hatshepsut, facing out from the temple, there stands an Iunmutef priest dedicating the offerings followed by two male priests and finally, with both arms raised, the god's wife.

The third ritual begins with the caption: 'Adoring god for the Ennead and for the kings of Upper and Lower Egypt and giving great praise by all the populace'. Eight figures follow in two registers: the god's wife and three priests, and below, a male *henuty*, two female *henutet*, and a male figure called 'all the populace'. The caption to the next scene is unclear. It is followed by two registers of three figures each, labelled in the upper register: nobles, companions, and *henuty* (all male figures), and below, a female *henutet*, and two male figures representing 'all the populace'. Next a group of male priests, led by the god's wife, have entered the sacred lake of the temple to be purified. The whole is captioned 'going down to be purified by the priests and the god's wife in the cool lake. Entering the temple' (fig. 42). Only properly purified people could pass beyond the open courtyard of a temple. Finally, the god's wife and three priests enter the sanctuary in the wake of Hatshepsut the king, who performs the rites before the statue of Amun-Ra. In practice the king would not always have been present to conduct the ritual; instead it would have been carried out by a priest. An obvious question is, did this have to be a male priest or could the god's wife perform the rites? Whatever the answer, these unusual scenes make it clear that the god's wife had an active role in temple ritual, and like male priests entered the sanctuary of the god.

The office of god's wife had been endowed by king Ahmose with its own domain, which possessed land and had a staff of male officials to administer it.[23] It is possible that the various musical performers associated with the cult of Amun at Thebes were attached to this institution. The owning of property made the office a powerful one, and the god's wife probably had real authority in the cult. The prestige conferred by the post would explain why Ahmose Nefertari, Hatshepsut and Neferura so often used 'god's wife' as their sole title. In fact, Hatshepsut may have used its authority to build up her political position, since it was her preferred title during her regency when she must have been gathering support for her eventual claim to the throne.[24]

Neferura continued to use the title in the same way as her mother, and although we do not understand what Hatshepsut intended for her daughter, the position of god's wife was clearly meant to remain important. Why then, with the advent of the sole rule of Thutmose III, did the title apparently go into abeyance until the end of the reign? During the New Kingdom it never regained its previous prestige. Instead, holders used the title infrequently in their royal titularies and seldom as their sole title, while from the reign of Amenhotep III to the end of the Eighteenth Dynasty there was no royal god's wife at all. It seems possible that Thutmose III deliberately reduced the importance of the office. Hatshepsut's political power may in part have derived from using the authority of the priestly office of god's wife, since the religious and political spheres were not separated in ancient Egypt as they are in most modern societies. Thutmose III may have felt the need to strip the office of any meaningful authority, so that no other woman could use it again to advance a claim to political power.

The significance of the term 'god's wife of Amun' is not fully understood. At face value it might be taken to mean a woman wedded to the service of Amun acting as his wife, and therefore unmarried to a human husband. However, in the Eighteenth Dynasty there is no doubt that many of the holders, like Ahmose Nefertari and Hatshepsut, were married and bore children. This may

62 Part of the *Book of the Dead* belonging to Hunefer and his wife who are shown adoring the rising sun.

have been irrelevant to their role in temple ritual. A second title 'god's hand', which sometimes follows that of 'god's wife', refers to the hand with which the creator god masturbated to produce the first divine pair, Shu and Tefnut. Because 'hand' is grammatically feminine in ancient Egyptian, it was easy to personify the hand as a goddess, and by the Eighteenth Dynasty this deity was often identified as Hathor. Clearly, then, the titles 'god's wife' and 'god's hand' have sexual reference, but how this translated into temple cult is unknown. Nevertheless, we can conjecture that the holder was probably responsible for rituals meant to stimulate the god sexually, so that he would continually re-enact the original creation of the universe and thereby prevent the world from falling back into chaos.

The title 'god's wife' reappeared in the Nineteenth Dynasty royal family and continued in use through the Twentieth. At first it was just one of many titles and seems to have carried little discernible importance. There are apparently no scenes showing the holder carrying out any functions connected with the office. In the reign of Ramses VI his daughter Aset was installed as god's wife, and we have a funerary stela[25] and a fragmentary pyramidion which belonged to her.[26] On both of these she is called 'king's daughter, divine adoratrice, god's wife'. There is no evidence that she was ever married, unlike most of her predecessors. However, her successors were all unmarried daughters of either kings or high priests of Amun who eventually came to select their successors by

63   Part of the *Book of the Dead* belonging to the musician of Amun Heretwebekhet.

adoption. Aset may have been the first of these celibate god's wives.

With the collapse of the New Kingdom at the end of the Twentieth Dynasty, subsequent dynasties ruled from the north, while Thebes and the south were for all practical purposes under the authority of the chief priest of Amun. The office of god's wife came to be used by kings to maintain some authority at Thebes. The god's wife would be the celibate daughter of a king, who thus could not establish her own dynasty, so that when she died, the reigning king's daughter could succeed. Supposedly she would be loyal to her father and look after his interests.

When at the end of the Third Intermediate Period the rulers of Kush began to extend their authority into Egypt, Kashta persuaded the incumbent god's wife Shepenwepet I, daughter of Osorkon III/IV of the Twenty-Third Dynasty, to adopt his daughter Amenirdis as her heir (fig. 43). The latter eventually functioned as god's wife under the subsequent kings Piy, Shabako and Shabitko of the Twenty-Fifth Dynasty. She in turn adopted a daughter of Piy, Shepenwepet II, who held the office after her in the reigns of Shabitko, Taharqo and Tanutamani. In her turn, she adopted Amenirdis II, a daughter of Taharqo, to follow her. However, Tanutamani was driven from Egypt by Psamtek I, founder of the Twenty-Sixth Dynasty, who now needed to secure Thebes. After intense negotiations with Amenirdis II, the adopted heir of the incumbent, Psamtek persuaded her to adopt his eldest daughter, Nitiqret (fig. 44).

We are lucky enough to have a stela recording the installation of Nitiqret.[27] It includes all the property and endowments that she brought with her to add to the domain of the god's wife, and it gives us an idea of how wealthy the institution must have become by this time. Psamtek I says: 'I have given to him [Amun] my daughter to be a god's wife and have endowed her better than those who were before her. Surely he will be gratified with her worship and protect the land of him who gave her to him.' The stela goes on to describe Nitiqret's departure for Thebes and her reception there. 'Departure from the king's private apartment by his eldest daughter clad in fine linen and adorned with new turquoise. Her attendants about her were many in number . . . They set forth happily to the quay in order to head southwards for the Theban nome. The ships about her were in great numbers . . . all being laden up to their gunwales with every good thing of the palace . . . Putting to land at the quay of the city of the gods Thebes. Her front hawser was taken, and she found Thebes with throngs of men and crowds of women standing and jubilating to meet her . . . Now after she came to the god's wife Shepenwepet, the latter saw her and was pleased with her.'

Her endowment is then listed. From seven nomes in Upper Egypt she received: '1800 arouras of fields together with everything that comes forth thence in country and in town, together with their dry land and their canals.' Similarly she received 1400 arouras from four nomes of Lower Egypt. Every day she was to receive from the fourth priest of Amun, his eldest son, and his wife, and from the first and third priests of Amun a total of 600 *deben* of bread, 11 *hin* (a *hin* is just under half a litre) of milk, $2^1/6$ cakes, $2^2/3$ bundles of herbs. Monthly she would receive 3 oxen, 5 geese, 20 *heben* of beer, and the yield of 100 arouras of fields. Various temples gave her 1500 *deben* of bread. Altogether she received 2100 *deben* of bread daily, and 3200 arouras of fields (over 2000 acres) in eleven nomes.

64 Funerary stela showing the rites before the tomb performed over the coffins of the male owner, his wife and his parents.

The adoption of Nitiqret also shows the political power of the office of god's wife, through which the allegiance of Thebes was changed peacefully from the Twenty-Fifth Dynasty to the Twenty-Sixth. The last two holders of the title were also unprecedentedly chief priestess of Amun, and thus the long-established supremacy of the god's wife in the Theban area was acknowledged. The Persian conquest of Egypt brought the Twenty-Sixth Dynasty to an end and along with it, for the time being, the office of god's wife. All this time, the domain of the god's wife had been administered by male officials, foremost of whom were the stewards.[28] They were clearly very powerful and wealthy men, leaving many fine statues, stelae, and tombs. It is unclear how authority was divided between god's wives and their stewards.

The iconography of the god's wife is of great interest. In the Eighteenth Dynasty there was a distinction between the costume of the god's wife as priestess and as a royal woman. After the Eighteenth Dynasty, the priestly attire almost completely disappears, and god's wives are mostly shown wearing queenly insignia. During the Nineteenth Dynasty and the first part of the Twentieth, the god's wife was also a queen, but from the reign of Ramses VI onwards, she was a king's daughter rather than a king's wife; nevertheless, she continued to wear queenly insignia, including the double feathers, horns and disk, vulture headdress, uraeus and double uraeus (figs. 43, 45, 46). Her titularies, however, were developed to imitate the king's use of a double cartouche, which contained his prenomen and given name. Each god's wife received a prenomen, usually containing the name of Mut, the consort of Amun, to be used alongside her given name. A cartouche of the god's wife could be venerated by an official in the same way as the king's cartouche.

Many of the scene types featuring the god's wife were taken over from the king's iconography.[29] She is shown directly before the god, adoring, offering, presenting *maat* or four calves, and conducting foundation rites, all of which were rituals exclusive to the king until this time. In addition, deities are shown purifying her, crowning her (fig. 44), embracing her, suckling her and offering her life (fig. 46) in scenes that normally form part of the legitimisation of kingship.

Part of the function of the god's wife was to play her sistrum before the god (fig. 45), so as to pacify him and avert his potential anger, and also to stimulate him in her role as god's hand, so that he would for ever keep the fertility of the universe from flagging. Her extraordinary role was confined to the Theban area and she does not appear on monuments from outside this region.

FURTHER READING

H. Fischer, 'Priesterin', *Lexikon der Ägyptologie* 4, Wiesbaden, 1982, 1100–105.

M. Gitton, *L'épouse du dieu Ahmès Néfertary*, 2nd ed., Paris, 1981.

M. Gitton, *Les divines épouses de la 18e dynastie*, Paris, 1984.

G. Robins, 'The god's wife of Amun in the 18th dynasty in Egypt' in: A. Cameron and A. Kuhrt (eds.) *Images of Women in Antiquity*, London and Canberra, 1983, 65–78.

CHAPTER NINE

Personal religion and death

Votive stelae and cloths

Temple cult served the state religion, which functioned on a cosmic level to maintain the order and working of the universe. While individuals might participate as personnel in the rituals, these latter were not addressed to personal needs.[1] From the Middle Kingdom on, private people could set up votive statues and stelae in temple precincts in order to establish a link between the individual and the temple. Many of these statues have survived and show a wide variety of forms and experimentation. Among the commonest types are seated statues, block statues, kneeling statues offering a stela or naos, or standing statues carrying a standard. We also find scribe statues, a type already known among funerary statues of the Old Kingdom. Women were not eligible to own scribe statues, nor do they usually have stelophorous, naophorous or standard-bearing statues. In general, ownership of temple statues was a male prerogative, although women might be included in some form or other on those statues dedicated by men.

By contrast, women, as well as men, could and did erect votive stelae in temples. These are stelae which often have a text based on the formula: 'Giving praise to [a deity], kissing the ground before [the same or another deity] for the *ka* of [the dedicator]'. The scene usually shows the dedicator offering to or adoring the deity or deities named (figs. 47, 48). The formula and scene-type tend to be similar irrespective of the gender of the owner, except for the substitution of feminine grammatical gender where necessary in the text, and of a female figure for a male one in the scene. Sometimes the first person singular pronoun is written with a male figure as though the speaker were male not female, showing that the male form was the dominant one and that it was not always adjusted for a female dedicator. In addition to owning votive stelae, women may accompany men on theirs, in which case the men are the primary dedicators (fig. 49). The number of surviving stelae belonging to men far outstrips those of women. For instance, of the twenty-four votive stelae found in the area of the sphinx at Giza, twenty were dedicated by men alone and none solely by women. Taking primary and secondary dedicators together, men outnumber women by thirty-five to six. Of seventeen votive stelae that came from the temple of Ptah at Memphis, eleven were dedicated by men alone and

65 False door stela belonging to Meretites.

66 False door stela of Iry and his wife Inet.

only two by women. Counting all the figures depicted on the stelae, twenty-five are male and seven are female.[2]

Who were the women who dedicated their own votive stelae? Sometimes they have no title, sometimes they are called 'mistress of the house' and sometimes they are a 'musician' of a particular deity. While we can surmise that they are members of the elite class, we are ignorant of whether the women commissioned these stelae out of their own resources, which some women certainly had, or whether their husbands and sons were financially responsible for them. The fact that far more votive stelae are known for men than women could be taken either way. As a class, elite women might simply have had fewer resources to put into such monuments, as compared with men who had regular incomes from their official positions. On the other hand, if the stelae were paid for by male relatives, we can imagine that these men would give priority to their own monuments, leaving less to spend on the women of their family. Those men who included their wives and sometimes other female relatives on their own votive stelae might thus have avoided having to provide them with separate stelae. When women do have their own stelae they are only exceptionally accompanied by their husbands. This is due to two basic rules of decorum that apply on all types of monuments. First, the owner of a monument must occupy the primary place in the decoration. Second, women, with only a few exceptions, take a subordinate position in relation to their husbands. Therefore, if a woman is the owner of a monument the primary place is hers, and her husband cannot be shown because he would be forced to appear in a secondary position.

There is a remarkable round-topped stela from Deir el-Medina which is owned by a woman but shows members of her family including her husband (fig. 50).[3] It is divided into several registers. In the lunette at the top, the mistress of the house Bukhanefptah adores Nebethetepet, a goddess closely associated with Hathor. The text specifically says that the stela was 'dedicated by . . . Bukhanefptah'. Below are four lines of a prayer praising Nebethetepet and asking for the goddess's mercy, spoken by Bukhanefptah. The bottom two registers contain the family members. The first is headed by the workman in the royal tomb, Kasa. He is given no kinship term relating him to Bukhanefptah in the lunette, but is identified merely by name and title as though he owned the stela. He is followed immediately by a female figure labelled 'his wife, the mistress of the house, Bukhanefptah', so that she appears twice on this stela. In this second manifestation she is related by the possessive pronoun 'his' to Kasa, thus satisfying the rules of decorum. However, the remaining thirteen figures are all identified as 'her son/daughter' and 'her brother/sister'.

We meet one of the sons again on a stela belonging to Kasa on which Bukhanefptah also appears.[4] There the son is called 'his son', showing that Kasa is his father. However, on this second stela a gender distinction is made between the children, the sons being called 'his son' and the daughters 'her daughter'. This occurs on other monuments too, so on a statue of a husband and wife dedicated by their daughter which is now in the British Museum, the girl is called 'her daughter' on the mother's side of the seat and 'his daughter' on the father's side.[5] A lot more work needs to be done on such monuments to provide a thorough analysis that would help identify ownership and patterns of filiation to mother and father through the use of the masculine or feminine personal pronoun.

It is interesting that while women are not barred from dedicating votive stelae to male deities, they frequently prefer female ones like Hathor, Isis, Mut the consort of Amun, the snake goddesses Meresger and Renenutet, or the deified queen Ahmose Nefertari. Some male-owned stelae that include women show the man adoring a male deity while the women adore a female one (fig. 51). Although it is by no means always the case, there is a tendency for gender distinction to govern the deities honoured by men and women.

A number of votive stelae from Deir el-Medina contain prayers which express awareness that the dedicators have transgressed against a deity, who has therefore punished them and who is consequently begged to show mercy. While many of these prayers are by men, a few concern women. One was dedicated by Iytnefret, wife of the workman Sennedjem who lived in the reign of Ramses II (fig. 52).[6] Iytnefret is shown kneeling at the bottom of the stela followed by a smaller figure representing her grandson. Nothing in the text says why he is there. Perhaps he commissioned the stela, but takes a subordinate place because the stela is for her; it may be that the rules of decorum were relaxed between grandmother and grandson, with her extreme seniority in generation as well as age giving her primacy. Her prayer asks the deity to 'Be merciful, for you have caused me to see darkness by day because of those words of the women. Be merciful to me that I may see your mercy. By the mistress of the house Iytnefret, true of voice.' The phrase 'you have caused me to see darkness by day' is a common one in these prayers expressing the burden of guilt. It is tantalising that we have no idea what the cause of all this, 'those words of the women', actually was.

A similar type of stela was dedicated by the workman Wennefer who is shown in the lunette worshipping a male deity (fig. 53).[7] However, the prayer is written on the main body of the stela next to two kneeling women and a naked boy, identified as the mistress of the house Nebetnehet, her son Nebansu, and her daughter the mistress of the house Meritamun. The prayer itself relates to Nebetnehet: 'You have caused me to see darkness of your making. Be merciful to me that I may see you. For the *ka* of the mistress of the house, Nebetnehet.' This would seem to be a stela dedicated by a husband for his wife.

A comparable stela of this type was dedicated by a son for his mother (fig. 54).[8] In the lunette the scribe of Amun, Pay kneels before the god Khons. Below, the mistress of the house Wadjetrenpet kneels with the text of a prayer to Khons: '... Behold you cause me to see darkness of your making. May you be merciful to me and I will recount it. How sweet is your mercy, Khons, to the poor women of your city. For the *ka* of the mistress of the house Wadjet-renpet.' This is followed by the statement: 'It is her son who made this stela in the name of his lord Khons, the scribe Pay. He says: "Turn your face. Do mercy"', thus reinforcing his mother's plea.

We have already seen that one of the most important deities for women was Hathor, goddess of love, sexuality, and fertility. She had a major cult place on the west bank at Thebes at Deir el-Bahri, and during excavations there many votive offerings from the New Kingdom were found, including fertility figurines and model phalli. Unfortunately most of these are uninscribed, so we have no idea of the gender of the donor or whether some were dedicated jointly by, for example, husband and wife. While only a few votive stelae were found at Deir el-Bahri, more were dedicated by women than men. A small faience votive plaque shows a woman libating before the Hathor cow, and was presumably presented by a woman. An unusual type of votive offering also found here consisted of painted textiles showing the principal donor, often with other figures, before a form of Hathor (fig. 55). Most of these have little text, but the gender of the donor can be told from the figure. Out of thirty-five known surviving textiles, none seems to have been dedicated by a man alone, while

67   False door stela of Kaihap and his wife Meretmin.

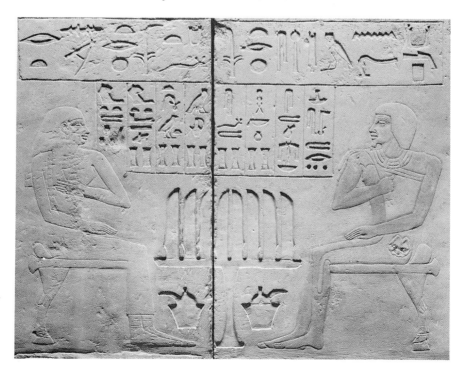

68 (*left*) Old Kingdom funerary statue of Nefretmin.

69 (*right*) Old Kingdom funerary statue of a man, his wife and son.

seventeen are dedicated by a woman alone. Out of all the figures on the cloths there are seventy-four women and thirty men. The shaven heads and the costumes of the men suggest that they are priests, perhaps serving in the cult of Hathor. Thus the cloths give evidence of a preponderance of female donors, emphasising their close connection with the goddess.[9]

Visits to the temple

Although most individuals had little personal interest in the state religion, clearly they visited temples and shrines to make votive offerings, and we can assume that women went too. The prayer of Bukhanefptah on her stela described above says of Nebethetepet: 'For all people come to you in crowds, men and women alike.' Further confirmation is found on a statue which was originally set up at Deir el-Bahri.[10] The text is specifically addressed to women: 'O people of Thebes, noble ladies as well as poor girls, all who come at (any) time to Djeseret (= Deir el-Bahri) . . .' The statue is of a well-known type, usually called intermediary, which carries texts promising to intercede with a deity on behalf of an individual in return for offerings. This one undertakes to petition Hathor on behalf of women for 'happiness and a good husband'.

Letters from the late Twentieth Dynasty also show that individuals would visit temples and pray to the gods. When Djehutymose, scribe of the necropolis at Thebes, was away from home, he sent a message to a number of women: 'Please call upon Amun to bring me back, for I have been ill since I arrived north and am not in my normal state. Don't set your minds to anything else. As soon as my letter reaches you, you shall go to the forecourt of Amun of the Thrones of the Two Lands taking the little children along with you and coax him and tell him to keep me safe.'[11] The temple is the mortuary temple of Ramses III where the workmen were living by this time. They were to go to the forecourt because this was the only place in the temple where the general populace could enter. Beyond it, only purified temple personnel could go. The letter assumes that women and also children will go to the temple to pray to the god.

Domestic cult

Because of the lack of information about houses, little is known of domestic cult.[12] However, at Deir el-Medina there is evidence of household altars, of wall paintings of Bes and Taweret, and of niches to hold stelae within the homes of the workmen. During excavation of the houses, statues, stelae, offering tables and basins dedicated to Taweret were also found.[13] We have already discussed fertility figurines. A good number of these have been recovered from settlement sites, including the Middle Kingdom town at Kahun and the New Kingdom site of Amarna as well as that of Deir el-Medina. It seems likely that these figurines were offered during rites at the household altar, or perhaps kept there to ensure the continuity of the family through the birth of children.

The rites practised in the domestic cult may have included offering food, libations and flowers at the altar, as in other Egyptian cults. The prominence of the deities Taweret and Bes, known to be connected with female matters, the fertility figurines, and the depictions of the birth pavilion, discussed in Chapter Four, suggest that women of the family had an important part to play, especially at Deir el-Medina where the men were away for days at a time.

One phrase meaning 'to marry' was 'to found a house', and referred to the new couple's setting up their own home. While there is absolutely no evidence, it is perhaps not too far-fetched to imagine that one of their first actions would have been to establish the altar and celebrate their union with their family and friends.

Women in funerary cult

From predynastic times the Egyptians had believed in an afterlife, and we know that by the Old Kingdom individuals set up their funerary cult to function after their deaths. Ideally a man's eldest son performed the rites, bringing food to the tomb and doing all that was necessary to ensure the survival of the deceased in the next world. We shall see that it was believed that women shared in the same afterlife as men and had the same needs for their burial and cult.

Here I will touch on the part played by living women in the funerary cult alongside men.

In the Old Kingdom women could serve as funerary priests.[14] Even the title 'overseer of funerary priests' is known for a woman. However, the evidence for female funerary priests dies out with the Old Kingdom. In the Middle and New Kingdoms women could dedicate funerary stelae showing themselves performing ritual for the deceased, for example, offering or libating (fig. 56). They could also dedicate funerary statues, often to parents or husbands. We do not know whether they commissioned and paid for these monuments themselves. Since women could own property, and take part in business activities and control their own financial affairs, it is possible that some of their independent income was spent on funerary monuments for parents or husbands.

In the tomb scenes, wives and daughters commonly offer to the deceased owner, in many cases holding out sistra and *menit*-necklaces which through their reference to Hathor promised rebirth to the dead man (fig. 57). Because of the association of Hathor with music, a number of tombs contain scenes showing dances performed in her honour, in which women played a major part.

When it comes to the last rites before the tomb when the opening of the mouth ritual was performed, New Kingdom and later scenes show the officiating priest to be male. The wife is often shown mourning at the foot of the coffin, and groups of male and female mourners accompany the funeral procession to the tomb.[15] In many cases female mourners outnumber the male ones (fig. 58), and it is possible that in addition to members of the family, there were also female professionals. A stela from Deir el-Medina was dedicated by a woman and her daughter who both use 'mourner' as a title, suggesting that this was their occupation.[16] Other women at funerals impersonated the two goddesses Isis and her sister Nephthys, who were mourners *par excellence* because they had lamented the murdered god Osiris.

The burial of women
Women shared in the same afterlife as men expected to enjoy, and they received burials basically similar to those of men. Little is known of the funerary customs of the non-elite, and the following sections will be based on the evidence left by the scribal class, particularly the upper ranks who could afford tomb chapels.

The actual body, together with all the funerary equipment that accompanied the deceased, was placed in a deep shaft cut into the ground. The shaft was then filled up and supposedly not entered again. The highest-ranking members of the bureaucracy had a second part to their tomb: the tomb chapel, which contained the entrance to the burial shaft. It was either free-standing, as often in the Memphite necropolis, or rock-cut, as at Thebes. Here was where the funerary cult would be carried out. Beginning in the Old Kingdom the walls would be covered with decoration, including a false door and later stelae, and from the Middle Kingdom onwards, statues representing the deceased would be visible within the chapel. The false doors, stelae, and statues formed focal points for the cult where the living could make contact with the dead.

In the majority of cases, these tomb chapels were owned by male officials. Their decoration revolved around the owner, and the women of his family, who were often shown too, took a subordinate place, even though other members of the family (including women, and almost always the owner's wife) would have been buried in shafts beneath the chapel. It was very rare for a private woman to own a tomb chapel. One case is a Middle Kingdom tomb chapel at Thebes belonging to the vizier's mother Senet, which we have already met in Chapter Five.[17] Very little of the decoration takes into account the fact that the owner is a woman. It is likely that Senet was not responsible for her own tomb chapel, but that her son commissioned it for her.

It is an interesting question why women from the upper ranks of elite families did not have their own chapels. One answer could be that ownership was a privilege that came from holding bureaucratic office of a certain rank, so that women would theoretically be excluded. Another could be that only officials above a particular rank were ever wealthy enough to put so much of their resources into their burials. Possibly the burial of a wife was the husband's responsibility. If that were the case, it might have been unthinkable for a

70 (*left*) Old Kingdom funerary statue of Katep and his wife Hetepheres.

71 (*right*) Old Kingdom funerary statue of a man, his wife and son.

married woman, however wealthy, to build her own chapel, or if she did, one might surmise that she had to bow to convention and let her husband or son take the primary place. This leads one to wonder what happened to an unmarried woman or a divorced one who did not remarry. Perhaps she was buried within the tomb of a male relative. If she had to arrange for her own burial, the evidence shows that this would not have included a tomb chapel.

At Deir el-Medina the workmen built their own tombs with decorated chapels and burial chambers, outside the village. The fact that they worked on them themselves in their spare time explains why these men who were not high officials were able to have chapels. People of equivalent rank in the rest of Egypt would have been unable to aspire to such heights. The decoration of the chapels is somewhat unusual in both style and content, but it still centred on the male tomb owner, although his family was also depicted (fig. 59). We know from wills at Deir el-Medina that women could inherit tombs. There is no evidence in the chapels of the decoration being altered to reflect a female owner, and possibly what was inherited was the right to be buried in a tomb, rather than the right to change the decoration in the chapel.

The suggestion that women were provided for by male relatives, and that it went against convention for them to make their own arrangements, is supported by evidence from funerary stelae. In contrast to votive stelae set up in temples, funerary stelae were associated with tombs or with cenotaphs, that is, tomb chapels without a burial, which would have taken place elsewhere. Such stelae were usually decorated with scenes showing the deceased before a table of offerings, sometimes with family members performing the rites, or later, the deceased before various deities, most frequently Osiris, the god of the dead. They are similar to some of the scenes found in tomb chapels. While it is not unknown for women to have funerary stelae, the majority were owned by men who occupied the principal place in the scenes (figs. 56, 72).

From at least the Old Kingdom the body of a deceased woman received the same sort of treatment as that of a man, and was buried with similar types of funerary equipment. Once the technique of mummification had been developed, women too were mummified to preserve their bodies for eternity. The body was placed in a coffin or set of coffins (fig. 60), and the viscera in canopic jars. With the introduction of shabtis in the Middle Kingdom, women were also provided with these funerary figurines. From the New Kingdom heart scarabs were placed over the heart of the dead person. They were inscribed with a text designed to prevent that organ from testifying against the deceased at the time of judgment, and women were given them as well as men.

From the New Kingdom onwards, it also became common to put a copy of the *Book of the Dead* into the tomb to guide the owner through the dangers of the underworld. Surviving copies show these could belong to women as well as men (fig. 61). Those made for men could include wives in a secondary position (fig. 62), but owing to rules of decorum, those adapted for women do not

72 Funerary stela of Ramose showing the owner and his wife Tetpu adoring Osiris, Isis and Nephthys in the upper register, and below receiving offerings from his son on the left, and incense and libations from his daughter on the right.

usually portray a husband. More copies of the *Book of the Dead* seem to have been owned by men than women, and in the Late Period, at least, men are much more likely to have longer, and therefore more expensive, versions than women. One vignette in the *Book of the Dead* shows the owner of the document harvesting grain. We have seen that in tomb scenes showing peasants at the harvest, only men actually wield a sickle, while women pick up the fallen ears (fig. 36). In *Books of the Dead* made for women we find that often a female figure is simply substituted for the male figure cutting grain in this scene, but occasionally a male figure is shown instead of a figure of the female owner (fig. 63), suggesting that some artists recognised that cutting grain was not a task normally carried out by women.[18]

Other items such as jewellery, clothes, wigs, and furniture are also found with both male and female burials. Despite this, it is a fact that more canopic jars, shabtis, heart scarabs, and *Books of the Dead* are known for men than for women. It is also common for men's funerary equipment to be richer than that of women. This suggests either that men were responsible for both sets and spent more on their own, or that women contributed their own equipment but had fewer resources with which to do so. Unfortunately no systematic study has been made to compare male and female funerary equipment from the point of view of cost, nor to see if there are gender distinctions between male and female burials.

The procession taking the deceased to the tomb and the accompanying rites performed over the mummy at the tomb entrance have already been mentioned. The body in its coffins and sarcophagus was dragged by oxen to the tomb, often with the canopic chest brought separately. Lines of men carried the funerary equipment, and groups of women (and less often men) wept and wailed, mourning the deceased. Outside the tomb the *sem*-priest in a leopard skin, usually the eldest son, performed the opening of the mouth rite to enable the mummy to live, while a lector priest read the ritual, and offerings were made (fig. 58). Although this is not shown, one can assume that when the rites were completed, the deceased and all the equipment were lowered into the shaft which was then filled in, and perhaps the funerary cult was then instigated in the chapel. The family and guests at the funeral probably ate a meal there, as they would continue to do once a year at the Beautiful Festival of the Valley.

Most of the scenes in tomb chapels depict the burial of the male owner. However, there is evidence that the same rites and ceremonies were carried out for women when their time of burial came. In the tomb of Senet, mentioned earlier, the use of feminine pronouns in the accompanying texts makes it clear that it is her funeral procession which is shown, not that of her son. Otherwise, the scene differs little from one composed for a man. The same is true of funeral processions in *Books of the Dead* belonging to women. In the Memphite tomb of Horemheb, a fragmentary scene shows a female coffin, presumably that of Horemheb's wife, with rites being performed over it.[19] A contemporary late-Eighteenth Dynasty relief belonging to a man called Ptahmose includes a scene showing the funerary rites being carried out before the coffin of a woman called Ray.[20] In some Ramesside scenes, two coffins are sometimes shown at the tomb entrance, one being the owner and the other probably his wife. Similarly, some stelae show the funerary rites being performed over several mummies, in one case identified as the male owner, his wife, and his parents (fig. 64). Such scenes, of course, telescope separate burials into one event, but they leave us in no doubt that women were buried with the same funerary rites as men. However, perhaps due to notions of decorum in art, while the mourning wife is often shown kneeling by her husband's coffin (fig. 58), scenes where a distraught husband mourns his wife do not seem to occur.

False doors and funerary stelae

Once the burial had taken place, a funerary cult on behalf of the deceased was established and supposedly performed in perpetuity in the tomb chapel, or at the mouth of the burial shaft for those who had not been able to have a chapel. In the Old Kingdom, the focal points for the funerary cult in tomb chapels were the false doors, and the statues in the serdab, a separate room which only communicated with the chapel by a slit or slits in the wall. The false door was where the living and the dead could meet. There was no way through in this world, but the spirit of the dead person could step through from the world beyond to enjoy the offerings brought by the funerary priests. The jambs and lintels of a false door were commonly decorated with titles, names and figures of the deceased, while above the lintel a rectangular stela usually depicted the dead person seated before a table of offerings. There could be more than one false door in a chapel. Many show the male owner alone. Sometimes he shares the door with his wife, while in other cases the wife has a door of her own. The decoration of these monuments is governed by rules of decorum. We can see this if we look at the rectangular slab stela above the lintel of the door.[21] When a door is owned by one person only, whether male or female, the primary position for the figure of the deceased is to be seated on the left hand side (that is, the viewer's left) facing to the right (fig. 65). When a man and a woman share a door, the man almost always takes this position, relegating the woman to sit on the subordinate side of the offering table (fig. 66). In a handful of examples, the male and female figures are reversed, and the woman takes the dominant place (fig. 67). Unfortunately, there is nothing in the texts or titles of the people concerned to show why this should be so, but it surely has some significance pertaining to the relative status of the man and woman.

The statues in the serdab provided a possible dwelling place for the spirit of the deceased, which could then look out through the communication slits into the tomb chapel, watch the rites being performed and smell the burning incense which was an integral part of Egyptian religious rites. More than one

73 Funerary stela of the musician of Amun Takha, who adores Osiris, Isis and Nephthys in the upper register, and below receives water from Hathor, the goddess of the west.

statue of an individual could be included, and sometimes one man owned a whole series of statues. In addition, images of other family members could be placed in the serdab. The wife of the tomb owner might have her own separate statue (fig. 68), or form part of a group statue with her husband that could also include images of children (fig. 69). When husband and wife are grouped together, the man is most frequently the dominant figure. If both are figures equal in size, the man is often on the more important right hand side of the group, that is, the viewer's left. There are, however, many exceptions (fig. 70); as with false doors, the positions may be making a statement about the status of the woman in relation to that of the man, but unfortunately little can be inferred from the inscriptions. In other statue groups the man is on a larger scale than his wife: for instance, the wife may squat as a small figure at his feet (fig. 69), or stand while he is seated so that although the figures are the same height, his is on a larger scale (fig. 71). There is also evidence that seated figures are of higher status than standing ones.

With the collapse of central government at the end of the Old Kingdom, far fewer fully decorated tomb chapels were built. More often the chapel was a small mud-brick structure which was undecorated except for one or more stelae set up in it. Funerary stelae developed from the rectangular slabs on false doors, which had normally shown a seated figure in front of offerings. In the First Intermediate Period it was more usual to show standing figures of the tomb owner, with or without his wife, holding a staff in one hand and a sceptre in the other, deriving from figures on the jambs of the false door and elsewhere in Old Kingdom tomb decoration. Most of these stelae have now lost their contexts. While many show men alone, others show a man accompanied secondarily by his wife, and a number show a woman alone. This is almost certainly not evidence that some women had their own tomb chapels, but rather that their husbands erected separate stelae for them in their chapels.

74   Funerary statue of Tetisonb dedicated by her son.

By the Middle Kingdom and throughout the New Kingdom the motif of the owner seated before a table of offerings returns to stelae, while from the middle of the Eighteenth Dynasty, scenes showing the owner offering to or adoring gods begin to become common for the first time (fig. 72). These funerary stelae were usually set up just outside or inside the tomb chapel. Sometimes they were erected in a cenotaph, that is, a chapel without a burial, most notably at Abydos in the Middle Kingdom. Abydos was sacred to Osiris, god of the dead, and the idea of the cenotaph was to link the owner and his family with the cult of Osiris for all eternity, even though they were buried elsewhere.

The majority of all funerary stelae were owned by men, that is, a man is most frequently the primary figure on the stela, and other figures appearing on it are usually related to him (figs. 56, 72). When he is accompanied by his wife or mother, she is shown seated beside him, rather than opposite him as in the Old Kingdom slab stela. According to the conventions of Egyptian two-dimensional art, the couple are spread out along the baseline so that one figure does not obscure the other. The 'forward' position is the primary one, and this is occupied by the man, while his wife or mother takes the subordinate position 'behind' (fig. 72). On the few occasions when the woman occupies the dominant position, the man is neither her husband or her son.[22] There are funerary stelae that belong to women only (fig. 73). Often they are dedicated by a female relative such as a daughter or sister. Compared to those owned by men, they form a very small proportion of the whole corpus. One must suppose that the rules of decorum would generally make it impossible for a woman owner to be accompanied by a husband or son. Thus we cannot tell whether women owning stelae were married or unmarried. One stela dedicated to a daughter by her parents suggests that she died young and was probably not yet married.[23] Other stelae dedicated by a woman's children indicate that she had been married at some point. Since we lack the original context of funerary stelae owned by women, it is dangerous to speculate on their significance.

From the Middle Kingdom onwards, statues of the deceased were placed in the tomb chapel. A niche was cut in the back wall on the axis of the chapel to contain the main statues, before which rites would be carried out. Sometimes in rock-cut tombs these were not free-standing but were carved from the rock. Others which were free-standing have long since been removed from their original contexts. While male statues once again predominate, there are also a considerable number which show only a woman (fig. 74). These were probably meant to form a pair with a statue of a man. Many funerary statues, however, depict a couple, with the man, as before, placed on the dominant right hand side (fig. 75). Again there are a number of exceptions (fig. 76), but the reason for these is not understood. In some cases, such dyads may have been made as pairs to be placed facing one another in the tomb. The change in the position of the two figures could then have been designed so that each was opposite an image of the same sex.

The funerary rites for women

Although women took second place to men on funerary monuments, they nonetheless shared at all times in the funerary cult. Documents from the Old Kingdom onwards show that a male official was responsible not only for setting up his own cult and carrying out that of his father, but also for the cults of his mother and wife. In a First Intermediate Period letter to the dead, a husband tells his wife: 'I have not garbled a spell before you, while making your name to live upon earth', and he promises to do more for her if she cures him of his illness: 'I shall lay down offerings for you when the sun's light has risen, and I shall establish an altar for you'. The woman's brother also asks for help, and he says: 'I have not garbled a spell before you; I have not taken offerings away from you'.[24] In another letter to the dead, a son threatens his difficult mother: 'Who

75 New Kingdom funerary statue of a couple.

76   New Kingdom funerary statue of Maya and Merit.

then will pour out water for you?'[25] In the New Kingdom *Instruction of Any*, the young scribe is advised: 'Libate for your father and mother, Who are resting in the valley (necropolis)'.[26]

One of the commonest texts on funerary monuments and other equipment from the Old Kingdom onwards is the so-called *hetep di nesu* offering formula, designed to secure necessities in the afterlife for the deceased. A typical Middle Kingdom example runs: 'An offering which the king gives (to) Osiris, lord of Busiris, the great god, lord of Abydos, that he may give invocation offerings of bread and beer, cattle and fowl, alabaster and clothing, and all good and pure things on which a god lives, to the *ka* of the revered one, Senusret, justified.'[27] When the text was recited the power of the words was such that the request was transformed into reality in the afterworld. In contexts where men are dominant, such as tomb chapels and stelae, the formula appears to be written in favour of the men only, but if there are women associated with them, it is likely that they were also meant to benefit. Certainly on objects belonging only to women, such as coffins or statues, the formula is written in favour of the female owner.

From the late Old Kingdom on, deceased men identified themselves with Osiris by prefixing their name with that of the god, in order to gain eternal life. Women could also do the same, even though Osiris was a male deity, because there was no true female equivalent. This seems to epitomise the position of women in relation to death. Their funerary equipment, monuments, texts, and rituals are all adapted from male forms by changing male pronouns in texts and male figures in scenes to female ones, and by applying rules of decorum in representation. There do not seem to be any major individual forms that developed specifically for women without male equivalents. All this notwithstanding, it is clear that men and women were assumed to enjoy the same afterlife and to require the same necessities to do so.

FURTHER READING

S. D'Auria, P. Lacovara and C. Roehrig, *Mummies and Magic: The Funerary Arts of Ancient Egypt*, Boston, 1988.

H. Fischer, *Egyptian Women of the Old Kingdom and of the Heracleopolitan Period*, New York, 1989, 2–9.

G. Pinch, *Votive Offerings to Hathor*, Oxford, 1993.

A. J. Spencer, *Death in Ancient Egypt*, Harmondsworth, 1982.

CHAPTER TEN

Images of women in literature and art

So far in our study of private women in Egyptian society, we have tried to reconstruct something of the reality of their lives. By now it should have become apparent that while some of the problems involved in this exercise arise from a lack of evidence, others are due to the incompleteness and biases of the surviving material. Because most texts were written by men of the scribal class from a male point of view, and most monuments were commissioned and executed by men, there are inherent distortions that make it dangerous to accept the material at face value as a truthful account of women's lives in society. However, neither the literary compositions nor the monuments of this elite group of men were created at random, but rather they reflect the male scribal ideal of society. Thus by studying this material we can get an idea of the male ideals concerning women and their place in society, and of the types of female behaviour that might have fallen outside the prescribed limits.

Literary texts
The *Wisdom Texts*, which give advice to young scribes on how to comport themselves in society, are also concerned with their behaviour towards wives and mothers, giving us an elite male view of the place of women.[1] In the *Instruction of Any* the author advises the reader to hold his mother in honour because she bore and raised him. This can be set alongside other texts from scribal literature to show that ideally the mother was a figure to be respected and honoured by her children (see Chapter Five).

When it comes to a man's wife, *Wisdom Texts* from all periods make it clear that it was her duty to have children. The New Kingdom *Instruction of Any* also reveals that she was in charge of the household: 'Do not control your wife in her house when you know she is efficient. Do not say to her: "Where is it? Get it!" When she has put it in the right place.' However, this passage also suggests that a husband had the right to become angry if his wife was not efficient. She may have been called 'mistress of the house', but her husband probably had ultimate authority.

Wives and mothers were women within the family circle who were to be treated honourably if they fulfilled the duties society expected of them. The *Wisdom Texts* also warn of women outside the family who have the potential to

77 Scene from the burial chamber of Sennefer showing the purification of the owner and his wife Merit.

be dangerous. In the *Instructions of Ptahhotep* the reader is cautioned against approaching the women in another household, while the *Instruction of Any* advises: 'Do not go after a woman, Let her not steal your heart.' In the same text a woman who is an outsider is also seen as a possible temptress, dishonourably trying to trap another man when she is already married. Thus, the male view of society reflected in the didactic literature divides women into two groups, the honourable and the dishonourable.[2]

Dishonourable women also feature in narrative stories. One Middle Kingdom story centres on the unfaithful wife of a magician, and the punishment meted out by the husband to the woman and the man involved.[3] From the New Kingdom we have already met the story of the unfaithful women in the *Two Brothers*. First the elder brother's wife tries to seduce the younger brother. Later in the story the wife of the younger brother abandons him to become the wife of the king of Egypt, and then repeatedly attempts to betray her former husband to his death. Another dishonourable woman appears in the *Tale of Truth and Falsehood*.[4] Here, a woman satisfies her lust for the handsome Truth who is in a bad way, having been falsely accused in court by Falsehood, blinded as a punishment, and cast out. Subsequently, the woman fails to treat Truth honourably, even though she bears him a son; she makes him her doorkeeper, a menial job outside the house proper.

This literary evidence suggests that men had a dual perception of women. They were either honourable wives and mothers within the family unit, producing children and ensuring continuity of the family; or they were dishonourable wives who betrayed their husbands with other men, or outsiders who threatened to entrap a man and destroy his family. In other words, women were perceived as honourable when they conformed to the norms of society and as dishonourable when they stepped outside them. To balance the picture, a similar conformity to the social ideal was expected for men, as the *Wisdom Texts* teach. Here, the ideal is the silent man who shows moderation, while the hot-headed man is frowned upon. One text describes unfavourably the type of man who gets drunk and quarrelsome and does not distinguish between mar-

78 Youthful and mature images of the Old Kingdom vizier Khentika called Ikhekhi.

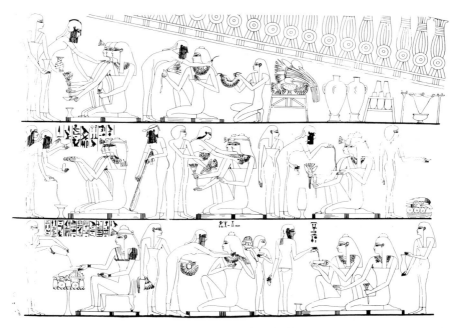

79   Part of the banquet scene from the tomb of Rekhmire.

ried and single women in his amorous affairs.[5] This was definitely not acceptable, and we have seen that complaints against an individual sometimes included the accusation that he had affairs with married women. Thus, in the
Egyptian model of society both men and women were expected to conform to
certain modes of behaviour. The picturesque non-conformist of modern times
was not encouraged.

Ideal male conduct is also reflected in the autobiographical texts that men
composed for their funerary monuments from the time of the Old Kingdom
onwards.[6] While some of these give information about the career of the individual, many simply ring the changes on stereotypic formulae in order to
record that he lived a life without blemish. By contrast, although a few short
'autobiographical' epithets occasionally occur in inscriptions with reference to
women, they mostly refer to their relationships with husbands and children.
Two rare statements in which a husband praises his wife survive from the Old
Kingdom. In one we are told: 'She did not utter a statement that repelled my
heart; she did not transgress while she was young in life.' The other calls the
wife: 'One who speaks nicely and sweetens love in the presence of her husband.'
Fischer interprets this as meaning that 'she was submissive and virtuous.'[7]

One genre of literary texts, the love poetry of the New Kingdom, gives a
very different image of women.[8] The poems are concerned not with the married state, but with the relationship between young lovers. They are clearly
meant to be erotic, and contain both specific and punning allusions to sex. The

question arises whether these poems represent a fantasy world or reflect social realities. The couples are unmarried yet enjoy sexual intercourse. Was sex before marriage acceptable? The theme of the poems is physical love, but how important was love, as opposed to economic and social factors, when it came to making a marriage? These poems are definitely good entertainment, but we cannot be sure that they are an accurate guide to social mores.

Many of the poems are cast in a form where the speaker is a woman, and it is sometimes suggested that they were composed by women. If this could be proved, it would be very exciting. Unfortunately, a male poet may take on a female persona, as happened regularly in certain genres of Chinese poetry, so that the question of authorship must remain undecided.

Representation of male and female figures

Egyptian art is basically idealising. This has much to do with its function in temples and tombs. Since artistic production was seen as akin to the act of creation, so that anything represented could be regarded as existing in some way in the worlds of the gods and the dead, non-ideal forms tended to be avoided. Thus, formal figures comprising those of the king, deities, and officials and their families are of standard idealised types which exclude any indication of sickness, deformity, old age, or any other negative quality. The ideal form for women is characterised by a youthful beauty in which the figure is always slender (figs. 36, 77); neither pregnancy nor the spreading waistline that many women must have had after years of childbearing is part of the image. There is indeed little distinction between the generations, and a man's wife and mother receive what is basically the same treatment. Men too are shown with a slender, youthful image (figs. 36, 77), but they also have a second one with no counterpart among the representation of women, in which the figure is fuller, with enlarged breast or explicit rolls of fat under the chest (figs. 75, 76, 78). This represents a mature and successful official who has achieved a sedentary lifestyle with access to plenty of food. It is not applicable to women, because they could not hold office. The equivalent to a successful bureaucrat might have been a woman who had borne many children, but this is not reflected in the female image.

There are other distinctions between male and female figures. In the majority of cases, the woman's skin is coloured a light yellowish-brown, while the man's is painted a much darker reddish-brown (figs. 36, 77). This could be an artistic device to symbolise what we have seen from other evidence: the tendency for women to be occupied indoors and men out of doors. The lighter colour for women would then indicate that they were less exposed to the sun. This is perhaps supported by evidence from the Old Kingdom, where some images of mature officials have the lighter skin associated with women. It could be meant to signify that they had reached a point in their careers when they could sit comfortably in their office all day and send their subordinates out to do the footwork. The colour differentiation between men and women could also be a matter of status, by which a man showed that he was wealthy enough to keep his wife from having to do outside work. The use of the two contrasting colours in relation to gender is obviously a convention, and while it may in part be based on reality, the situation with regards to skin colour in life is likely to have been far more complex.

Male and female figures are also distinguished by their proportions (figs. 36, 77). In general, female figures have a higher small of the back than male ones, and are also narrower across the shoulders and waist, with more delicate limbs. These are distinctions found in nature: in a man and a woman of the same height, the woman will have slenderer bones, including vertebrae, and thus narrower shoulders and limbs, and a shorter spinal column with a higher small of the back. While the proportions of the human body in art are not constant throughout Egyptian history, these gender differences are almost always observed. In life, too, women generally have less muscle than men, and this distinction was also incorporated into the art. In the Old Kingdom, the early Middle Kingdom and the Late Period in particular, emphasis was put on the musculature of male figures shown in the youthful form. This is not something that was ever associated with female figures, which are always portrayed as less physically strong than those of men. Accordingly, women seldom appear in hunting scenes as observers, let alone participants. Apart from the royal family at Amarna, they are not shown driving chariots. Compared with men they are usually shown in a passive stance (fig. 36, 77), and their clothing until the mid-Eighteenth Dynasty is depicted as much more restrictive than male costume (fig. 77). The whole combines to suggest that men were expected to be far more active than women, at least in the elite male ideal of society.

Costume

Part of the artistic image of both men and women is their costume. From the Old Kingdom until the mid-Eighteenth Dynasty women wore a tight-fitting sheath dress. This is a simple garment that falls from just below the breasts to just above the ankles, being held up by two shoulder straps. On statues the straps cover the breasts (fig. 74), but in accordance with the conventions of two-dimensional art, the single breast depicted in profile is exposed in painting and relief (fig. 77). In most cases the dress hugs the body with no slack, so that the wearer appears to be hobbled. Most formal female figures have their feet almost together. When a figure needs to be shown in movement, the dress is extended just enough to allow this, as though it were elasticated (fig. 1). Women are also portrayed sitting and kneeling in this garment, which still clings to the outline of the body (figs. 57, 79). It is clear that the image is an artistic one and not one that could have existed in reality.

Such an image ensures that the shape of the body is not obscured by the dress. Egyptian clothes were mostly made from linen which tends to sag rather

80   Fragment of a banquet scene from the tomb of Nebamun.

than cling. Surviving dresses consist of a body made from a tube of material sewn up one side, supported not by straps but by a bodice with sleeves.[9] These garments would tend to be baggy, and would conceal rather than reveal the wearer's body. By contrast, the sheath dress displays every curve of the body, including the erogenous zones of stomach, buttocks, thighs, pubic triangle and breast, thus putting emphasis on the sexuality of the figure (figs. 56, 57, 71, 77).

Male costume in art from the Old Kingdom to the Eighteenth Dynasty, compared with female, is more varied. Frequently it consists of no more than some form of kilt wrapped round the waist and ending above the knee (figs. 56, 69, 70). From the Middle Kingdom onwards, a longer transparent overskirt may be worn over the kilt (fig. 36). The mature male image often has a longer calf-length skirt, but this never hugs and constricts the legs like the sheath dress (fig. 78). The torso, arms and lower legs are frequently left uncovered, although jewellery is often worn on the chest and arms. Later, the upper part of the body may be covered by a transparent shirt through which the outline of the body may be seen (fig. 77). Although the general shape of the body is revealed, there is one point of contrast with female figures: the kilt on most formal male figures conceals the genital region. In addition, the impressions conveyed by the images of the two are completely different. While the female sheath dress would have been very restrictive, the various forms of the male kilt would all have allowed the wearer to move freely. This fits in with the concept of men being more active than women.

During the Eighteenth Dynasty, probably beginning in the reign of Amenhotep II and certainly by that of Thutmose IV, the image of female costume in
art began to change. First, dresses became longer, then less tight, and finally
gave way to a loose pleated form obtained by draping a rectangular sheet of
linen round the body. While the shape of the body remained clear in three-
dimensional representations, in two dimensions it was mostly obscured, apart
from the breast, by the looseness of the garment (fig. 84). By the Amarna
period, however, the form of the female body including the pubic triangle was
again made visible by the simple expedient of treating the material as transparent and showing the details of the body beneath it (fig. 13). This became the
normal way of rendering the human female figure (figs. 48, 61, 73). Goddesses
continued to be shown in the sheath dress until the end of pharaonic civilisation (figs. 72, 73).

About the same time that the image of female costume was changing, or
perhaps just after, male dress in art began to alter also. The amount of material
used in garments increased and the whole became more complex. By the
Amarna period, men were usually shown with their torso covered, with short
sleeves, and a calf-length or longer pleated skirt tied in a complex arrangement
with an extra fold of material falling down in front. This type of elaborate
costume continued to develop, and remained in use over the following centuries. While certain parts of the garment were shown as transparent so that
the torso and lower legs could be seen, the region over the genitals was always
opaque, and was usually covered by more than one layer of material (fig. 62).
Thus the emphasis on female sexuality, in contrast to male, survived the
change in artistic representation of costume.

The new loose costume for women in art would seem to place no more
limitations on the wearer than that worn by men. It is an intriguing question
whether this altered image reflected a change in real costume, or a change in
society's perception of women. For instance, from the Nineteenth and
Twentieth Dynasties there is evidence that women took part in business affairs
and deputised for their husbands in their official duties, and one might argue
that they had more freedom to act on their own at this time. But, in the absence
of comparable material from earlier periods, we cannot be certain that women
were not already engaged in these activities.

Hairstyles

In addition to gender differentiation, the style of hair or wig associated with a
figure seems to have carried information about the wearer. For instance,
children wore their hair short, frequently with a longer sidelock falling from
the right-hand side of the head (figs. 3, 11, 51, 69, 71). Certain priests in the
New Kingdom who enacted a filial role in ritual wore a plaited sidelock to
indicate this filial status. In these instances, the lock was attached to an elabor-

ately curled wig, to indicate that adult status was also held. In the Nineteenth and Twentieth Dynasties, adult royal children wore a loose sidelock over a wig, presumably to mark on the one hand their filial relationship with the king, and on the other, the fact that they were no longer children. Private, married women most often wore a tripartite hairstyle that fell below the shoulders, with a lock passing each side of the face in front of the shoulders, and the rest falling behind (figs. 52, 56, 57, 62, 65, 66). A second style with long hair, usually called the enveloping wig, was also worn by married women (figs. 36, 77). It differed from the tripartite wig in that the hair covered the shoulders all the way around without any division. This style became more popular than the tripartite during the reigns of Thutmose III to Amenhotep III in the Eighteenth Dynasty. Both styles, however, remained in use by elite women throughout the New Kingdom and after. The tripartite wig was also worn by women in subordinate positions (fig. 79). It may have been an indicator less of class than of maturity.

81 (*left*) Spoon decorated with the figure of a naked adolescent girl playing the lute.

82 (*right*) Cosmetic pot carried by the figure of a naked adolescent girl wearing a Bes amulet round her neck.

In tomb chapels and on stelae a different style of hair was often worn by daughters of the owner who seem to have reached adult status but were perhaps not yet married. The mass of hair was less weighty and fell to just below the shoulder, with ringlets on either side of the face somewhat separate from the thicker strands at the rear (fig. 57). The same style could be worn by young maidservants (fig. 79), and perhaps indicated that they too were at a stage of life somewhere between childhood and mature adulthood. In the late Eighteenth Dynasty and Ramesside period, the same stage of development may have been indicated by an elaborate sidelock worn over a wig. Other important phases in a woman's life were associated with distinctive hairstyles, such as those depicted for pregnant women (fig. 20), women in the birth pavilion (fig. 22), and lactating women (fig. 27; Chapter Four). Further systematic research needs to be done on material from all periods to uncover the social significance of different styles for the hair. While there is enough evidence at the moment to make it virtually certain that meaning was encoded, we are still far from understanding the system. Literary and artistic evidence has already suggested that elaborate hairstyles and the dressing of female hair had an erotic significance.[10]

The motif of the naked adolescent girl

One female image that appears in the art of the New Kingdom is rather different from anything we have looked at before, and this is the motif of a nearly naked adolescent girl. In most cases she wears only jewellery and a girdle round her hips, often with an elaborate hairstyle. The image is found in tomb chapels of the second half of the Eighteenth Dynasty representing musicians, dancers (fig. 35), and serving girls (fig. 80). It also decorates ritual spoons (fig. 81),[11] cosmetic pots (fig. 82),[12] mirrors, bowls (fig. 83),[13] and similar objects used in daily life and subsequently placed in a burial, which is how they come to be preserved today. The virtual nakedness of the girl, and the various hairstyles, suggest that the image has a sexual connotation. This interpretation is supported by other considerations. First, there is a connection with Hathor, the goddess of sexuality associated with music and dance. Like the musicians and dancers in tomb chapels, some of the figures on domestic objects carry or play a musical instrument (figs. 81, 83). Because of their shape, mirrors have a solar connection which links them to Hathor, and naked girl figures often form the handles.[14] A few figures have images of Bes tattooed or painted on their thighs (fig. 83), and one wears a Bes amulet around her neck (fig. 82). We have seen that Bes was associated with sexuality, and thus with Hathor. Second, there is a likeness to fertility figurines, which also frequently wear elaborate hairstyles, jewellery, and a hip girdle (fig. 17). The sexual connotations of both cannot be doubted, and the naked girl motif may have been meant to incorporate a function similar to that of the figurines. This would help to ensure in life the fertility of the owner, and the continuity of the

83   Blue faience bowl decorated with the figure of a naked girl playing the lute, with a Bes figure tattooed or painted on her thigh.

family, while in the tomb it would aid the rebirth of the deceased.

It is interesting that there is no real male counterpart to the naked girl image. Male servants and musicians appear in tomb scenes (fig. 80), and male figures are found on ritual spoons and cosmetic objects, but they always have their genital region covered, and they do not give the impression of being adolescent. Indeed, in the New Kingdom adult male figures are rarely naked whatever their status. It was different in the Old and Middle Kingdoms, when peasants were frequently shown, if not completely naked, at least stripped down for work with their genitals exposed. By contrast, the officials overseeing them are always kilted with their genitals covered. Thus a distinction may have been made between those who engaged in physical labour and took off their garments to do so, and their supervisors who remained fully clad. Since the latter were of higher standing, the distinction between naked and clad could have differentiated between low and high status.

Children of both sexes were usually depicted without clothes (figs. 59, 69). On occasion, however, they are shown dressed. It is doubtful if they really went round with nothing on, partly because winters can be very cold in Egypt, and partly because some children's clothes have survived.[15] The nudity of children seems to be an artistic image which makes a statement about age and status. If dress marked the adult, then it was logical for children, who as yet had no place in adult society, to be shown naked. When they were considered to be adult they were depicted clad, and from then on the male genital region was usually covered.

Sex and sexual allusion

Despite the stress on female sexuality in art, the actual act of sexual intercourse is generally avoided in formal scenes contained in temples and tomb chapels. In representations of the divine birth of the king, intercourse between the god and the queen is symbolised by the couple sitting together on a bed while the god hands the queen the sign of life (fig. 10).[16] In the cycle of temple scenes portraying the death and resurrection of Osiris and the conception of Horus, Osiris is shown impregnating Isis who hovers over him in the form of a bird, but in the main divine protagonists are rarely depicted engaging in intercourse. Although copulation is not depicted explicitly in tomb chapels, scenes can, in addition to their overt meanings, encode allusions to fertility and the interaction of the sexes by symbols and puns. One of the functions of the tomb was to provide an appropriate setting for rebirth into the next world. We have already seen that birth and rebirth were closely connected, so that Hathor was concerned with both, and sexuality was linked to rebirth as well as to birth. It is, therefore, not surprising to find, amongst a whole series of references appropriate to the rebirth of the owner, ones with a sexual meaning.

Two common scenes found in tomb chapels from the Old Kingdom to the end of the Eighteenth Dynasty are usually placed next to each other, so that they form one double scene. In one half the male owner hunts birds with a throwstick, and in the other he triumphantly spears two fish (fig. 84). The whole is set against a marsh backdrop. The owner hunts and fishes from a light

84   Scene from the tomb of Menna showing the owner accompanied by his family spearing fish and hunting birds with a throwstick.

papyrus boat with his wife and children in attendance, apparently contradic-
ting the general rule that women do not accompany men in their sporting
activities. On the surface the scene depicts the tomb owner and his family
enjoying an outing in the marshes, but this may not be its only meaning.
Further analysis reveals the presence of a series of mythological references,
actions representing the triumph of order and life over chaos and death, and
various symbols and possible puns which encode meanings relating to the
rebirth of the tomb owner.[17] In the fishing scene, the tomb owner spears one or
sometimes two tilapia fish. This fish is well-known as a symbol of rebirth in
Egyptian art, and is in addition associated with Hathor. The tilapia also has
mythological connections, since it is said to accompany and protect the sun
god on his daily journey. The possession of the tilapia by the tomb owner
recalls part of spell 15 of the *Book of the Dead* by which the deceased hopes to
take his place in the sun bark: 'You see the tilapia in its (true) form at the
turquoise pool', and 'I behold the tilapia in its (true) nature guiding the speedy
boat in its waters.'

The fowling scene represents the triumph of order over chaos. The wild
birds of the marshes represent the forces of chaos. By bringing them down with
a throwstick, the tomb owner overcomes chaos and establishes order. It is for
this reason that fowling was to be one of the activities of the resurrected Osiris,
who ultimately triumphed over his murderer Seth, the god of chaos and death.

The marsh setting in both scenes may provide an allusion to Hathor who,
when she appears in the form of a cow, usually emerges from a papyrus thicket.
It may also recall the primordial swamp from which the mound of creation
arose, thus linking the tomb owner's hopes of rebirth with the original act of
creation, the birth of the world. In addition the marsh provided plenty of
lotuses, a flower which was a major symbol of rebirth on account of the myth
that the young sun god came forth from a lotus. A spell in the *Book of the Dead*
'for being transformed into a lotus' is illustrated by a man's head coming out of
a lotus, symbolising both the daily appearance of the young sun and, by
analogy, a promise of rebirth for the deceased just as the sun is reborn. In these
scenes the accompanying members of the owner's family often carry lotus
flowers in profusion. The women represent the female principle of the universe, while the children are concrete symbols of fertility, the result of interaction between male and female.

It may also be possible to read sexual allusions through visual puns. The act
of throwing a throwstick in ancient Egyptian is *qema*; for the Egyptians this
would recall the word *qema* meaning 'to create' or 'to beget'. In the same way
the word for spearing fish is *seti* which resembles another word *seti* meaning 'to
impregnate'. Through these puns the actions of the tomb owner can be read as
having meanings appropriate to his rebirth.

These two scenes, then, in which women are almost always present, may not
simply show the whole family participating in sporting activities. In addition,

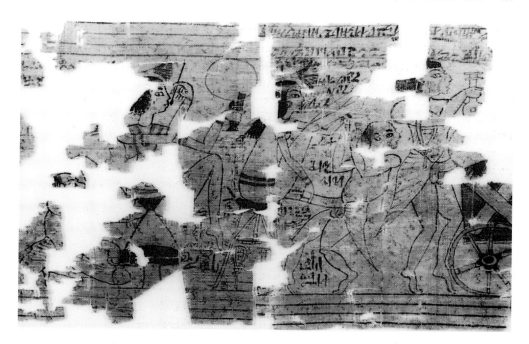

85   Detail from the Turin erotic papyrus.

they set the scene for the tomb owner's rebirth, with the female figures playing an important role as representatives of the female generative principle of the universe. Another scene common in the Eighteenth Dynasty, which may carry a similar meaning, is the banquet scene which shows the deceased and guests participating in a ritual meal,[18] although no one eats (figs. 79, 80). Both male and female guests often hold lotuses; they also wear them made into floral collars, and the women put them in their hair. Servants, sometimes depicted as naked adolescent girls, may pour drinks, and this action could be read as a sexual pun, since 'to pour' and 'to impregnate' are both *seti*.

If sexual intercourse was not part of the general repertory of formal art, quick sketches of men and women coupling are known from ostraka and other graffiti.[19] More accomplished is a papyrus from Deir el-Medina, now in the Egyptian Museum in Turin, which shows a series of scenes involving women and men in sexual situations in which intercourse is clearly the aim (fig. 85).[20] The figures of the women all resemble the naked adolescent girl image, being naked with elaborate hairstyles, jewellery, and a hip girdle. By contrast, the male figures are kilted, but this is inadequate to hide their enormous genitals, thereby breaking the rules of decorum in formal art. Not only do the women resemble fertility figurines or the naked girl image, but some of the scenes also contain the sistrum and mirror of Hathor, and the lotus of rebirth. It is difficult to tell what the exact purpose of the papyrus was, but it clearly belongs to a genre that is otherwise not represented in our sources.

FURTHER READING

A. Depla, 'Women in ancient Egyptian wisdom literature' in: L. Archer *et al.* (eds.) *An Illusion of the Night*, forthcoming.
M. Fox, *The Song of Songs and Ancient Egyptian Love Songs*, Madison, Wisconsin, 1985.
G. Robins, 'Some images of women in New Kingdom art and literature' in: B. Lesko (ed.) *Women's Earliest Records from Ancient Egypt and Western Asia*, Atlanta, 1989, 105–16.
G. Robins, 'Problems in interpreting Egyptian art' *Discussions in Egyptology* 17 (1990), 45–58.

Conclusion

In this book I have tried as objectively as possible to assess from the tantalisingly limited evidence the position occupied by women in ancient Egypt; what was expected of them and what was denied to them; what under favourable circumstances they could achieve and contribute to society; and what men thought of them, as seen in the various texts that survive, and in inscriptions and representations on funerary and votive monuments. The evidence shows that the main roles of Egyptian women were to bear children, to run the household and manage its economy, to help accumulate wealth through the exchange of surplus goods (often of their own production), to weave textiles which were fundamental for clothing, and to produce flour and bread basic to the Egyptian diet. In divine worship the special function of women was to provide music, singing and dance in the service of the presiding deity of the temple, whether god or goddess. The 'god's wife' or 'divine adoratrice' achieved high status in the cult of Amun-Ra at Thebes, and in the Late Period the holder of the office came to have supreme power there.

In the main, however, women did not achieve executive power. The rare event of a woman on the throne was alien to the Egyptian concept of kingship, and when Hatshepsut became king, presumably through force of character, her successor did his best to obliterate her presumption from the monuments. Women were excluded from the literate bureaucracy, and while boys went to school, girls did not. A father would want his son to become a scribe, but a daughter's expectations lay in marriage and motherhood. Women could in their own right acquire wealth, by personal effort or by inheritance, and in theory they were equal with men under the law, but a woman without the protection of a man was probably in many cases at risk from exploitation.

The subordinate status of women was epitomised on monuments by their being placed almost always in the less honorific position when they were shown with their husbands or sons. Nevertheless, in Egyptian art, in contrast to that of Neo-Assyria or classical Greece for example, women figured prominently as part of the family, and this can be taken as recognition by men of the important contributions made by women to society and of their active part in it. One can perhaps go further. The student of classical Greek art may suspect that the ancient Greeks never really liked women at all. Egyptian art gives rise to no such doubts. The beauty of the youthful female form has never been more acutely realised, and even if ancient Egyptian men felt both superior to and afraid of women, the texts and monuments that they have left behind also reveal that they loved and respected them. Nevertheless, one must not allow the high visibility of women within Egyptian art to obscure the fact that gender distinction existed as part of the formal structure of Egyptian society, and that in general women occupied a secondary position in relation to men throughout ancient Egyptian history.

References

CHAPTER ONE
Royal women and queenship
1 Silverman 1991, 58–73.
2 Robins 1981; Troy 1986.
3 Fischer 1973, 16–18.
4 Robins 1983a.
5 Loewe 1974.
6 Helck 1969; Redford 1975.
7 Janssen and Dodson 1989, 136.
8 Allen 1991.
9 Kitchen 1982, 100, 110–11.
10 Schulman 1979.
11 Winlock 1948.
12 Schulman 1979, 183.
13 Schulman 1979, 183.
14 Schulman 1979, 183 n.30.
15 Schulman 1979, 183.
16 Schulman 1979, 177–9.
17 Schulman 1979, 193.
18 Schulman 1979, 179.
19 Schulman 1979, 191–2.
20 Blankenberg-van Delden 1969, 18, 129–33.
21 Schulman 1979, 186 n.41.
22 Schulman 1979, 187 n.41.
23 Schulman 1979, 179 n.11.
24 Schulman 1979, 178 n.3.
25 Schulman 1979, 183 n.32.
26 Kitchen 1982, 110; Wente 1990 no.34; Reiser 1972, 57–8.
27 Kitchen 1979, 320, 381.
28 Janssen and Dodson 1989.
29 De Buck 1937, 152–64.
30 Parkinson 1991, 50.
31 Lichtheim 1973, 19.
32 Reiser 1972; Kemp 1978.
33 Brunner 1964.

CHAPTER TWO
Queens, power and the assumption of kingship
1 James 1973, 306; see also Vandersleyen 1971, 129–96.
2 Gitton 1981.
3 Edwards 1965, 25, pl.11 no.2.
4 Sethe 1927, 59–60.
5 Brunner 1964.
6 Dorman 1988.
7 Redford 1967, 57–64.
8 Egyptian Museum, Cairo, CG 34013.

9 Newberry 1943; Zivie 1982.
10 Nims 1966.
11 Blankenberg-van Delden 1969, 16, 21–56.
12 Green 1988.
13 Harris 1973a,b; Samson 1978.
14 Allen 1991.
15 Harris 1974; Reeves 1988.

CHAPTER THREE
Marriage
1 Valbelle 1985, 56–7.
2 Eyre 1984, 100.
3 Helck 1956, 1369.
4 After Pestman 1961, 8.
5 Pestman 1961, 8–9.
6 After Pestman 1961, 8.
7 After Pestman 1961, 8.
8 Lloyd 1983, 305.
9 Allam 1973, no.272; Janssen 1982a, 119.
10 Janssen 1982b, 256.
11 Bierbrier 1980, 101.
12 Pestman 1961, 17.
13 After Pestman 1961, 22.
14 Ward 1986, 65–9.
15 Černý and Peet 1927.
16 Peet 1930, pl.34, p. 15 11.4 & 7.
17 Peet 1930, pl.27, p. 3 11.8–9 & 13.
18 After Ward 1986, 66.
19 Ward 1986, 65–9.
20 Peet 1930, pl.34, p. 15 1.7.
21 Pestman 1961, 65.
22 Gardiner and Sethe 1928, 8–9; see also M. Guilmot 1973.
23 Ockinga and al-Masri 1988, 11 n.36; Simpson 1974b, 104.
24 E.g. Kanawati 1976, 149–60.
25 After Peet 1920, 18.
26 Whale 1989, 247–8, 272–3.
27 Gardiner 1910, 92.
28 Allam 1973, no.272; Janssen 1982a, 120.
29 Whale 1989, 264.
30 Černý 1945.
31 Eyre 1984.
32 Eyre 1984, 100.
33 Eyre 1984, 94.
34 Eyre 1984, 94.

35 Černý 1929.
36 Černý 1929, pl.43, 11.2–4.
37 Janssen 1982a, 115.
38 Janssen 1982a, 115.
39 Eyre 1984, 95 with n.25.
40 Lichtheim 1976, 137.
41 Parkinson 1991, 68.
42 Parkinson 1991, 68–9.
43 Lichtheim 1976, 207.
44 Simpson 1973, 16–19.
45 Pestman 1961, 56.
46 Janssen 1982a, 120.
47 McDowell 1990, 115.
48 Janssen 1988, 135.
49 Janssen 1988, 135.
50 Whale 1989, 244–5.
51 Parkinson 1991, 55.
52 Ward 1963, 431.
53 Whale 1989, 253.
54 Whale 1989, 253.

CHAPTER FOUR
Fertility, pregnancy and childbirth
1 Lichtheim 1976, 136.
2 Lichtheim 1973, 58.
3 Lichtheim 1973, 69.
4 Iversen 1939, nos.IV,V,VI,VII.
5 Pinch 1983.
6 Gardiner 1930.
7 Schott 1930.
8 Bierbrier 1982a, 32; Černý 1973, 325.
9 Theban Tomb 336.
10 Janssen 1982a.
11 Gardiner 1940, but for another interpretation see Cruz-Uribe 1988, and in reply Allam 1990.
12 Wente 1990, no. 206.
13 Hall 1986, 55 and fig.42.
14 Simpson 1973.
15 Depla forthcoming.
16 Lichtheim 1980, 128.
17 Lichtheim 1980, 128.
18 Lichtheim 1976, 200.
19 Lichtheim 1976, 212.
20 Faulkner 1969, 120.
21 Lichtheim 1976, 220.
22 Wreszinski 1909, 47 no.199; see also Iversen 1939, 14.
23 Sandison 1975.

24 Sandison 1975.

25 Brunner-Traut 1970a;
Brovarski, Doll and Freed
1982, 293.

26 Westendorf 1980.

27 Westendorf 1966, 144–5.

28 Bourghouts 1978, 40 no.63.

29 Lichtheim 1976, 141.

30 Lichtheim 1976, 200.

31 Lichtheim 1973, 219.

32 Lichtheim 1973, 220–2.

33 Barns 1956, 27 pl.18 1.28.

34 Bourghouts 1978, 39–40
nos.62–3.

35 Bourghouts 1978, 39–40 no.62.

36 Bourghouts 1978, 40 no.63.

37 Bourghouts 1971, 30.

38 Bourghouts 1978, 39
nos.60,61.

39 Lichtheim 1976, 108.

40 Erman 1901, F.

41 Brunner-Traut 1955; Janssen
and Janssen 1990, 4.

42 Janssen and Janssen 1990, 7–8.

43 Lichtheim 1973, 221.

44 Kemp 1979.

45 Barnes 1956, 27, pl.18 1.21f.

46 Barnes 1956, 27 pl.18 1.23f.

47 Lichtheim 1976, 138.

48 Lichtheim 1980, 58–9.

49 Wente 1990, 141–2 no.184.

50 Barnes 1956, 26, pl.17 1.15.

51 Erman 1901; Parkinson 1991,
129.

52 Erman 1901, B.

53 Borghouts 1978, 42 no.66;
Erman 1901, D.

54 Erman 1901, E.

55 After Parkinson 1991, 129–130
no.49a; Erman 1901, P.

56 Parkinson 1991, 130 n.1.

57 Erman 1901, L.

58 Erman 1901, N.

59 Erman 1901, Q.

60 Steindorff 1946, 50.

61 Altenmüller 1965.

62 Edwards 1960.

63 Edwards 1960.

64 Lichtheim 1980, 128.

65 Janssen 1982b, 255.

66 Manniche 1987, fig. 26; Bryan
1991, pl. 2 figs. 6a,b.

67 Wente 1967, 28.

68 Janssen and Janssen 1990, 17.

69 Lichtheim 1976, 169.

70 Maruéjol 1983.

71 Erman 1901, I.

72 Brunner-Traut 1970b;
Brovarski, Doll and Freed
1982, 293–4.

73 Janssen and Janssen 1990, 19.

CHAPTER FIVE
The family and the household

1 Lichtheim 1976, 143.

2 Lichtheim 1976, 203–5.

3 Lichtheim 1976, 207.

4 Kemp 1989, 151–3.

5 Winlock 1955.

6 Kemp 1989, 294–8.

7 Ikram 1989.

8 Kemp 1989, 294–6; see also
Brovarski, Doll and Freed
1982, 25–34.

9 Badawy 1968, 113–15.

10 Kemp 1987a, 41–2.

11 Kemp 1987a, 41.

12 Peet and Woolley 1923, 60–61.

13 Kemp 1979.

14 Kemp 1986, 5.

15 Peet and Woolley 1923, 62.

16 Kemp 1986, 6.

17 Kemp 1986, 7, 1987a, 10.

18 Peet and Woolley 1923, 63.

19 Kemp 1986, 7.

20 Kemp 1987a, 40–1.

21 Kemp 1987b, 26.

22 Kemp 1986, 20–7.

23 Badawy 1968, 65–8.

24 Wente 1990, no.170.

25 Gabra 1976, 48.

26 James 1962.

27 Kemp 1989, 157–8; Parkinson
1991, 111–12 no. 38.

28 Kemp 1989, 156.

29 Černý 1929, 254.

30 Valbelle 1985, 57.

31 McDowell 1991.

32 Bierbrier 1980; Robins 1979.

33 Davies 1920.

34 Lichtheim 1973, 170.

35 Hayes 1955, 105.

36 James 1962.

37 Kemp 1989, 297 fig.99.

38 Černý 1929, 246.

39 Lichtheim 1976, 205.

40 Gardiner 1935.

41 Peet 1930, pl.31 p. 10 1.15.

42 Peet 1930, pl.32 p. 11 1.7–8.

43 Kemp 1989, 257–8.

44 Peet 1930, 90.

45 Lichtheim 1976, 141.

46 Parkinson 1991, 73.

47 After Gardiner and Sethe
1928, 4.

48 Parkinson 1991, 74, 76.

49 Parkinson 1991, 73–6.

50 Bakir 1952.

CHAPTER SIX
Women outside the home

1 Baines and Eyre 1983, 81–5.

2 Ward 1986, 16–17.

3 Fischer 1976, 77.

4 Graefe 1981, 41–2 (j200).

5 Ward 1989, 35.

6 Wente 1967, 28.

7 Bryan 1984.

8 Davies 1913, pl.26.

9 Ward 1986, 24–8.

10 Fischer 1989a, 15–16.

11 Fischer 1989a, 14–15.

12 Ward 1986, 3–8.

13 Fischer 1976, 79.

14 Nord 1970; Drenkhahn 1976.

15 Helck 1939, 66–70,

16 Ward 1989, 36.

17 Ward 1989, 36–7.

18 Simpson 1974a, pl.63.

19 Smither and Dakin 1939, 164,
pl.21 no.4.

20 Wente 1990, 96.

21 Wente 1990, 108.

22 Eg. Ward 1982, 73 nos.
595–601, 101 nos.841–2, 104
no.860, 178 no.1542.

23 Kemp 1989, 223.

24 Ward 1982, 67 nos.557, 559, 94
no.787, 149 no. 1286.

25 Fischer 1989a, 10.

26 Hayes 1955.

27 Kemp 1989, 297 fig.99.

28 Davies and Gardiner 1948,
pl.35.

29 Hall 1986, 48–56.

30 Brunner-Traut 1958.

31 Fischer 1989a, 6.

32 Lichtheim 1973, 216–17.

33 Wente 1990, 141.

34 Quirke 1990, 133.

35 Hayes 1955.

36 Caminos 1954, 250.

37 Caminos 1954, 51 (8,2), 55.

38 Caminos 1956, 10 B2, 5.

39 Lichtheim 1976, 190.

40 Gardiner 1941b, 1948a,b;
Katary 1989.

41 Gardiner 1941a, 52.

42 Gardiner 1941a, 22–37.

43 Wente 1990, no.290; Janssen
1986.

44 McDowell 1990, 222.

CHAPTER SEVEN

*The economic and legal position
of women*

1 Goedicke 1970.
2 Parkinson 1991, 110 no.36.
3 Harris 1971, 304–5.
4 Hayes 1955, 114–23.
5 Quirke 1990, 148–9.
6 I would like to thank Andrea
  McDowell for allowing me to
  read her unpublished paper
  'Women's economic position in
  the New Kingdom'.
7 Janssen 1975, 460.
8 Janssen 1975, 279 no.11, 281.
9 Černý and Gardiner 1957,
  pl.51 no.1.
10 Allam 1973, no.183.
11 Černý and Gardiner 1957,
  pl.86 no.1.
12 Černý and Gardiner 1957,
  pl.51 no.2.
13 Gardiner 1906.
14 Gardiner 1935.
15 Janssen 1975.
16 McDowell 1990, 135.
17 Černý 1945.
18 Černý and Peet 1927.
19 Allam 1973, no.233.
20 Janssen and Pestman 1968;
  quotations are after their
  translations.
21 Wente 1990, no.351.
22 McDowell 1990, 124.
23 Wente 1990, no.199.
24 Fairman 1938, pl.11 no.3. My
  thanks to Andrea McDowell
  for drawing my attention to
  this stela and allowing me to
  see her translation.
25 Katary 1989.
26 Gardiner 1905; Gaballa 1977.
27 Bierbrier 1982a, 104–7.
28 McDowell 1990, 160, 251.
29 McDowell 1990.
30 McDowell 1990, 160.
31 McDowell 1990, 151–2.
32 Lichtheim 1973, 172.
33 Lichtheim 1988, 104.
34 Lichtheim 1980, 27.
35 Ockinga and al-Masri 1988,
  37–8.
36 Lichtheim 1988, 139.
37 Lichtheim 1973, 100.
38 Lichtheim 1976, 151.
39 Lichtheim 1976, 161.
40 Lichtheim 1988, 139.
41 Lichtheim 1988, 23.
42 Lichtheim 1973, 89.
43 Baines and Málek 1980, 204.
44 Cruz-Uribe 1989.

CHAPTER EIGHT

Women and temple ritual

1 Fischer 1982.
2 Galvin 1984.
3 Ward 1986, 20–21, 34–5.
4 Brovarski, Doll and Freed
  1982, 256.
5 Davies 1923, pl.14.
6 Lacau and Chevrier 1977, pl.9
  blocks 61 and 66; 1979,
  198–202, paras. 295–300.
7 Lacau and Chevrier 1977, pl.9
  block 130; 1979, 203–4, paras.
  303–5.
8 Epigraphic Survey 1980, pl.59.
9 Foucart 1935, pl.31.
10 Davies and Gardiner 1948,
  pl.14.
11 Davies and Gardiner 1948,
  pl.15.
12 Davies 1927, pl.5.
13 Épron 1939, pl.56.
14 Wente 1990, no.93.
15 Nord 1981; Bryan 1982.
16 Scharff 1924, 45, pl.9.
17 Bryan 1990.
18 Caminos and James 1963,
  pl.38.
19 BM 1280.
20 Gitton 1981; Gitton 1984;
  Gitton and Leclant 1977.
21 Gitton 1981, frontispiece.
22 Gitton 1976.
23 Gitton 1981; Graefe 1981.
24 Robins 1983b.
25 Petrie 1896, pl.19.
26 Bierbrier 1982b.
27 Caminos 1964.
28 Graefe 1981.
29 Fazzini 1988, 19–21.

CHAPTER NINE

Personal religion and death

1 Baines 1991.
2 Pinch 1993.
3 Černý 1958, no.7.
4 James 1970, pl.37 no.2.
5 BM EA 29.
6 Černý 1958, no.6.
7 Tosi and Roccati 1972,
  no.50051.
8 Tosi and Roccati 1972,
  no.50052.
9 Pinch 1993.
10 Hall 1914, pl.40.
11 Wente 1990, no. 295.
12 Kemp 1989, 305.
13 Bruyère 1952, 72–82.
14 Fischer 1989a, 13.
15 Werbrouck 1938.
16 Tosi and Roccati 1972,
  no.50053.
17 Davies 1920.
18 I would like to thank Malcolm
  Mosher, Jr. for information on
  Late Period *Books of the Dead*,
  and for a fruitful discussion
  and correspondence on the
  topic of *Books of the Dead*
  owned by women.
19 Martin 1989, pl.125 no.112a.
20 Bierbrier 1982b, 9–10, pls.4–5.
21 Fischer 1989a, 2–3.
22 Robins 1990a, 92 no.54.
23 Hall 1914, pl.49.
24 Parkinson 1991, 142.
25 After Gardiner and Sethe
  1928, 4.
26 Lichtheim 1976, 137.
27 Gardiner 1957, 170.

CHAPTER TEN

*Images of women in literature
and art*

1 Depla forthcoming.
2 Troy 1984.
3 Simpson 1973, 16–19.
4 Lichtheim 1976, 211–14.
5 te Velde 1977, 55–6.
6 Lichtheim 1988.
7 Fischer 1989a, 3.
8 Lichtheim 1976, 181–193;
  Simpson 1973; White 1978;
  Fox 1985.
9 Hall 1986.
10 Derchain 1975.
11 Brovarski, Doll and Freed
  1982, 207–9.
12 Brovarski, Doll and Freed
  1982, 204–5.
13 Brovarski, Doll and Freed
  1982, 141–2, 144–5 no.143.
14 Brovarski, Doll and Freed
  1982, 184–8.
15 Hall 1986.
16 Brunner 1964.
17 Derchain 1976; Westendorf
  1967.
18 Manniche 1987.
19 Manniche 1977, 1987.
20 Omlin 1973.

Bibliography

Abbreviations

ASAE *Annales du Service des Antiquités de l'Égypte*, Cairo.

BES *Bulletin of the Egyptological Seminar*, New York.

BSFE *Bulletin de la Société française d'Égyptologie*, Paris.

CdE *Chronique d'Égypte*, Brussels.

GM *Göttinger Miszellen*, Göttingen.

JARCE *Journal of the American Research Center in Egypt*, New York.

JEA *Journal of Egyptian Archaeology*, London.

JNES *Journal of Near Eastern Studies*, Chicago.

LÄ *Lexikon der Ägyptologie*, Wiesbaden.

MDAIK *Mitteilungen des Deutschen Archäologischen Instituts Abteilung Kairo*, Mainz.

SAK *Studien zur Altägyptischen Kultur*, Hamburg.

ZÄS *Zeitschrift für Ägyptische Sprache und Altertumskunde*, Berlin.

ALLAM, SCHAFIK 1973
Hieratische Ostraka und Papyri aus der Ramessidenzeit, Tübingen.

ALLAM, SCHAFIK 1981
'Quelques aspects du mariage dans l'Égypte ancienne' *JEA* 67, 116–35.

ALLAM, SCHAFIK 1986
Some Pages from Everyday Life in Ancient Egypt, Giza.

ALLAM, SCHAFIK 1989
'Women as owners of immovables in pharaonic Egypt' in: B. Lesko (ed.) *Women's Earliest Records from Ancient Egypt and Western Asia*, Atlanta.

ALLAM, SCHAFIK 1990
'A new look at the Adoption Papyrus (reconsidered)' *JEA* 76, 189–91.

ALLEN, J. P. 1991
'Akhenaten's mystery coregent and successor' *Amarna Letters* 1, 74–85.

ALTENMÜLLER, H. 1965
Die Apotropaia und die Götter Mittelägyptens: eine typologische und religionsgeschichtliche Untersuchung der sogenannten "Zaubermesser" des Mittleren Reichs, Munich.

BADAWY, A. 1968
A History of Egyptian Architecture: The Empire, Berkeley and Los Angeles.

BAINES, J. 1991
'Society, morality, and religious practice' in: B. E. Shafer (ed.), *Religion in Ancient Egypt: Gods, Myths, and Personal Practice*, Ithaca and London, 123–200.

BAINES, J. AND EYRE, C. J. 1983
'Four notes on literacy' *GM* 61, 65–96.

BAINES, J. AND MALEK, J. 1980
Atlas of Ancient Egypt, Oxford.

BAKIR, ABD EL-MOHSEN 1952
Slavery in Pharaonic Egypt, Cairo.

BARNS, J. 1956
Five Ramesseum Papyri, Oxford.

BIERBRIER, M. L. 1980
'Terms of relationship at Deir el-Medina' *JEA* 66, 100–7.

BIERBRIER, M. L. 1982a
The Tomb-Builders of the Pharaohs, London.

BIERBRIER, M. L. 1982b
Hieroglyphic Texts from Egyptian Stelae etc. Part 10, London.

BLACKMAN, A. M. 1924
The Rock Tombs of Meir IV, London.

BLANKENBERG-VAN DELDEN, C. 1969
The Large Commemorative Scarabs of Amenhotep III, Leiden.

BOURGHOUTS, J. F. 1971
The Magical Texts of Papyrus Leiden I 348, Leiden.

BOURGHOUTS, J. F. 1978
Ancient Egyptian Magical Texts, Leiden.

BROVARSKI, E., DOLL, S. K. AND FREED, R. E. 1982
Egypt's Golden Age. The Art of Living in the New Kingdom, 1558–1085 BC, Boston.

BRUNNER, H. 1964
Die Geburt des Gottkönigs, Wiesbaden.

BRUNNER-TRAUT, E. 1955
'Die Wochenlaube' *Mitteilungen des Instituts für Orientforschung* 3, 11–30.

BRUNNER-TRAUT, E. 1958
Der Tanz im Alten Ägypten, Glückstadt.

BRUNNER-TRAUT, E. 1970a
'Gravidenflasche. Das Salben des Mutterleibes' in: A. Kuschke and E. Kutsch (eds.) *Archäologie und Altes Testament*, Tübingen, 35–48.

BRUNNER-TRAUT, E. 1970b
'Das Muttermilchkrüglein. Ammen mit Stillumhang und Mondamulett' *Die Welt des Orients* 5, 145–64.

BRUYÈRE, B. 1952
Rapport sur les fouilles de Deir el Médineh (1935–40), Cairo

BRYAN, B. M. 1982
'The etymology of ḥnr "group of musical performers"' *BES* 4, 35–54.

BRYAN, B. M. 1984
'Evidence for female literacy from Theban tombs of the New Kingdom' *BES* 6, 17–32.

BRYAN, B. M. 1990
'The tomb owner and his family' in: E. Dziobek and Mahmud Abdel Raziq, *Das Grab des Sobekhotep Theben Nr.63*, Mainz am Rhein, 81–8.

BRYAN, B. M. 1991
The Reign of Thutmose IV, Baltimore and London.

DE BUCK, A. 1937
'The judicial papyrus of Turin' *JEA* 23, 152–64.

CAMINOS, R. 1954
Late-Egyptian Miscellanies, London.

CAMINOS, R. 1956
Literary Fragments in the Hieratic Script, Oxford.

CAMINOS, R. 1964
'The Nitocris adoption stela' *JEA* 50, 71–101.

CAMINOS, R. AND JAMES, T. G. H. 1963
Gebel es-Silsilah I, London.

ČERNÝ, J. 1929
'Papyrus Salt 124 (Brit.Mus. 10055)' *JEA* 15, 243–58.

ČERNÝ, J. 1945
'The will of Naunakhte and the related documents'
JEA 31, 29–53.

ČERNÝ, J. 1958
Egyptian Stelae in the Bankes Collection, Oxford.

ČERNÝ, J. 1973
A Community of Workmen at Thebes in the Ramesside Period, Cairo.

ČERNÝ, J. AND GARDINER, A. H. 1957
Hieratic Ostraka 1, Oxford.

ČERNÝ, J. AND PEET, T. E. 1927
'A marriage settlement of the twentieth dynasty' *JEA* 13, 30–39.

CRUZ-URIBE, E. 1988
'A new look at the Adoption Papyrus' *JEA* 74, 220–23.

CRUZ-URIBE, E. 1989
in: B. S. Lesko (ed.) *Women's Earliest Records from Ancient Egypt and Western Asia*, Atlanta, 136–7.

DAVIES, N. DE G. 1905
The Rock Tombs at El-Amarna II, London.

DAVIES, N. DE G. 1913
Five Theban Tombs, London.

DAVIES, N. DE G. 1920
The Tomb of Antefoker, Vizier of Sesostris I, and of his Wife, Senet (No.60), London.

DAVIES, N. DE G. 1923
The Tombs of Two Officials of Thutmosis the Fourth, London.

DAVIES, N. DE G. 1927
Two Ramesside Tombs at Thebes, New York.

DAVIES, N. DE G. 1930
The Tomb of Ken-Amun at Thebes, New York.

DAVIES, N. DE G. 1943
The Tomb of Rekh-Mi-Re at Thebes, New York.

DAVIES, N. DE G. AND GARDINER, A. H. 1948
Seven Private Tombs at Kurnah, London.

DEPLA, A. S. M. forthcoming
'Women in ancient Egyptian wisdom literature' in: L. Archer *et al.* (eds.) *An Illusion of the Night*.

DERCHAIN, P. 1975
'La perruque et le cristal' *SAK* 2, 55–74.

DERCHAIN, P. 1976
'Symbols and metaphors in literature and representations of private life' *Royal Anthropological Institute News* 15, 7–10.

DORMAN, P. F. 1988
The Monuments of Senenmut, London.

DRENKHAHN, R. 1976
'Bemerkungen zu den Titel ḥkr.t nswt' *SAK* 4, 59–67.

EDWARDS, I. E. S. 1960
Hieratic Papyri in the British Museum 1, London.

EDWARDS, I. E. S. 1965
'Lord Dufferin's excavations at Deir el-Bahari and the Clandeboye Collection' *JEA* 51, 16–28.

EPIGRAPHIC SURVEY 1980
The Tomb of Kheruef, Theban Tomb 192, Chicago.

ÉPRON, L. 1939
Le Tombeau de Ti I, Cairo.

ERMAN, A. 1901
Zaubersprüche für Mutter und Kind aus dem Papyrus 3207 des Berliner Museums, Berlin.

EYRE, C. J. 1984
'Crime and adultery in ancient Egypt' *JEA* 70, 92–105.

FAULKNER, R. O. 1969
The Ancient Egyptian Pyramid Texts, Oxford.

FAZZINI, R. 1988
Egypt: Dynasty XXII–XXV, Leiden.

FISCHER, H. G. 1973
'An eleventh dynasty couple holding the sign of life' *ZAS* 100, 16–28.

FISCHER, H. G. 1976
Egyptian Studies I: Varia, New York.

FISCHER, H. G. 1982
'Priesterin' *LÄ* 4, 1100–105.

FISCHER, H. G. 1985
Egyptian Titles of the Middle Kingdom, New York.

FISCHER, H. G. 1989a
Egyptian Women of the Old Kingdom and of the Heracleopolitan Period, New York.

FISCHER, H. G. 1989b
'Women in the Old Kingdom and the Heracleopolitan Period' in: B. Lesko (ed.) *Women's Earliest Records from Ancient Egypt and Western Asia*, Atlanta.

FOUCART, G. 1935
Tombes thébaines. Nécropole de Dirâ' Abû' n-Nága. Le tombeau d'Amonmos (quatrième partie), Cairo.

FOX, M. V. 1985
The Song of Songs and Ancient Egyptian Love Songs, Madison, Wisconsin.

GABALLA, G. A. 1977
The Memphite Tomb-Chapel of Mose, Warminster.

GABRA, G. 1976
'Preliminary report on the stela of *Ḥtpi* from el-Kab from the time of Wakhankh Inyotef II' *MDAIK* 32, 45–56.

GALVIN, M. 1984
'The hereditary status of the titles of the cult of Hathor' *JEA* 70, 42–9.

GARDINER, A. H. 1905
Inscription of Mes, Leipzig.

GARDINER, A. H. 1906
'Four papyri of the 18th dynasty from Kahun' *ZAS* 43, 27–54.

GARDINER, A. H. 1910
'The tomb of Amenemhet, high priest of Amon' *ZAS* 47, 87–99.

GARDINER, A. H. 1930
'A new letter to the dead' *JEA* 16, 19–22.

GARDINER, A. H. 1935
'A lawsuit arising from the purchase of two slaves' *JEA* 21, 140–46.

GARDINER, A. H. 1940
'Adoption extraordinary' *JEA* 26, 23–9.

GARDINER, A. H. 1941a
'Ramesside texts relating to the taxation and transport of corn' *JEA* 27, 19–73.

GARDINER, A. H. 1941b
The Wilbour Papyrus 1, Oxford.

GARDINER, A. H. 1948a
The Wilbour Papyrus 2, Oxford.

GARDINER, A. H. 1948b
The Wilbour Papyrus 3, Oxford.

GARDINER, A. H. 1957
Egyptian Grammar, 3rd edition, Oxford.

GARDINER, A. H. AND SETHE, K. 1928
Egyptian Letters to the Dead, London.

GITTON, M. 1976
'Le rôle des femmes dans le clergé d'Amon à la 18e dynastie' *BSFE* 75, 31–46.

GITTON, M. 1981
L'épouse du dieu Ahmès Néfertary, 2nd ed., Paris.

GITTON, M. 1984
Les divines épouses de la 18e dynastie, Paris.

GITTON, M. AND LECLANT, J. 1977
'Gottesgemahlin' *LÄ* 2, 792–812.

GOEDICKE, H. 1970
Die Privaten Rechtsinschriften aus dem Alten Reich, Vienna.

GRAEFE, E. 1981
Untersuchungen zur Verwaltung und Geschichte der Institution der Gottesgemahlin des Amun vom Beginn des Neuen Reiches bis zur Spätzeit I, Wiesbaden.

GREEN, L. 1988
'Queens and princesses of the Amarna Period: The social, political, religious and cultic role of the women of the royal family at the end of the 18th dynasty', unpublished doctoral thesis, Toronto.

GUILMOT, M. 1973
'Lettre à une épouse défunte (Pap. Leiden I, 371)' *ZÄS* 99, 94–103.

HALL, H. R. 1914
Hieroglyphic texts from Egyptian Stelae, etc in the British Museum. Part V, London.

HALL, R. 1986
Egyptian Textiles, Aylesbury.

HARRIS, J. R. (ed.) 1971
The Legacy of Egypt (2nd ed.), Oxford.

HARRIS, J. R. 1973a
'Nefertiti Rediviva' *Acta Orientalia* 35, 5–13.

HARRIS, J. R. 1973b
'Neferneferuaten' *GM* 4, 15–17.

HARRIS, J. R. 1974
'Kiya' *CdE* 49, 25–31.

HAYES, W. C. 1955
A Papyrus of the Late Middle Kingdom in the Brooklyn Museum, New York.

HELCK, H.-W. 1939
Der Einfluss der Militärführer in der 18. ägyptischen Dynastie, Leipzig

HELCK, W. 1956
Urkunden der 18. Dynastie Heft 18, Berlin.

HELCK, W. 1969
'Die Tochterheirat ägyptischer Könige' *CdE* 44/87, 22–6.

IKRAM, S. 1989
'Domestic shrines and the cult of the royal family at el-Amarna' *JEA* 75, 89–101.

IVERSEN, E. 1939
Papyrus Carlsberg No.VIII, with some Remarks on the Egyptian Origin of some Popular Birth Prognoses, Copenhagen.

JAMES, T. G. H. 1953
The Mastaba of Khentika called Ikhekhi, London.

JAMES, T. G. H. 1962
The Hekanakhte Papers and other early Middle Kingdom Documents, New York.

JAMES, T. G. H. 1970
Hieroglyphic Texts from Egyptian Stelae etc. Part 9, London.

JAMES, T. G. H. 1973
'Egypt: From the expulsion of the Hyksos to Amenophis I' in: I. E. S. Edwards *et al.* (eds.) *Cambridge Ancient History* 2 part 1, 3rd ed., Cambridge, 289–312.

JANSSEN, J. J. 1975
Commodity Prices from the Ramesside Period, Leiden.

JANSSEN, J. J. 1982a
'Two Personalities' in: R. J. Demarée and J. J. Janssen (eds.) *Gleanings from Deir el-Medina*, Leiden, 109–131.

JANSSEN, J. J. 1982b
'Gift-giving in ancient Egypt as an economic feature' *JEA* 68, 253–8.

JANSSEN, J. J. 1986
'A notable lady' *Wepwawet* 2, 30–31.

JANSSEN, J. J. 1988
'Marriage problems and public reactions (P. BM 10416)' in: J. Baines *et al.* (eds.) *Pyramid Studies and other Essays presented to I. E. S. Edwards*, London, 134–7.

JANSSEN, J. J. AND DODSON, A. 1989
'A Theban tomb and its tenants' *JEA* 75, 125–38.

JANSSEN, R. M. AND JANSSEN, J. J. 1990
Growing up in Ancient Egypt, London.

JANSSEN, J. J. AND PESTMAN, P. W. 1968
'Burial and inheritance in the community of the necropolis workmen at Thebes' *Journal of the Economic and Social History of the Orient* 11, 137–170.

JÉQUIER, G. 1920
L'Architecture et la decoration dans l'ancienne Égypte I, Paris.

KANAWATI, N. 1976
'Polygamy in the Old Kingdom' *SAK* 4, 149–60.

KATARY, S. 1989
Land Tenure in the Ramesside Period, London and New York.

KEMP, B. J. 1978
'The harim-palace at Medinet el-Ghurab' *ZÄS* 105, 122–33.

KEMP, B. J. 1979
'Wall paintings from the workmen's village at el-Amarna' *JEA* 65, 47–53.

KEMP, B. J. 1986
Amarna Reports III, London.

KEMP, B. J. 1987a
Amarna Reports IV, London.

KEMP, B. J. 1987b
'The Amarna workmen's village in retrospect' *JEA* 73, 21–50.

KEMP, B. J. 1989
Ancient Egypt: Anatomy of a Civilization, London and New York.

KITCHEN, K. A. 1979
Ramesside Inscriptions, Historical and Biographical II, Oxford.

KITCHEN, K. A. 1982
Pharaoh Triumphant: The Life and Times of Ramesses II, Warminster.

LACAU, P. AND CHEVRIER, H. 1977
Une chapelle d'Hatshepsout à Karnak I (text), Cairo.

LACAU, P. AND CHEVRIER, H. 1979
Une chapelle d'Hatshepsout à Karnak II (plates), Cairo.

LICHTHEIM, M. 1973
Ancient Egyptian Literature 1, Berkeley, Los Angeles, London.

LICHTHEIM, M. 1976
Ancient Egyptian Literature 2, Berkeley, Los Angeles, London.

LICHTHEIM, M. 1980
Ancient Egyptian Literature 3, Berkeley, Los Angeles, London.

LICHTHEIM, M. 1988
Ancient Egyptian Autobiographies chiefly of the Middle Kingdom: A Study and Anthology, Freiburg.

LLOYD, A. 1983
'The Late Period, 664–323 BC' in: B. Trigger *et al. Ancient Egypt: A Social History*, Cambridge, chapter 4.

LOEWE, M. 1974
Crisis and Conflict in Han China, London.

McDOWELL, A. G. 1990
Jurisdiction in the Workmen's Community of Deir el-Medina, Leiden.

McDOWELL, A. G. 1991
'Agricultural activity by the workmen of Deir el-Medina' in: *Sixth International Congress of Egytology, Abstracts of Papers*, 1991, 52.

MANNICHE, L. 1977
'Some aspects of ancient Egyptian sexual life' *Acta Orientalia* 38, 11–23.

MANNICHE, L. 1987
Sexual Life in Ancient Egypt, London.

MARTIN, G. T. 1989
The Memphite Tomb of Horemheb Commander-in-Chief of Tutankhamun I, London.

MARUEJOL, F. 1983
'La nourrice: un thème iconographique' *ASAE* 69, 311–19.

NAVILLE E. 1896
The Temple of Deir el-Bahari II, London.

MOUSSA, A. M. AND ALTENMÜLLER, H. 1977
Das Grab des Nianchchnum und Chnumhotep, Mainz am Rhein.

NEWBERRY, P. E. 1943
'Queen Nitocris of the sixth dynasty' *JEA* 29, 51–4.

NIMS, C. 1966
'The date of the dishonoring of Hatshepsut' *ZÄS* 93, 97–100.

NORD, D. 1970
'ḥkrt-nsw = "king's concubine"?' *Serapis* 2, 1–16.

NORD, D. 1981
'The term ḥnr: "harem" or "musical performers"?' in: W. K. Simpson and W. M. Davies (eds.) *Studies in Ancient Egypt, the Aegean, and the Sudan*, Boston, 137–45.

OCKINGA, B. G. AND AL-MASRI, YAHYA 1988
Two Ramesside Tombs at el-Mashayikh Part 1 *The Tomb of Anhurmose – the Outer Room*, Sydney.

OMLIN, J. 1973
Der Papyrus 55001 und seine satirische-erotischen Zeichnungen und Inschriften, Turin.

PARKINSON, R. B. 1991
Voices from Ancient Egypt. An Anthology of Middle Kingdom Writings, London.

PEET, T. E. 1920
The Mayer Papyri A & B, London.

PEET, T. E. 1930
The Great Tomb Robberies of the Twentieth Dynasty 1–2, Oxford.

PEET, T. E. AND WOOLLEY, C. L. 1923
The City of Akhenaten Part 1, London.

PESTMAN, P. W. 1961
Marriage and Matrimonial Property in Ancient Egypt, Leiden.

PETRIE, W. M. F. 1896
Koptos, London.

PINCH, G. 1983
'Childbirth and female figurines at Deir el-Medina and el-Amarna' *Orientalia* 52, 405–14.

PINCH, G. 1993
'*Votive Offerings to Hathor*', Oxford.

QUIRKE, S. 1990
The Administration of Egypt in the Late Middle Kingdom, New Malden, Surrey.

REDFORD, D. 1967
History and Chronology of the Eighteenth Dynasty of Egypt: Seven Studies, Toronto.

REDFORD, D. 1975
'Studies on Akhenaten at Thebes. II. A report on the work of the Akhenaten Temple Project of the University Museum, The University of Pennsylvania, for the year 1973–4' *JARCE* 12, 9–18.

REEVES, C. N. 1988
'New light on Kiya from texts in the British Museum' *JEA* 74, 91–101.

REISER, E. 1972
Die königliche Harim im Alten Ägypten und seine Verwaltung, Vienna; rev. D. Nord *JNES* 34, 1975, 142–5.

ROBINS, G. 1979
'The relationships specified by Egyptian kinship terms of the Middle and New Kingdoms' *CdE* 54/108, 197–217.

ROBINS, G. 1981
'Egyptian queens in the 18th dynasty up to the end of the reign of Amenhotpe III', unpublished doctoral thesis, Oxford.

ROBINS, G. 1983a
'A critical examination of the theory that the right to the throne of ancient Egypt passed through the female line in the 18th dynasty' *GM* 62, 67–77.

ROBINS, G. 1983b
'The god's wife of Amun in the 18th dynasty in Egypt' in: A. Cameron and A. Kuhrt (eds.) *Images of Women in Antiquity*, London and Canberra, 65–78.

ROBINS, G. 1986
'The role of the royal family in the 18th dynasty up to the end of the reign of Amenhotpe III: 1. Queens' *Wepwawet* 2, 10–14.

ROBINS, G. 1987
'The role of the royal family in the 18th dynasty up to the reign of Amenhotpe III: 2. Royal children' *Wepwawet* 3, 15–17.

ROBINS, G. 1989
'Some images of women in New Kingdom art and literature' in: B. Lesko (ed.), *Women's Earliest Records from Ancient Egypt and Western Asia*, Atlanta.

ROBINS, G. (ed.) 1990a
Beyond the Pyramids: Egyptian Regional Art from the Museo Egizio, Turin, Atlanta.

ROBINS, G. 1990b
'While the woman looks on: gender inequality in the New Kingdom' *KMT* 1 no.3, 18, 21, 64–5.

ROBINS, G. 1990c
'Problems in interpreting Egyptian art' *DE*, 17, 45–58.

SAMSON, J. 1978
Amarna, City of Akhenaten and Nefertiti: Nefertiti as Pharaoh, Warminster.

SANDISON, A. T. 1975
'Empfängnisverhütung' *LÄ* 1, 1227–8.

SCHARFF 1924
'Briefe aus Illahun', *ZÄS* 59, 20–51.

SCHMITZ, B. 1976
Untersuchungen zum Titel S3–NJSWT 'Königssohn', Bonn.

SCHOTT, S. 1930
'Die Bitte um ein Kind auf ein Grabfigur des frühen Mittleren Reichs' *JEA* 16, 23, pl.10 no.4.

SCHULMAN, A. 1979
'Diplomatic marriage in the Egyptian New Kingdom' *JNES* 38, 177–93.

SETHE, K. 1927
Urkunden der 18. Dynastie Heft 1, 2nd ed., Berlin.

SILVERMAN, D. 1991
'Divinity and deities in ancient Egypt' in: B. E. Shafer (ed.), *Religion in Ancient Egypt: Gods, Myths, and Personal Practice*, Ithaca and London, 7–87.

SIMPSON, W. K. (ed.) 1973
The Literature of Ancient Egypt, New Haven and London.

SIMPSON, W. K. 1974a
The Terrace of the Great God at Abydos, New Haven and Philadelphia.

SIMPSON, W. K. 1974b
'Polygamy in Egypt in the Middle Kingdom?' *JEA* 60, 100–5.

SMITHER, P. C. AND DAKIN, A. N. 1939
'Stelae in the Queen's College Oxford' *JEA* 25, 157–65.

STEINDORFF, G. 1946
'The magical knives of ancient Egypt' *Journal of the Walters Art Gallery* 9, 1946, 41–51, 106–7.

SWEENEY, D. forthcoming
'Women's correspondence from Deir el-Medinah' *Acts of the VIth International Congress of Egyptology*, Turin.

TOSI, M. AND ROCCATI, A. 1972
Stele e altre epigrafi di Deir el-Medina n.50001–n.50262, Turin.

TROY, L. 1984
'Good and bad women' *GM* 80, 77–82.

TROY, L. 1986
Patterns of Queenship in Ancient Egyptian Myth and History, Uppsala.

VALBELLE, D. 1985
'Les ouvriers de la tombe'. Deir el-Medineh à l'époque ramesside, Cairo.

VANDERSLEYEN, C. 1971
Les guerres d'Amosis, Brussels.

VELDE, H. TE 1977
Seth God of Confusion, Leiden.

VERCOUTTER, J. 1965
'La femme en Égypte ancienne' in: P. Grimal (ed.) *Histoire mondiale de la femme*, Paris.

WARD, W. A. 1963
'Notes on some Semitic loan-words and personal names in Late Egyptian' *Orientalia* 32, 413–36.

WARD, W. A. 1982
Index of Egyptian Administrative and Religious Titles of the Middle Kingdom, Beirut.

WARD, W. A. 1986
Essays on Feminine Titles of the Middle Kingdom and Related Subjects, Beirut.

WARD, W. A. 1989
'Non-royal women and their occupations in the Middle Kingdom' in: B. Lesko (ed.) *Women's Earliest Records from Ancient Egypt and Western Asia*, Atlanta.

WENTE, E. F. 1967
Late Ramesside Letters, Chicago.

WENTE, E. F. 1990
Letters from Ancient Egypt, Atlanta.

WERBROUCK, M. 1938
Les pleureuses dans l'Égypte ancienne, Brussels.

WESTENDORF, W. 1966
'Beiträge aus und zu den medizinischen Texten' *ZÄS* 92, 128–54.

WESTENDORF, W. 1967
'Bemerkungen zur "Kammer der Wiedergeburt" im Tutankhamungrab' *ZÄS* 94, 139–50.

WESTENDORF, W. 1980
'Isisknoten' *LÄ* 3, 204.

WHALE, S. 1989
The Family in the Eighteenth Dynasty of Egypt. A Study of the Representation of the Family in Private Tombs, Sydney.

WHITE, J. B. 1978
A Study of the Language of Love in the Song of Songs and Ancient Egyptian Poetry, Missoula, Montana.

WINLOCK, H. 1948
The Treasure of the Three Egyptian Princesses, New York.

WINLOCK, H. 1955
Models of Daily Life in Ancient Egypt, New York.

WRESZINSKI, W. 1909
Der Grosse Medizinische Papyrus des Berliner Museums (Pap.Berl.3038), Leipzig.

ZIVIE, C. M. 1982
'Nitokris' *LÄ* 4, 513–14.

Illustration acknowledgements

1 Temple of Deir el-Bahri, Thebes, From Naville, 1896, pl. 49 left, EES.

2 Karnak, 18th Dynasty, Archives Lacau A XV 5, by permission of the Centre Wladimir Golenischeff.

3 Karnak, 18th Dynasty, Luxor Museum, from Karol Myśliewiec *Eighteenth Dynasty before the Amarna Period*, Iconography of Religions XVI, 5, Leiden 1985, pl. 1 no. 1, by permission of E. J. Brill.

4 TT 192, 18th Dynasty, Epigraphic Survey 1980, pl. 42 right, courtesy of the Oriental Institute of the University of Chicago.

5 TT 192, 18th Dynasty, Epigraphic Survey 1908, pl. 49, courtesy of the Oriental Institute of the University of Chicago.

6 Medinet Habu, Thebes, Cairo Museum, 18th Dynasty, from Jequier 1920, pl. 77.

7 18th Dynasty, Pelizaeus-Museum 53b, photo Pelizaeus-Museum Hildesheim.

8 18th Dynasty, Ägyptisches Museum, Berlin, inv. no. 15699, courtesy of the Ägyptisches Museum.

9 *Chapelle rouge* of Hatshepsut block 26, detail, Karnak, 18th Dynasty, author's photograph.

10 Temple of Deir el-Bahri, Thebes, 18th Dynasty, Naville 1896, pl. 47 right, EES.

11 Thebes, 18th Dynasty, BM, EA 174.

12 Serabit el-Khadim, Sinai, 18th Dynasty, Cairo JE 38257, by courtesy of the Egyptian Museum, Cairo.

13 Amarna, 18th Dynasty, Ägyptisches Museum, Berlin inv. no. 14145, courtesy of the Ägyptisches Museum.

14 Amarna, 18th Dynasty, University College London 038, courtesy of the Petrie Museum, University College London.

15 Tomb of Panehsy, Amarna, 18th Dynasty, Davies 1905, pl. 8, EES.

16 Amarna, 18th Dynasty, Museum of Fine Arts, Boston 64. 521 left, Egyptian Curator's Fund, Courtesy, Museum of Fine Arts, Boston.

17 (a) Ägyptisches Museum, Berlin inv. no. 9583, courtesy of the Ägyptisches Museum.
(b) Sanctuary of Hathor, Faras, Nubia, 18th Dynasty, BM 51236
(c) Thebes, New Kingdom, BM, EA 2371.

18 Middle Kingdom, Ägyptisches Museum, Berlin inv. no. 14517, courtesy of the Ägyptisches Museum.

19 BM EA 35813.

20 18th Dynasty, BM EA 30459.

21 18th Dynasty, Brooklyn Museum 37. 710E, courtesy of the Brooklyn Museum.

22 Deir el-Medina, New Kingdom, BM EA 8506.

23 Middle Kingdom, BM EA 18175.

24 TT 93, 18th Dynasty, Davies 1930, pl. 9 right.

25 Middle Kingdom, Queen's College, Oxford cat. no. 1113, courtesy of the Visitors of the Ashmolean Museum, Oxford.

26 Tomb of Niankhkhnum and Khnumhotep, Saqqara, 5th Dynasty, Moussa and Altenmüller 1977, pl. 26 (a) left, by courtesy of the German Institute of Archaeology, Cairo.

27 18th Dynasty, Louvre AF 6. 643, photo copyright RMN.

28 TT 280, Middle Kingdom, Egyptian Museum JE 46723, courtesy of the Egyptian Museum, Cairo.

29 Peet and Woolley 1923, pl. 16, taken from Miriam Stead *Egyptian Life* London 1986.

30 After Badawy 1968, 65 fig. 34.

31 TT 217, 19th Dynasty, from Davies 1927, pl. 30.

32 Grave 604, Sidmant, Middle Kingdom, Ashmolean Museum 1921.1423, courtesy of the Griffith Institute, Ashmolean Museum, Oxford.

33 TT 52 (Nakht), 18th Dynasty, MMA 15. 15.19e, facsimile painting by Nina Davies, detail. All Rights Reserved, the Metropolitan Museum of Art, New York.

34 Tomb D no. 2 at Meir, Blackman 1924, pl. 10, EES.

35 Tomb of Nebamun at Thebes, 18th Dynasty, BM EA 37984.

36 TT 52 (Nakht), 18th Dynasty, MMA 15.5.19b, facsimile painting by Nina Davies. All Rights Reserved, the Metropolitan Museum of Art, New York.

37 *Chapelle rouge* of Hatshepsut block 66, Karnak, 18th Dynasty, author's photograph.

38 TT 192 (Kheruef), 18th Dynasty, Epigraphic Survey 1980, pl. 59, courtesy of the Oriental Institute of the University of Chicago.

39 TT 51 (Userhat), 19th Dynasty, Davies 1927, pl. 5 lower register.

40 Tomb of Ti, Saqqara, 5th Dynasty, from Epron 1939, pl. 56 detail.

41 *Chapelle rouge* of Hatshepsut block 37, Karnak, 18th Dynasty, author's photograph.

42 *Chapelle rouge* of Hatshepsut, parts of blocks 140 and 292, Karnak, 18th Dynasty, author's photograph.

43 25th Dynasty, BM EA 46699.

44 Karnak, year 9 or Psamtek I, 26th Dynasty, Louvre E 26.905, photo copyright RMN.

45 Karnak, 26th Dynasty, BM EA 835.

46 Karnak, 26th Dynasty, BM EA 1519 right jamb.

47 Deir el-Medina, 19th Dynasty, BM EA 1516.

48 Probably Thebes, 19th Dynasty, Kestner Museum, Hanover 2938, courtesy of the Kestner Museum.

49 19th Dynasty, BM EA 65355.

50 Deir el-Medina, 19th Dynasty, Bankes Stela no. 7. Černy 1958, no. 7, courtesy of the National Trust, Kingston Lacy, Bankes Collection.

51 18th Dynasty, BM EA 1297.

52 Deir el-Medina, 19th Dynasty, Bankes stela no. 6, Černy 1958, no. 6, courtesy of the National Trust, Kingston Lacy, Bankes Collection.

53 Deir el-Medina, New Kingdom, Museo Egizio, Turin 50051, courtesy of the Museo Egizio, Turin.

54 Deir el-Medina, New Kingdom, Museo Egizio, Turin 50052, courtesy of the Museo Egizio, Turin.

55 Deir el-Bahri, 18th Dynasty, BM EA 43215.

56 18th Dynasty, Turin cat. 1611, courtesy of the Museo Egizio, Turin.

57 TT 100 (Rekhmire), 18th Dynasty, from Davies 1943, pl. 63.

58 Book of the Dead belonging to Ani, 19th Dynasty, BM EA 10470/6.

59 TT 359, 20th Dynasty, courtesy of the Griffith Institute, Ashmolean Museum, Oxford.

60 Thebes, 18th Dynasty, BM EA 48001.

61 20th Dynasty, BM EA 10472/4.

62 19th Dynasty, BM EA 9901.

63 Deir el-Bahri, Thebes, 21st Dynasty, Cairo 14–7/35–6, courtesy of the Egyptian Museum, Cairo.

64 Thebes, 19th Dynasty, BM EA 305.

65 4th Dynasty, BM EA 1228.

66 Giza, 5th Dynasty, BM EA 1171.

67 Saqqara, 5th Dynasty, BM EA 1848.

68 Meidum or Dahshur, 6th Dynasty, BM EA 65430.

69 Saqqara (?) late 5th – early 6th Dynasty, Brooklyn Museum 37.17E, courtesy of the Brooklyn Museum.

70 Saqqara, 5th Dynasty, BM EA 1181.

71 Old Kingdom, Brooklyn Museum 49.215, courtesy of the Brooklyn Museum.

72 19th Dynasty, Museo Archeologico di Firenze, inv. no. 2522, courtesy of the Museo Archeologico.

73 19th–20th Dynasty, Museo Archeologico di Firenze, inv. no. 2591, courtesy of the Museo Archeologico.

74 18th Dynasty, Kestner Museum 1935.200.106, courtesy of the Kestner Museum, Hanover.

75 BM EA 36.

76 Tomb of Maya, Saqqara, Leiden, Rijksmuseum van Oudheden AST 3, courtesy of the Rijksmuseum van Oudheden.

77 TT 96, 18th Dynasty, from Karol Myśliwiec *Eighteenth Dynasty Before the Amarna Period*, Iconography of Religions XVI, 5, Leiden 1985, pl. 40 no. 1, by permission of E. J. Brill.

78 Tomb of Khentika, Saqqara, James 1953, pl. 7 lower left, EES.

79 TT 100, 18th Dynasty, from Davies 1943, pl. 64.

80 18th Dynasty, BM EA 37986.

81 18th Dynasty, University College London 14365, courtesy of the Petrie Museum, University College London.

82 18th Dynasty, Gulbenkian Museum of Oriental Art, University of Durham, courtesy of Durham University Oriental Museum.

83 18th–19th Dynasty, Leiden, Rijksmuseum van Oudheden AD 14, courtesy of the Rijksmuseum van Oudheden.

84 TT 69, 18th Dynasty, MMA 30.4.48, facsimile painting by Nina Davies. All Rights Reserved, Metropolitan Museum of Art, New York.

85 Deir el-Medina, New Kingdom, Museo Egizio, Turin 2031, courtesy of the Museo Egizio, Turin.

Index

Figures in italics refer to illustrations